A RELUCTANT TRAVELLER IN RUSSIA

A Reluctant Traveller in Russia

BY TADEUSZ Wittlin

RINEHART & COMPANY, INC.

NEW YORK

TRANSLATED FROM THE POLISH
BY NOEL E. P. CLARK

Contents

TO THE MEMORY OF MY MOTHER

A RELUCTANT TRAVELLER IN RUSSIA

Author's Note

A tourist wishing to visit the United States of America, or any country in Western Europe, has only to buy his ticket, collect his papers, his money, and then, armed with a suit-case, climb aboard his boat, 'plane or train. Should he be heading for a more exotic destination—the African jungle, for example—he will need to provide himself with maps, compass, revolver, sun-helmet and inoculations. Either way, the preparations involve no great difficulty.

The traveller who desires to visit the Soviet Union, on the other hand, is frustrated by insurmountable obstacles, for the Soviet Embassy categorically denies the right of access to any applicant for a visa who is not well vouched for and approved of by the authorities in Moscow. Such a person may either be invited to come on a visit or, at any rate, given permission to travel. No sooner does such a tourist find himself in Soviet territory, however, than he receives the immediate attention of propaganda officials from the Travel Bureau and likewise a few secret agents who tail their guest to ensure that he sees only what he is shown.

It is hard enough to see Russia even this way, nor have many the chance to do so. There remains, however, another method of viewing the dictatorship of the proletariat. No passport, visa or money is required. One merely needs to fall into the clutches of the Soviet Security Police.

By doing so you can pass through villages, towns, districts—even republics. You can watch the aurora borealis in Siberia or gaze on the green fields of Kazachstan, talk with countless individuals of every class, race and creed who have been hunted down and imprisoned by reason of their convictions or their origins. And only thus, albeit in the company of secret agents but without the protection of propaganda officials, can one get to know the true face of Russia.

That was, in fact, how I, myself, saw Russia when, fleeing from German-occupied Warsaw, I thought I would try to get to France through the eastern part of Poland which was occupied by the Russians.

ONE

Gulliver's Dream

I am a little boy, only seven years old. I am sitting on a low stool at the feet of my mother who is holding an open book with illustrations. In a colourful picture, the giant Gulliver is asleep on the ground while round him swarm tiny Lilliputians, binding him down with ropes no thicker than thread. Every separate hair of his tousled head has been firmly lashed to a stake no thicker than a match-stick. The mysterious giant is sleeping peacefully but when he wakes up his captive hair will cause him no little pain. Before he does get up, however, I am already twelve. I am in class during a dull arithmetic lesson and under the lid of my desk I am holding a book: *Winnetou, the Redskin Gentleman*. In the illustration, Indians have tied two white hunters to the stake and are about to scalp them. A neat, practised slit round the forehead and the white travellers will have been deprived of their hair. I take a closer look at the picture and see that one of the white men surrounded by redskins is none other than Gulliver. I am just going to cry out when I wake up. I rub my eyes and—help! they're scalping me! Scalping me, although I am not tied to a stake but lying on the ground like Gulliver.

Sleep departs, but the reality remains. I lie there motionless, so as not to lose my hair or, who knows, perhaps even my head. All round me, the men have been up and about some time, a few of them lacing their boots, others buttoning jackets, tidying their bunks or going out with their bowls to get soup or coming back with a hunk of brown bread. Tramp of snow-covered boots, noise of shouting and the voices of several hundred men dressed in padded coats and pants. I had slept soundly, worn out by the previous day's work, and had not heard reveille—a vicious order from the group commanders: 'On your feet!' Now I found I could not get up, and, still half asleep, I could not make out what was wrong with me. I felt as if I had been scalped or as though every hair of my head were tied to an invisible stake. The slightest movement of my head caused me pain.

'Hey, Toporov!' I called to a comrade near by. 'There's something wrong with me. I can't move.'

'Maybe you're ill,' he answered. 'I'll tell the group leader at roll-call. They'll cart you off to hospital and it's always nicer to die in a hospital than a hut,' he added lightly, as though advising me to send my boots to the shoe-maker instead of patching them up myself.

'But in the meantime I can't move my head. I can't understand what's the matter with me.'

Toporov drew closer, pressed his thick fingers to my forehead, then, passing his hand round the back of my head, burst into roars of laughter.

'Wait a minute, I'll cure you,' he said cheerfully. He went to his bunk and took a piece of glass wrapped in cloth from the kit-bag behind his pillow. Then he began to snip the ends of my hair. There was no need to call a doctor; this strange indisposition was a case not for a doctor, but for a barber. While I had been asleep my cap had fallen off and my hair had frozen to the wall.

Once freed, I leapt from my bunk and went to get

breakfast before my detachment marched out to work.

The dream about Gulliver and the Indian chief, gentle legacy from the years of my care-free childhood, was swiftly engulfed in the grey mist of a Siberian dawn.

*

'Hey, soldier! We've chopped down the third tree. What about a smoke?'

'Go ahead,' said the guard.

Dropping my saw, I sat down on a fallen tree trunk, and, pulling out a little bag containing coarse shag and a few strips of newspaper, was soon engrossed in rolling a primitive cigarette. The other members of our woodcutters' commando did likewise: dry, sharp crackle of a match, sweet, biting tang of smoke—glorious repose.

Tobacco was the most precious commodity in camp. It increased one's strength and lengthened one's life. If a man tried to slack while work was in progress the guards would shout at him or set the dogs upon him, but if one asked for permission to smoke they never refused. Thanks to that, one could sit down, embark on the lengthy procedure of rolling a cigarette, spit and have a root. Tobacco, therefore, was worth even more than food. Everyone smoked—even those who, hitherto, had never tasted a cigarette.

The woodcutters squatted in a circle and enjoyed their smoke. Markin, a swarthy Cossack, drew so deeply at the thick, black vapour that he coughed till he cried, and there wafted about him the magnificent fragrance of violets.

'Hey, Markin! Where did you get that?' asked Baklanov.

'Get what?' asked Markin with a crafty smile and knowing perfectly well what Baklanov meant.

'The violets.'

'In the shop,' he answered reluctantly.

'Any left there?'

'There was yesterday—maybe there's still some left to-day.'

When work was finished in the clearing, those in the secret went to look at the storekeeper's window before supper.

'Listen, Volkov, have you any eau de Cologne?'

'There's a few bottles left, but not enough for everyone.'

'Of course not. How much is it?'

'Official price, state-controlled. It's on the bottle, seven roubles thirty—no less, no more. You know I can't take more than that.'

'But you can take a woollen scarf?'

'Certainly, I can take a scarf.'

'Put a bottle by for us and, after supper, we'll bring the scarf and the money.'

'Fair enough.'

Seven roubles, a laughably small sum in the world of the free, was a huge amount in camp, where no one had any money. Several men had to club together to raise the necessary sum. There was less difficulty about the woollen scarf. True, none of the collaborators could deprive himself of such an article for the good of the rest, for the simple reason that none of them possessed a scarf, but that did not worry them—they could steal one from an intellectual.

Late that evening, the four friends sat down to their drinking on a double bunk in the corner. In front of them was a small bottle full of a yellow liquid. The bottle bore a black label gaily adorned with many flowers and the legend in French—'Eau de Cologne.' This was printed as one word in Russian letters of gold.

Nikita and Terentiej brought with them a couple of metal cups, Alcosha sacrificed a piece of bread crust which he first charred on the stove, while Baklanov presented a handful of cotton wool which, to judge by its dirty grey colour, had not come from the hospital but probably from the lining of his coat or trousers.

The cotton wool was inserted between two slices of burnt bread and the unusual sandwich was held over one of the metal cups while the violet scent was carefully poured through it. The fragrant perfume when filtered through the wool and the charcoal was rendered a little more fit for consumption.

The process of distillation having been repeated several times, the spirit, which was some twenty per cent. alcohol, was pronounced drinkable. The communal vessel was passed in turn from one to the other, from hand to hand, from lip to lip. They drank in harmony as honest men, not one of them cheating by so much as a sip. A cigarette concluded the celebration and the gathering broke up sleepily as the participants retired to their bunks. Soon the hut was filled with whistling snores and the fragrant scent of spring flowers.

In far away Moscow, the greatest cosmetic factory in the Soviet Union produces a gorgeous perfume called 'Breath of Stalin.' If the breath of a simple Cossack in Siberia, drinking eau de Cologne at seven roubles a bottle, could diffuse the scent of woodland violets, just think what fantastic aromas must fill the Kremlin when the Leader breathes—for, doubtless, he drinks the most exclusive of Soviet perfumes.

The sun's white disc, full as the May moon, was slowly suffused with colour. First it glowed faint red, then turned to a blaze of crimson—scattering golden sparks that set alight the grey canopy of cloud. The cheering rays of the sun's orb illumined the solemn quiet of the landscape, flooding the heavy trampled earth of the compound with brilliance. All was green and colourful. Berries grew in clusters on the high bushes and broad ferns caressed your knees as you walked among them.

Beyond the vast quagmire, so bright a shade of brown and yellow that it appeared red in the distance, blue fields of heather stretched out to the fringe of a melancholy wood of white birches behind which again lay the infinite forest of whispering pines, reaching to the sky.

Looking the other way, one could see the snow-bound slopes of the Urals, gleaming silver in the distance.

July in Siberia.

Some kind of greenish-yellow bird, no larger than a sparrow, swooped out of the sky. Silent and dignified it strutted about like a farmer surveying his land.

When the first shift marched out to work in the forest, the sun lit the steep left slope of the hut roof. It was night. As the group they had relieved marched back into camp, less than an hour later, the sun's rays would be warming the right-hand slope of the roof. It was day. There is little other difference between day and night in Siberia during the summer.

You could not just fall asleep as soon as work was finished, however exhausted you might be. You had first to get your bread and soup, and sip a little boiling water to warm yourself up.

I made for the cook-house carrying my mess-can. A heavy, smoke-blackened cauldron suspended by a few twists of wire attached to a wooden cross-beam hung over the red hearth which lame Vasia fed with logs from time to time. He wore a pair of dilapidated black boots and padded black pants, tattered black gloves, a black padded jacket, patched all over, and a black cap with ear-flaps, the peak of which was pulled down half over his nose. His beard was tucked into his collar, that was likewise black. Vasia's face was thick with soot and grime and covered all over with a day's old growth of fuzzy, grey hair. Hobbling about in front of the fire, he looked like the devil incarnate. Although he had been a prisoner for many years, he never complained. His work, after all, was not too exacting. Moreover it was dry and warm, therefore pleasant. Nor was he ever troubled by hunger, and he was well clad into the bargain. What more could he ask for?

'Hello, there, Vasia!' I greeted him. 'Give me some hot water.'

'Hello, lad.' He reached for my mess-can through the wooden stakes of the fence and poured in a quart of steaming hot water with the aid of a huge ladle.

'Nice weather, we're having, eh? Real summery it is to-day. Lovely and warm,' he said.

'Yes, it's fine enough.'

'You know, that's what I like about Siberia, it's always nice and warm. You don't get much more than eleven months of perishing cold and then it's summer, summer all the way, and you're as warm as toast.'

Pleased with this gem of wit, he grinned broadly, exposing a row of decayed stumps under his black moustache.

I took hold of the mess-can with both hands and raised it to my lips. Its pleasant warmth made my face ruddy, and after a few draughts of the soft warm water my spirits rose. Life began once more to be worth living.

'Thanks, Vasia, good-bye.'

'Cheerio! If you want any more, come round again.'

I hobbled away from the cauldron towards a low shack where a queue of labourers like myself were waiting for bread. I went and stood on the end of the queue, pulling from under my jacket the little bag which hung on a long tape round my neck and which I had sewn together myself from the remnants of an old pair of drawers. Then I drew off my right-hand glove with my teeth and fished out my bread card, issued the day before by my section leader. When at last I was in possession of a brick of black bread, I went round to the cook-house where I received a paltry helping of precious pea soup. Having collected my breakfast, I returned to the hut, leaned my weight against the heavy log door which hung on two straps in lieu of hinges, and in I went.

In the middle of that huge room, surrounded by plain wooden benches, stood the immense circular stove, thundering and trembling with the fire inside it.

There were bunks running round the long walls which were made of thin boards that let in the gnawing cold at dawn through innumerable chinks. Three feet above the first row of bunks was a second floor, as it were, above that a third and, finally, a fourth.

It was silent and there seemed to be plenty of room. Half the occupants had been marched out to work on the day shift. The rest were asleep, fully clothed, thin blankets thrown over them, caps pulled crookedly over their eyes and their boots and mess-cans under their pillows.

Only a few of the men were actually busy, either sorting out the belongings they kept in wooden boxes or repairing their underclothes.

A prisoner who managed to make sure of a top-floor bunk was very well off. Up there, he had enough light to see by and the air was a bit fresher. Besides that, nobody trod on him and he could look down from his perch and survey every inch of the hut. The only trouble was getting up there, but the knack came with practice.

I put down my bread and soup on the edge of a first-tier bunk and began the ascent, reaching up to the second tier with my hands and easing my body up with my knees. After carrying my food up a stage, I repeated the whole performance until at last I arrived in my eyrie where I sat down to rest. There on the bunk next to mine lay Baklanov.

Baklanov was a thorough scoundrel. He never wore a fur cap with ear-flaps, not even in the coldest weather, but sported instead a chauffeur's cap with an oil-cloth cover, and he was never cold. His ears were not even red. Right now he was wearing only one shoe, holding the other between his knees, and with the help of a stone hammering long wooden nails into the sole. He had a handful of nails in a red rag spread out beside him.

'How are you?' he greeted me cheerfully, keeping his eyes on his work. He stabbed the sole of his shoe with a piece of wire, thrust a nail into the hole prepared for it, and banged it home with the stone.

'See how it's going?' he asked.

'Ahm,' I conceded. My mouth full of bread moistened with pea soup to the consistency of clay, I was incapable of expressing my appreciation at greater length. But even that was sufficiently eloquent.

Again he made a hole with the sharp wire and inserted a white wooden nail, which wobbled there, like a soldier hesitating on the brink of a shell hole, wondering whether or not to jump in, till a smack with a stone hammer buried it up to its neck. Suddenly from outside, like the echo of Baklanov's hammer blows amplified a thousandfold, came the sound of iron being beaten and uproar broke loose in the camp.

'What's all that?' I asked.

'The alarm,' he calmly replied, reaching for another

white nail. 'They're banging that old bit of rail. That means fire. Something's burning somewhere.'

The sound of the alarm became ever more persistent. The rhythm of the blows on that piece of iron rail which hung on a post near the sentry-box grew more and more disquieting. First booming like a gong, then roaring like thunder, it worked itself up to a passionate climax and wailed like a church bell rocking in despair at the threat of danger, or like a chained she-wolf being beaten to death.

'Let 'em bang away,' said Baklanov, in a low voice and to himself rather than to anyone else.

He interrupted his work, did up the shoe he was wearing, drawing the laces round his ankles, then carefully tied up the remaining nails in the red rag, which he hid under his pillow.

'Probably one of the huts on fire,' he added with a yawn. 'A spark flies out, catches something alight and there you have it. Hell, you could get to sleep if it weren't for the ruddy noise!'

Meanwhile panic had spread through the camp. Soldiers and guards were running about in all directions. The commandant was twirling the handle of the telephone in his office and shouting into the mouth-piece so loudly that he was clearly audible in the yard outside. The Alsatians were barking furiously and the camp security agents, who generally wore civilian clothes, had hastily donned uniforms and were now circling the prisoners with drawn revolvers.

All work stopped in the kitchens and the cook with his two aides, grey-haired emaciated women who looked like impoverished Jewish intellectuals, were standing in the doorway with their arms folded, surveying the scene. In the accountant's office, the cashier and his clerks pressed their livid noses to the window panes.

Prisoners working in the vicinity, carrying bricks for

the wall of the bath-house, had also stopped thinking about exceeding the norm and, smothered in red dust, were standing about watching curiously. All said and done, if the powers that be were sounding the alarm, there was no point in working as usual. In fact, the sound was the signal to down tools, or so one would have imagined, but it was hard to say. You never knew quite what they were up to. It might be a trick. The sick in hospital in baggy underclothes and blue smocks knelt on their beds listening attentively, while from the huts poured forth others, rudely awakened by the noise, with jackets undone and caps awry; the doors were thronged, and all stood looking around them with complete unconcern.

A fire.

But where? There was not a sign of flame or smoke. Then somebody in the crowd round the sentry-box threw up his hand, as though pointing at a 'plane in the sky.

'Aaaaa!' breathed the men surrounding him. Far away, beyond the black swamp and the yellow morass, beyond the field of purple heather and those twelve treacherous kilometres which we had to cover to and from work each day, there on the edge of the tundra, over the tips of the giant pines—there shimmered a faint haze of smoke.

The tundra was burning.

There were few left in the hut. There were three who lay snoring like samovars on the boil. They were White Russians, big as bears, gentle and hard working, Bible readers. Always amiable, active and eager to help one another, ever ready to share what was going. Condemned on account of their religious convictions, they were always together, working, eating and snoring, shoulder to shoulder. It took a great deal to wake them. So worn out were they from felling logs that the roof might have burned down over their heads and they would not have stirred. Apart

from them, only a few old men lay stretched in their corners. Perhaps even they were not quite so old, but their
grey hairs and the straggling growth of beard on their
pale faces, their sunken cheeks and the blank watery stare
in their yellow eyes, criss-crossed with crimson veins, made
them look ancient. These men were not sleeping, but sunk
in apathy. Had they suddenly heard that the guards were
all drowned and they were at liberty, they would have
known no joy. They were commonly referred to as 'being
on their way,' organically quite sound and in no need of
hospital treatment, but nevertheless completely exhausted
and, what was worse, and in such conditions most dangerous, broken in spirit.

Having long since ceased to take any interest in life,
their only hope and desire was for a swift, silent death that
might come in the night and spirit them off as they lay there
dreaming their warm, cosy dreams of the homes they had
lost, poor and inadequate homes, but they loved them; of
fond wives, sad and overworked, and of children who now
must be grown up, perhaps of their mothers, long dead
but in memory immortal, white angels full of tenderness.

So to dream for ever and ever was all they desired.
And soon death would come to them, or rather they with
outstretched hands would run to greet it, being already
'on their way.'

They used to die quietly, with a smile on their wasted
faces, lips slightly parted and practically always with eyes
closed. Now and again one would cry out briefly or sigh as
death was upon him, but only when the sharp frost crept
through the chinks in the hut walls or the icy wind blew.

Getting down from my bunk, I went and stood in the
open doorway of the deserted barrack watching what was
going on outside. Baklanov, however, remained where he
was. Taking no interest whatsoever in the exceptional

events of the day, he produced a tin comb and began running it through his pale blond hair.

'We'll soon be having a new workmate,' he said with a smile.

'How's that?' I asked.

'What do you mean, "how's that"? You just got here from the moon or something?' He stopped combing his hair and began to clean the comb with a splinter of wood ripped from the wall. 'That devil, Lunin, will be getting a "bushlat."'

(Lunin was the commandant of the camp and a 'bushlat' was the padded coat worn by deportees.)

'You think they'll put him inside?'

'What do you think they'll do with him? Give him the Order of Lenin?'

'But if the tundra catches fire twelve kilometres away from the camp . . .'

'Are you defending him or what?'

'Not a bit of it. I'm just amused; he's here, the fire's there and just because of that he'll be digging coal for a few years. What's he guilty of? The thing's a joke.'

'Sure it's a joke. And what are you guilty of, to be sitting here, eh?'

The argument was a good one.

On the other side of the swamp the merciless fire was slowly strangling the green vegetation. Under a blue-grey veil of smoke it crept forward, low in the grass, leaving destruction in its wake. With a crackle, it snapped the slender twigs from the bushes, leapt over the bilberry shrubs, which with an agonized hiss were instantly turned into black skeletons.

As a wolf might a sheep, the fire smothered and ravished the defenceless tundra. A terrifying and impenetrable wall of smoke and flame surged onwards. The feeble hawthorn, wrapped in the fatal embrace, perished swiftly in its mantle of scarlet berries. Only the juniper died a hero's death with a loud merry crackling, its perfume reviving happy memories of carefree boyhood days and school outings. The delicate bird-cherry sank in silent, breathless surrender, like a girl struck down by tuberculosis. She shuddered, grew pale, turned grey, then, wilting helplessly, fell face downwards on the ground, and breathed her last.

The fire thrust on relentlessly, like a giant grey bear, heavy and lumbering but merciless. For a moment, it seemed that it might make a halt, as it stood on its hind legs to pluck at the branches of trees in its path. First, it clutched at the foot of the trunk, as though to tear the tree out by the roots, to raise it aloft and shoulder it but, finding the weight too much, it buried its claws in the bark and strove to reach the boughs.

The graceful, majestic cedar was already aflame, filling the air with the sweet and saintly aroma of incense. Larches and stout oak saplings—a joy to behold such a short time before—were now in their death throes, waging a desperate struggle with the aggressor and, lapped in his awful embrace, they perished after a brief but valiant stand.

The green needles of the lofty pines turned russet, then black, only to sink with the charred branches into the silent grace of smouldering moss below. The sky was black with smoke. All around, the forest rocked and swayed like a ship in a stormy sea at night with its helm shattered and masts, struck by lightning, all ablaze. The crimson tongues of flame licked skywards as the fire, like a flood, swept over the tundra, draping it in a vast mantle of black.

In the heart of the forest, where we sometimes went to cut timber, there was an open space cleared by the woodmen's axes in the centre of which was the oval expanse of a great lake. The fire had stopped short at that point as though stayed by some invisible hand and there was the lake, blue and silent, with the azure window of the sky as ever mirrored on its surface. Had it not been for the unexpected guests who, in their panic to escape the pursuing fire, sought refuge in it, the lake would have been quite unaffected by the inferno raging around it. But on the smooth expanse of glistening water there now swam, side by side, a grey wolf and a white Siberian hare, a warder's dog that had snapped its leash, and a gentle reindeer, on whose broad antlers had settled a multi-hued butterfly, a green bird with a black beak and a large dragon-fly with gleaming transparent wings.

Made one by their common dread in the face of death, they swam together and, just as the reindeer swam close to the wolf, so six fellow convicts swam close to a guard, all seven having been caught unawares by the fire in the clearing. It was they, in fact, who later described the scene.

The wooden highroad through marsh and swamp, made of timber and bundles of brushwood cut and laid by convicts and which led through the heart of the forest to the edge of the open ground, disappeared without trace, devoured by the hungry fire, and the narrow gauge iron tracks which ran along it were melted and buckled by the heat.

From one section of the camp, eleven commandos, each a hundred strong, marched into the forest at dawn, while neighbouring centres dispatched forces of similar proportions. I didn't know how they proposed to rescue the tundra from this blazing inferno, but soon the wind, blowing from the direction of the smoke-screen, brought with it the sharp clatter of axes, like the crackle of rifle-shots.

The men who had thronged the yard to look at the

fire now started to move back to their huts. Did this mean
that the fire was out? On the contrary, it was raging more
fiercely than ever. That was why the commandant was demanding that they march out and fight it. He would have
a long time to wait before any squads set forth for the
forest. The law is the law and rules are rules. The authorities always said that everything was regulated by law.
Hence, when the prisoner had worked his daily shift of
twelve hours he was entitled to lie on his back and twiddle
his thumbs till it was time to start work again. The forest
was burning, was it? Let it burn!

At first the men muttered curses, but after a while
they lapsed into total silence.

Suddenly, the doors of the hut were flung open and
in rushed Vala. Her hemp-like hair, cut short, stuck out
from under a scarlet beret which stayed on her head by
some miracle. Her cheeks were red under their freckles,
her large eyes burning with emotion and the consciousness
of this solemn moment. There was no breath left in her
flat, boyish breast.

Vala had once been employed in the office of a shoe
firm in Tashkent, thousands of miles away in the warm
capital of the Uzbeck Republic. She had been given three
years' hard labour for defrauding the firm. As a member
of the Young Communists League, she was politically en-
lightened and having only been deported for a criminal
and not a political offence, she served as the local propagandist—a task which she performed with fanatical zeal.
From the moment the fire broke out, she had run from hut
to hut appealing to the men to form voluntary fire-fighting
squads.

'Comrades!' she began, jumping up on a bench.
'Brothers! Eagles! The forest is burning! A Soviet forest!
Our forest, our very own! A forest whose timbers go to

help build the ships of our glorious and invincible Red Fleet! Wood which will build the houses, schools and orphanages of so many Soviet towns. Wood for the tables and benches to furnish them! What if you are convicts, prisoners like myself? Have you ceased to be workers and peasants and sons of our great Motherland? No, say I, and again, no! When you have served your term, each of you will go back to his home and become a useful citizen of our great Nation. And when you see a new barn or a village social club and in it a library, a reading-room, or a wooden stage in the theatre, you will think to yourselves, "Maybe it's made out of wood I cut in the Urals! My punishment was of some use to my family and my comrades!" Brothers, do not allow this precious building material to fall a needless victim to the flames. Let us hasten to save this property of the Soviet. Let's race into the yard and fly like hawks in defence of our threatened nest!'

She stopped. There was no answer. Not a sound. The men had pretended not to hear the speech, turning their backs eloquently in her direction, pulling their caps down over their ears to shut out the sound of her terrifying voice and feigning sleep as they waited for her to shut up and go to the devil. They would have cursed her, only they felt sorry for her. Everyone liked her. Vala was young, always cheerful, willing to share her tobacco, clean, never coarse; nor did she let the commandant touch her, preferring Fedia who was an ordinary driver. How could they then insult her? Let her talk away, tire herself out and go.

Vala saw with helpless terror that her words and gesticulations had had no effect on anyone. Her hands fell to her sides in despair. She did not know whether to go through her speech again or to turn to some particular individual for assistance. But what was the use of repeating it? How could she hope for support from a line of indifferent backs? Only Baklanov was sitting there as before, with his legs crossed under him, comb in hand, looking at Vala with expressionless eyes. She turned to him, as her only listener.

'Hey, Baklanov!' she shouted, balancing on the bench. 'There's a fire! D'you understand? The forest is burning!'

'I understand,' he answered her, 'and what does that make me? A fireman?'

'No! But when your house is burning down you don't wait for the fire-brigade; you crawl up on the roof and try to put the fire out yourself, don't you?' she rejoined, glad at the thought of commencing a discussion on a well-rehearsed theme.

'Yes,' admitted Baklanov. 'When my house starts burning, I'll get up on the roof. Only just now, my house isn't burning.'

'Isn't it?' cried the girl. 'The forest is burning! What's the difference?'

'The difference is that the forest is not a house, neither is it mine.'

'Not yours?' screamed the girl in sublime indignation. 'Does it belong to a nobleman who would set his dogs on a poor peasant gathering a handful of fuel or have him shot like a wild beast by his gamekeeper? What nonsense you talk! It's a Soviet forest—and that means it belongs to you, me and all of us.'

Baklanov's curiosity was clearly aroused by the girl's final words. He grew serious, opened his eyes wide and asked in genuine amazement,

'All of us, you say?'

'Of course!' she shouted enthusiastically. 'It's a communal Soviet forest—our own property. I have a share in it, another bit is yours—every comrade has a part of it. And now it's on fire!'

'My bit, too?' asked Baklanov, rising to his knees.

'Your bit, too,' Vala assured him. 'You've a piece of forest out there and it's burning!'

'Well, if it's mine,' said Baklanov with a wave of his hand, 'let it burn—and to hell with it!'

TWO

Order and Orders

'And you, what had you done to get yourself here?'

Like flies buzzing about my head Baklanov's question would give me no peace. Memories of the lost two years kept forcing my drooping eyelids apart and held that benefactor sleep at bay.

It was a moonless night, the darkness impenetrable. I stumbled through the wood, constantly tripping over roots, bushes and twisted undergrowth. Twigs, needle-sharp, pricked my face. My boots had filled with water as I was crossing a broad stream; now they squelched at every step I hacked from the silent blackness, like a man cutting footholds in rock.

Far off, amongst the trees, the electric flash-lamps of the German frontier guards, through whom I had to steal, gleamed intermittently. I moved cautiously forward for a long time until the black curtain of trees parted to reveal a large clearing in the forest. Close by, a flicker of firelight crept over the topmost branches of the pines. Wriggling forward on my stomach, like a small boy playing Red Indians, I reached the last fringe of protective branches and peered through. The clearing was lit by a glowing red fire at which two sentries were toasting themselves. I made a broad detour, plunged into a maze of straggling thicket and, at last, in the chill light of dawn, I came to the outskirts of a market town.

Nothing but mud and swamp, pools of dirty water and scattered layers of sodden, rust-coloured straw. To the thatched roof of the huts had been fixed poles from which fluttered bits of red rag or paper. Near the well stood farm-carts, laden with straw and guarded by a soldier in a long grey coat with a thin leather belt. He wore a grey pointed cap of coarse cloth, embellished with a green star. His hands clasped a rifle topped by a thin bayonet of improbable length.

I stood still. One source of danger was safely behind me. Another, unknown, awaited me. The early morning mist hung thickly about the poor settlement, bestowing upon it all the sadness of autumn. Hungry and very tired, I moved on in search of more secure quarters. I needed to get away from the belt of frontier settlements where one might be stopped any time and sent back to one's starting-point.

From a side turning there emerged a straggling group of people on their way to the railway station. They were bound for a neighbouring township, somewhat further removed from the frontier zone. I joined them and soon the procession spread out, snake-like, along the permanent way. Every so often, at the points or by a bridge, we passed a soldier with rifle and bayonet. Some members of the procession would greet him joyfully with clenched fist raised in the Communist salute. The soldier would look at them impassively, as though they did not exist. That form of greeting had long been abolished by the Soviets; it was reserved for export only—as an expression of dissent for the use of workers in capitalist countries. The authorities in the Union had no wish to be greeted by threatening fists

upraised. But these people did not know that. They saluted
the soldier in the sure belief that they were understood
and, stumbling along the wooden sleepers, they hurried
towards the station gleaming white in the distance. Once
having reached their goal, they were to stand in streaming
rain all that day and the following night, until a merciful
goods train bore them away.

Packed in with the rest, I got out two days later at a
fair-sized station. It was daybreak and the rain was falling
steadily. An innumerable throng of passengers who had
travelled free of charge fought their way through the turn-
stile, completely ignoring the ticket-collector. No one had
a ticket. The railway official sat in his box, gazing helplessly
at the human river flowing steadily past him. I left the station, not knowing where to go or what to do. After looking
about me for a while, I set off along a broad street which
led me to the centre of the town. My one aim was to find
somewhere to rest. Anything was better than dragging
one's feet through that cold, cloying mud. I began a house-
to-house search for a place to spend the night or, at the
very least, some corner where I could lie down and rest
for a while. But that proved far from easy. People, at sight
of a stranger, slammed their doors in my face, without
waiting to hear what I wanted. The hotels and inns had
been filled long since. The town was vastly overcrowded.
I spent many hours climbing flights of stairs and crossing
from one street to another before an old woman allowed
me to leave my knapsack in her kitchen till I found a place.

I put down the heavy sack and, once out in the street,
made my way to the square which proved to be spacious.
At one time it might even have looked imposing. Now,
however, it resembled a country market-place with business
in full swing. Apart from two cafés which were thronged
and overflowing on to the pavements, this square was the

meeting-place for the whole town. The people were herded together and the air was full of their noisy conversation. Here families were reunited, dealers in currency flourished, saccharine and visas for Brazil were bought and sold. Smugglers were there too—in their distinctive blue skiing-caps with ear-flaps, taking letters for delivery across the line and bringing messages from the other side. Fairground noise and bustle. From the top of a high mast four loud-speakers blared out to the town the strains of a military march, scraped from an ancient record with a rough needle.

From time to time, I caught a glimpse of people I knew—lawyers, judges, engineers and doctors. Their faces were pinched and on their heads were cloth caps instead of hats, which the Soviet authorities considered the hall-mark of the bourgeoisie.

'Hullo there!' said somebody grabbing hold of my hand. 'Well, well, you must be doing all right these days!'

'Marvellously,' I answered. 'God alone knows where I'll spend the night!'

'Haven't you been to the Writers' Union?'

'No. Is there such a thing here?'

'Indeed there is. You get free dinners, a club-room and financial assistance.'

'Well, where is this place?'

'They have a registration office in the Town Hall. You have to go there and put your name on the list. My God, if only I were in your shoes!'

I was no longer listening. Taking leave of him, I ran to the Town Hall, a substantial building, visible a long way off. In front of it hung gigantic portraits of Lenin and Stalin like the appalling posters outside a small cinema. In the doorway stood a Soviet soldier with a rifle slung on his shoulder. He stopped me as I was about to enter.

'Got a pass?' he asked.

'No,' I admitted. 'I only arrived to-day, and I want to register.'

'No one is allowed in without a pass. Those are my orders and that's how it is.'

'Ah well, if that's how it is, it's just too bad. Do you know where I can get a pass?'

'On the first floor.'

'But how am I to get there if you won't let me in?'

'That's not my worry,' said the sentry. 'Meanwhile, stop blocking up the entrance and clear off, or else . . .' and he tapped the butt of his rifle significantly.

That argument was most convincing. I turned away humbly and went back to the square to tell the first acquaintance I met about this amusing incident. Contrary to my expectations, it provoked no merriment. Not even surprise. It was, apparently, an old story and here in the square were 'specialists' who hired out the necessary passes for a moderate sum. In next to no time, I found one of these accommodating gentlemen and the transaction was swiftly arranged. We set off together for the Town Hall. When we were close to the building, the purveyor of passes took a typed sheet from his wallet and handed it to me, telling me not to be long. He did not want to be kept waiting as he was expecting other customers. Up the steps I went and showed my pass to the sentry who admitted me without enquiring how I had come by it. I ran up to the first floor where I obtained, without any difficulty, a pass to enter the building in which I was standing.

That was the order, however, and that's how it was.

*

In the main hall which had been converted into the Secretariat of the Writers' Union, behind a large table littered with heavy volumes, sat three round-shouldered

young men. In place of shirts and collars they wore polo-
necked sweaters of coarse wool. Their black curly hair was
long and unkempt, and spectacles embellished their prominent noses. I walked up to the table and gave my name.
They had never heard of me—a mutual state of affairs
since I had never heard of them. I therefore mentioned
the titles of my books which would probably be available
in the local library. The presiding journalist entered my
name in a ledger, tore a page out of a receipt-book and
handed it to me, saying, as he did so,

'Here, comrade, is a ticket for a free dinner. Usually
we give out seven cards in advance for the week, but as you
haven't got a fixed address, you'd better report to us every
day. We'll be able to keep track of you that way.'

I left and went in search of the soup-kitchen. At the
far end of a long street of wooden huts, a queue of shabby
individuals proclaimed a free meal. I waited here awhile
before they let me enter a low, dark room where two long
benches were set on either side of a plain wooden table,
stained with tea and soup.

The cutlery consisted of several iron spoons attached
to the table by heavy chains. Two old women, in black coats
and equally sombre hats with imitation flowers to complete
the funereal effect, brought round tin bowls of barley with
perhaps a stray piece of meat, and earthenware cups of
hot water in which floated a few lonely ersatz tea-leaves.

During the meal, I saw a former friend of mine who
promptly offered to share his quarters with me. He lived in
a widow's house and was sure she would take in another
homeless man. The old lady agreed to lay down a mattress
for me each evening—in the passage. I gratefully accepted
this arrangement and brought my knapsack over as quickly
as I could.

When I arrived at the Town Hall next day to collect

my dinner-ticket, the man in the Union drew my attention to a notice painted on the wall in ink.

'Read this, comrade,' he said, 'and remember what it says.'

The notice informed all concerned that there was to be a Writers' Meeting at the Ritz Hotel that evening.

Before setting out, I carefully scraped the mud from my decrepit shoes, brushed the shaggy edges of my turn-ups, washed the collar of my shirt and, at the appointed time, presented myself at the hotel. When I asked the elegant porter in which room the Writers' Meeting was taking place, his tone of haughty contempt changed to one of fawning obsequiousness. Before I could fully grasp the reason for this change, the manager of the hotel, in person, came up at a trot to help me take off the very coat which served me at night as a blanket.

On entering the banqueting-hall, I stood still. It was as though I had crossed the threshold of another world.

The tables, disposed in the shape of a horse-shoe, glittered with snow-white serviettes, polished plates and an imposing array of silver cutlery. Flowers and giant baskets of fruit completed the picture.

Not quite. Platters piled high with fresh bread and whorls of sweet-smelling butter drew my eyes irresistibly. There were dozens of people in the hall. Apart from the President of the Union, the man who issued lunch-tickets, I saw and recognized several genuine writers, friends or acquaintances of mine in happier times.

Everywhere there was laughter and excitement induced by the brilliant lights and the waiting food.

'Reminds me of the good old days,' said someone, nodding at the bottles.

'Don't count your chickens . . .' laughed somebody else.

'Who's giving this party anyway, and why?' I asked.

'It's to get better acquainted with the Polish literary world,' said a poetess, sometime writer of patriotic tales for children and a keen opportunist. 'It's given by our new authorities,' she added unctuously.

I didn't know whether she was serious or putting on an act. Nor did I ask, having just noticed on many lapels and dress-fronts, little red stars with the hammer and sickle or a likeness of Stalin.

Minutes of waiting dragged slowly into hours. The chairman of the Association of White-Russian Writers, citizen Klimkovitch, was coming from Minsk by car, but his arrival had been delayed by the bad weather.

At last, just when the self-control of hungry people, forced to gaze on bread and butter for several hours, was near breaking-point, a sudden commotion and the noise of footsteps in the ante-room announced the arrival of the dignitaries. After a while, three Soviet officers entered with heavy, military strides. The first was Colonel Spasov, commander of the local Red Army garrison. Behind him came Major Prusak, master of life and death in the district, and third, Captain Gershman, the political officer, a powerfully built man with a fair collection of medals on his tightly belted Army blouse. Last came a thin, bald-headed civilian with an intelligent face, meanly dressed in a shiny, serge suit. This was our chairman, Klimovitch.

Then followed personal introductions, with the dignitaries coming up one by one to shake hands with all present. Finally, we took our seats and the banquet commenced. A multitude of waiters in tails, carrying dishes of mayonnaise salad, ran round the tables with the alacrity of slaves newly purchased.

'More?' asked one of them, piling my plate.

'Go ahead! Fill it right up, old boy,' I whispered conspiratorially, feeling I could control myself no longer and might start eating before the others had so much as raised their forks.

Not for many weeks, in fact not since I started my travels, had I seen such food and I had all but forgotten the existence of tables so sumptuously laden.

Our glasses were filled to enable the gathering to drink toasts. The Colonel set the ball rolling by stressing the merits of the Peasants' and Workers' Red Army in freeing nations from the yoke of capitalist oppression. Bravo! Bravo! Then the political officer foretold a new era of liberty for the pen. Bravo! Bravo! Then more food, fruit and wine. A band which had sprung from nowhere played the 'Internationale.' All present stood to attention. No sooner had the music ceased than someone yelled: Hurrah! Other voices took up the cry: Hurrah! Some youth or other climbed up on a chair and began reciting a piece of Russian propaganda verse.

Black coffee arrived and the banquet seemed to be over. The band played Russian tunes and a few people tried to dance, since there turned out to be two other women besides the poetess. The tables were suddenly deserted and the revellers, grouped in corners of the spacious hall, began eagerly smoking cigarettes brought round by the waiters and discussing, or rather, vying with one another in praise of everything which the Russian invader had brought into the country.

On a couch at the head of the table sat Gershman, the political officer, his chin in his hands. No less apathetically, I sat on my chair. With a nod and a smile he invited me to come and sit beside him.

'Well how do you like it with us?' he asked, as I took the place indicated.

I didn't know what he meant by the words 'with us.'

After all, he was in my country, not I in his; but perhaps the question referred to the banquet.

'Certainly it's very pleasant,' I answered evasively.

'I'd like to talk to you sometime,' he began. 'To-morrow, in the Town Hall, there'll be a meeting of your Union. You'll be there, eh? I shall be speaking and I've quite a lot to say. Between you and me, though, there won't be much time for chatting, but if you want anything explained or any doubts cleared up, I'll be glad to oblige.'

It seemed I was rather more sober than I had imagined. Perhaps it was a natural instinct for self-preservation which bade me weigh carefully every word I uttered in the presence of the Soviet dignitary.

'Don't forget, citizen'—I began slowly and thoughtfully, playing my words like chess-men—'I am a poet, I spend my time writing about flowers, love and the moon. Stands to reason, I don't know anything about politics.'

'I'll very gladly put you in the picture. What would you like to know?'

'Well, for one thing, I can never understand how the Soviet Union could possibly make an alliance with Hitler, a sworn enemy of Communism. Why, there's a line in the Nazi Party's anthem that says: "We'll shatter the Red Front." I could never make it out at all.'

'Couldn't you really?' said the officer with a condescending smile. 'It's really quite simple.'

'You don't say.'

'Of course it is. I suppose that even poets sometimes read the newspapers?'

'Oh, yes.'

'Well, you must be aware that France has a Socialist government and that there exists in France a legitimate Communist Party.'

'Yes, I know.'

'And if instead of making a pact with Hitler, we had made an alliance with the Left-wing French Government, would that have surprised you?'

'No.'

'Well now, it's all the same to us. France and Germany are both capitalist countries. It doesn't matter what sort of government is in power. The least dangerous régime from our point of view is the Fascist dictatorship, Hitler's régime to be precise. Tradition constitutes a much more serious threat to what we stand for. For that reason, England is our greatest enemy. The Fascist régime can only live as long as the dictator is there to inspire it. Hitlerism therefore will perish with Hitler. He's fifty years old now, so how much longer is he likely to live? Twenty or thirty years at the most, and that's the end of it. In England, on the contrary, the social order is not in the least dependent upon the King. It doesn't matter over there whether they have one king or another. What does matter, is that they have a tradition which is already several hundred years old and that's what's dangerous. We made an alliance with Hitler to help him fight a war against England. And when they're both done bleeding each other we can attack the winner. Now, do you get it?'

'Yes, I begin to see now. And what's going to happen to governments like the Swedish and Danish?'

'These governments are just like petty trading concerns. With big stores beside them they've no alternative but to go bankrupt. They can't compete. They've just got to close down.'

To have answered the political commissar's remarks as they merited would have involved me in a dangerous discussion. Instead, I asked him what were his views on art.

Meanwhile, though everyone thought that the feast

was over, fresh dishes were arriving. Waiters entered, bearing steaming plates of roast beef, macaroni and vegetables. There followed two lads dragging baskets of champagne bottles.

The discussion groups broke up, their members rushing back to the tables like hens lured by grain. The terrible gorging began anew to the accompaniment of delighted yells, clucking tongues, noisy swallowings, salvoes of champagne corks and the strains of the band blaring, 'If War Should Break Out To-morrow,' 'Katiusha,' 'The Three Tank-men,' and other Soviet ditties.

'As far as art is concerned,' the officer continued, 'I'm afraid you capitalist writers will find it hard to become writers of the Soviet kind. You see, art in the Soviet Union plays a role different to that which it plays in the degenerate countries of Western Europe. With us, art is not only there to give pleasure but also to teach and instruct. To instruct in the political sense, moreover. In the spirit of Marxist Socialism. Otherwise, it is not art. Your painter paints a wood or a field, some poppies or corn, believes he has fulfilled his duty as an artist and considers his painting a work of art. With us, it's quite different. Our way is that painting is only a work of art if, for example, a labourer is working in the field or Soviet tanks are shown emerging from the wood. Only then is the painter a true Soviet artist.'

'Our theatre has also a different role to yours,' interposed Comrade Klimkovitch who, having joined us silently, had been listening to our conversation. 'In capitalist countries the theatre is a privately controlled business. If a show—no matter how excellent—doesn't make a profit because the public don't like it, it's taken off and replaced by another work, often of no merit but calculated as a box-office success—merely in order to rescue the bank balance.

In the Union, where the theatre, like all art, is a means of distilling propaganda, once a show has satisfied the authorities that it is useful and is fulfilling its Socialist task, it will be played for a year or even more. It will be given the best directors and actors, first-class scenery, beautiful music, costumes, ballet, choirs—in short, it will be a lavish production and will stay on the bills as long as the authorities see fit. The audience? Well, if a factory employing five thousand workers gets five hundred or so tickets for distribution amongst the best workers, and those who get a ticket stop work at midday—do you think they won't be delighted to go?'

'But what if a worker, instead of going to the theatre, wishes to spend his free afternoon some other way?' I asked.

'Oh, no, my dear fellow,' replied the chairman. 'He gets the time off to go to the theatre, and for no other reason.'

'And he does go, I can assure you,' the officer added in support.

The three of us laughed heartily.

'Yes, but, he'll really *like* the performance,' said Chairman Klimkovitch, attempting to soften the impression made by the political officer's remark, 'since, as we said, it will be excellently produced and directed. We've got good actors, too.'

'Yes, I know,' I admitted.

'And the next day, workers chosen from another factory will go to see it, and so on. This keeps the theatres full all the time. Besides, our theatres being State-owned don't have to worry about a possible deficit in their budget. Thus they can, and must, fulfil their instructive purpose.'

'It's easy to understand why you know so little about all this, but I've heard that you're a talented writer and I'll try to make you one of ours,' the political officer consoled me. 'To-morrow, after the meeting, come and see me so that we can talk at greater length and I'll give you a few hints on how to write in the true Soviet spirit.'

'That's kind of you,' I said, knowing full well I would never make use of his invitation and that the only way out for me was to leave town as quickly as possible.

Champagne goes to the head quickly at the best of times, but when it is drunk on top of other wines and helped along with vodka . . . Toasts. More toasts. Bravo! Shouts and raucous laughter. The political officer drank *Brüderschaft* with the President of the Union, the issuer of lunch-tickets. They became the best of friends. The young official beamed with pride and pleasure, repeatedly shaking the hand of his Soviet protector as though he had discovered a long-lost brother. How was he to know that in less than twenty-four hours, his friend, Comrade Gershman, would thunder at him from the rostrum, brand him a renegade, and personally 'elect' an entirely new executive for the Union?

At the moment, however, no one could foresee the gathering storm-clouds. The band played indefatigably and no less so did the revellers drink. The enterprising poetess plumped down beside the political officer in order, a moment or two later, to land, most politically, on his knee. Colonel Spasov was also managing to amuse himself most dexterously with the young woman beside him. The third officer, not to be outdone by his comrades, had annexed the remaining lady and was noisily kissing her.

Somebody pulled the corner of the table-cloth, bringing the wine-glasses crashing to the floor . . . the tinkle of broken glass . . . a stream of wine . . . the dull thud of apples and oranges falling. . . . Suddenly, the two bulbs on the ceiling went out. They may have fused or been switched off. The band played the 'Cossack.' One of the women began to scream shrilly.

The scene became more and more revolting. It now resembled a film version of a Tsarist officer's orgy in the days when Russia was simply a church, a samovar and a Gipsy romance. All it needed was for somebody to smash the mirrors. If nobody did so the omission was probably due to the fact that there was not a single mirror in the entire hall. I had had enough. Unnoticed, I slipped out to the cloak-room and as I left the hotel the porter bowed low in farewell.

The clock on the tower struck some hour of the night or morning. Full of mayonnaise, my head whirling from the champagne, I hurried stumbling through the empty streets of the strange town—back to my kennel with its palliasse thrown in a dark passage.

My pockets bulged with slices of white bread filched from a literary banqueting table.

*

It is not always easy to raise a sufficiently large sum of money for a journey, especially when it has to be done in a hurry. Owning two overcoats, I decided to sell one. An unusual sort of market had spread itself over the uneven surface of the square, amid sheets of black mud and trampled snow. Immediately beyond the quiet, rural calm surrounding the farm-carts with their loads of yellow straw, where the acrid reek of horses mingled with that of sheepskin coats, there jostled a mob of vociferous traders. This was not the famous black-market where foreign currency, jewellery and passports were bought and sold. Such operations took place in cafés and restaurants. This market was the resort of ordinary people, ruined by the war, who went there to dispose of such things as they still possessed.

Men and women, until recently wealthy, were parting with their last belongings : warm, padded quilts and the pillows from under their heads. Those who, at one time, had made their living by trade of some sort managed, even here, to induce prospective buyers to take their wares at a satisfactory price. Thus, a poverty-stricken but glib salesman, extolling the virtues of an archaic gramophone with a bright blue trumpet, would get a better price for it than the white-haired widow of a professor, shamefacedly holding out a gold fountain-pen. Here everything conceivable was offered for sale, from the last word in luxury articles to the basic necessities of life. It was a deep chasm of squalor and misery, made to seem all the worse by the fact that those who had always known hunger now rubbed shoulders with people who, previously, had wanted for nothing.

The majority of the bargain-hunters belonged to the Red Army; soldiers and officers alike, chiefly on the prowl for wrist-watches. A wrist-watch in Russia is not only a rare phenomenon but also a sign of the highest culture, and consequently an object of pride. Quite frequently, in Russia, a pocket watch is altered and worn on the wrist. It is then strapped on top of the shirt-cuff, while the military wear them on the sleeves of their tunics. After all, evidence of such high civilization should be visible from afar in order to command the respect it deserves.

A luxurious, modern limousine disgorged three Russian girls on the fringe of the market. These women, probably the wives of the eminent persons entitled to the car, were dressed in sheepskin jackets and coats and wore high, peasant boots. Round their heads they had tied flowered kerchiefs, peasant fashion. They drove up to the market with a flourish which the wives of West European millionaires reserve for the best of fashion-houses. They scanned

the riches surrounding them and soon one bought a hat—
a green cap with a large scarlet wing attached. Concealing
her embarrassment with peals of shrill laughter, she tried
it on for size, then paid for it hurriedly and walked away.
She held her acquisition in her hands, lacking the courage
to put it to its proper use by placing it on her head. She
would have felt uncomfortable in it. Not because it was
hideous—after all, she had bought it, so she must have
liked it—but because it was certainly her very first hat.

Not far away, two Army officers were absorbed in a
thermos flask. One of them frankly admitted his conviction that it was a time-bomb. Its owner explained its use
and the officers marvelled greatly. They said they would
gladly buy it, but would never be able to master its in-
tricacies. When they were told that all they needed to do
was to fill it with hot water and screw on the cap, they refused to believe it.

Somebody had brought along a divan, so constructed
that, during the day, the bed-clothes could be placed inside
it as in a large box. An Air Force captain inspected it thoroughly. He said he would like to buy it only he feared that
while he was asleep in the box during the night, the spring
hinges might close and he would be suffocated. On hearing
that, at night, the bed-clothes were meant to be taken out
and spread on top of the divan, the officer replied that if
that was really the case, the material covering the divan
would hardly be of so fine a texture. Taking a look at the
curious crowd which by then surrounded them, the officer
decided that the salesman was making a fool of him by
trying to persuade him that anyone would take bed-clothes
out of a warm box and spread them on top in the cold.
Fearing he might become a laughing-stock if he bought
the thing, he stamped away, red in the face, like a schoolboy on whom the teacher has exercised his sarcasm.

THREE

The Triumph of the Male

The little town, situated close to the Lithuanian border across which thousands crept illegally, was crowded with new arrivals.

I got out of the train, meaning to look for someone to show me the way to an inn or hotel. The hesitation of a newcomer on the emptying platform drew the attention of the militiaman on duty. The slant-eyed sleuth, with a large revolver at his belt, clad in a navy coat and a cap in which crimson and blue were ill-combined, sensed that the stranger was there on no legal business. He bore down upon me.

'What are you after?' he asked.

'An inn.'

'What d'you want an inn for?'

'The usual reasons. I want to sleep in it.'

'Um . . .' He made a wry face. 'I don't like the look of you.'

'You don't have to. I'm not a girl. I don't much care for you either.'

Being in possession of all the necessary papers and hiding nothing illegal, I could well afford to be impertinent to this representative of the law. There was no other way to treat him, anyway. Such a man would have taken a meek demeanour for a sure sign of fear and weakness.

'All your papers in order?' he asked.

'Of course. Do you want to see them?'

'Not me, I don't. Come along!'

It appeared that he had power to arrest people even when their papers were in order. Since that was the case with me, I followed him to the militia post which occupied part of the station building. In the Soviet Union, every railway station has its detachment of militia and a lock-up. Probably for the convenience of passengers.

He led me into a room where I was confronted by the station sergeant, seated at a table.

'He doesn't know what he came here for,' the militia-man reported, indicating me to his superior with a nod of his head.

'That's nice,' the sergeant commented. 'Where have you come from?'

I told him.

'Who've you come to see?'

'My wife.'

'Where is she?'

'Here . . . somewhere.'

'Where does she live?'

'I don't know. I came here to find her.'

'Run away from you?' He waited for me to answer in the affirmative so that he could burst out laughing.

'No. On the contrary. She escaped from Germany and has taken refuge here, I believe.'

'H'm. What's your name?'

I gave him my name.

'Your first name?'

'Tadeusz.'

'Father's name?'

'Antoni.'

'Wife?'

'Sophy.'

'Not her first name! Her second name!'

'Since she's my wife, it must be the same as mine.'

'Got any papers?'

'Yes.'

'Give me them.'

I took out my Writers' certificate and pass. The sergeant, without bothering to read them, laid them in front of him on the desk and weighted them with an ink-pot.

'And what have you got in there?' He pointed to my knapsack.

'What everyone needs on a trip—food and clothes.'

'We shall see.'

I took the sack off my back. The sergeant slipped his hand inside and went over the contents.

'All right,' he admitted, somewhat disappointed. 'But you're not going to get away scot-free. Once you're in here, you don't get out so easily.' He picked up the wooden pen-holder and wiped the nib on the rim of the ink-pot. 'We'll just take down your particulars.'

He tore the two middle pages from a school-type exercise book, separated them, and began to write. At the top, he put the heading in large, printed lettes: PARTICULARS, and with a few figures, immortalized the day, the month, and the year. While absorbed in this task, he raised his cap by the peak several times as though greeting someone, only to scratch his head anxiously.

The militiaman who had brought me there, seeing that his superior had the case well in hand, considered his duty done and went out. The sergeant studied the papers in front of him and asked again:

'What do they call you?'

'Wittlin.'

'Hm . . . yes. Correct.'

Looking at the certificate, he began to copy out, or rather, to sketch out, my surname. He laboured equally hard over my Christian name. The work tired him greatly and he paused frequently to mop the perspiration from his forehead. When he dipped his pen in the ink-pot, prior to copying out my father's name, a large blob fell from the nib on to the paper. The sergeant, with a muttered curse, crumpled the sheet in his fist and threw it under the table. Then he grasped the pen and began anew on the second sheet. Worn out, however, by the first round, he decided to rest awhile and lit a cigarette which he greedily inhaled.

At last he overcame the word PARTICULARS, the date, place and his own name. He then began to struggle with the confession of the accused.

'Well, how was it?'

'How was what?'

'What brought you here?'

'A militiaman brought me. I had no wish to come here at all.'

'I know that! But what have you come to this town about?'

'I'm looking for my wife. I heard she was in this neighbourhood, only I don't know the exact address.'

'Wait a minute! Not so fast!'

And, dictating the words to himself, he wrote: 'The arrested party admits that he is looking for his wife because he does not know where she is.'

He lifted his hand, pen and all, to scratch his ear when, from the nib, another sombre drop slowly detached itself and fell, like a pigeon's visiting-card, on the paper below. That was too much. The sergeant swore drastically and flung the ball of crumpled paper at the opposite wall like a boy trying to smash a neighbour's window with a snowball. A moment later, he opened the exercise book once again to tear out two more pages but, struck by their virgin whiteness, he grew sorrowful at the thought of the sad fate by which they were threatened. He raised his eyes from the precious paper to look at me, the direct cause of this waste of valuable stationery. Then he shouted furiously:

'So you want a wife! Perhaps I'm to go and hunt out a wife for you? Get out of here, you!'

He jumped off his chair, thrust the papers into my hands and, catching me by the collar, propelled me towards the door, as though I were unwilling to leave of my own free will.

'Out of it! You bastard!' He was shaking with sudden fury.

He dragged me from the room and, although I was far from offering resistance, but doing everything possible to hasten our departure, he would not let go my collar till we were right outside in the snow.

'Looking for a wife, eh? And that's a reason for bothering the militia and interfering with important work? I'll show you!'

In an empty, snow-covered field, he told me in a voice of thunder to go to hell. And, turning round, he stormed back to his office.

In the frost-bound, snow-clad countryside, I stood alone. Free.

The little town had only one inn and this was, of course, filled to overflowing. I was in luck, however, for a guest was leaving that night. Promising to return later, I set out along the snow-covered street in the direction of the peasant Konarenko's cottage which passers-by pointed out to me. After knocking on the window, I had to wait several minutes before an old woman opened the door. In reply to my enquiry about the whereabouts of Konarenko, she reluctantly told me that he was out and said she had no idea when he would be back. I left a message for him to come and see me at the inn. The old woman muttered something under her breath and hastily withdrew, slamming the door.

The snow had an icy hardness and the frost, so sharp that it stung like fire, settled on my eyebrows and lashes, restricting my vision. I had to rub my nose and ears really hard to avoid being painfully frost-bitten.

I got to the inn and found that there was, in fact, room for me. The proprietress, a young, good-looking, jolly woman, was forthright in manner.

'I'm alone all day, as my husband works away from home,' she said, placing before me a glass of hot tea.

Her laughing eyes twinkled with health, fun and mischief, but lest I should misunderstand her, she hastily added:

'These stockings, now . . .' she stretched out a leg, 'that kerchief and a lot of other things besides were given to me by Russian officers. Love, free of charge, is all right for nightingales,' she ended philosophically, proving thereby that, although she had probably never read Marx, she was nevertheless a sworn materialist. A young sergeant with a mandolin walked in, smiled at the woman, gave me a friendly nod and sat down on the bed. Shortly afterwards, two other soldiers arrived. They did nothing in any way to conceal their obvious intimacy with our hostess.

The woman fixed the samovar and boiled some water for tea. Then the door opened again to admit a frontier guard with the face of a morose criminal. He seated himself on a stool between the bed and the cupboard and looked at me with distrust.

'When did you arrive?' he asked casually.

'This morning.'

'Staying long?'

'That depends.'

'On what?'

'On whether I find my wife who escaped from Germany and is living round here.'

'What's her name?'

On hearing it, he shook his head. He knew of no one of that name in the neighbourhood.

'What does she do for a living?'

'She's a school-teacher.'

The frontier guard shook his head again.

'What does she look like?'

I took a photo of a well-known actress from my wallet and held it out.

'Hm . . . she's all right,' he admitted.

The soldiers drew closer to look at the picture over the frontier guard's shoulder.

'Your wife?' asked the sergeant.

'Yes.'

'Not bad. But fancy coming such a long way to find her . . . what a fool!' He shrugged his shoulders. 'A wife never gets lost unless she wants to. Then no power on earth will find her. Is it worth while to freeze on the road and lose good money on her account? Have you the least idea where she is?'

'I've been told she's somewhere around this town.'

'Somewhere around! And if she's not here, what then?'

'I'll go back to where I came from. I work there.'

'Did you get special leave?'

'Yes, a few days.'

'To find your woman?'

'Yes.'

'What a fool you are! There's other fish. . . .'

'Yes, but you see I happen to love her.'

'She's very pretty.' It was the young hostess who spoke in support of me. She had also been looking at the photograph.

'There's plenty of pretty ones,' replied the sergeant, unable to understand how a man could devote time and money to finding someone he merely loved.

The samovar roared like a steam-engine. The soldiers set about the hot tea and began rolling tobacco in scraps of newspaper. The sergeant started strumming on his mandolin. When dusk fell they went off to get their dinner at the Army cook-house.

It was already dark when a sallow-faced man in a black sheepskin coat entered the inn.

'I'm Konarenko,' he roared at no one in particular. Then he greeted the hostess, as an old neighbour.

'Good, evening,' I said. 'I went round to see you this morning.'

'I know. My wife told me. That's why I'm here.'

We went outside, where we could talk more freely.

'Some friends gave me your address,' I said. We stood on an empty road running through snow-swept fields.

'Were you thinking of going to-night?'

'If possible.'

'Will you pay a hundred roubles?' he asked, looking at me out of the corner of his eye.

It was no use bargaining.

'Yes. I'll pay.'

'Wait outside the chemist's at ten o'clock. D'you know where it is?'

'No, but I'll find out.'

At the agreed hour I waited as arranged. My guide soon arrived.

'Got the money?' was his first remark. I gave him the grey-black note with its likeness of Lenin. He stuffed it in his quilted coat and we set off.

We trudged across the hard, lumpy surface of a frozen field, then turned down a forest path. The guide asked the time. It was close to eleven. We had to wait awhile. It would be easier to slip past the sentry posts at midnight while the guard was being changed.

We lit cigarettes under our coats and, shading the glow with our hands, inhaled the smoke. An infinity of time dragged past. There was nothing to talk about. We nipped the glowing ends off of our cigarettes and moved on. As we hurried along, our breath made grey clouds in the frosty air. Our route took us uphill and breathing became difficult. The guide reached out for my sack.

'Give it to me. It's hard going, here. I'll help you with it,' he kindly offered.

'No, thanks. I'll manage.'

'It's all right. I'll take it for a bit, then you can have it back.'

I let him have it, deciding to keep close enough to him to prevent him from running away with it. But Konarenko was not contemplating theft. 'That'll be easier for you now,' he said. All of a sudden an unpleasant feeling came over me: it was as though by taking my sack the peasant was seeking to bind me to him. We made our way slowly through thick woods. The heavy, biting frost made such going particularly difficult and we had to stop and rest.

'Another kilometre and I'll take you there, straight as
a die,' whispered the guide, breathing the cold air deeply.

We recovered our breath a little and set off once
more. Coming out of a forest of tall pines, we struck off
along a well-trodden, winding path. It led us to a clearing
in which a small hut, like an ice-safe or a pitch-burner's
dwelling, half buried in the earth, loomed through the
darkness. It was too late to withdraw. Konarenko had kept
his word. He had led me over, straight as a die—and into
a post of Soviet frontier police.

*

I was arrested by the guards, taken to a large sunken
shed and locked inside. In the darkness, I tripped over a
body. More than two hundred people, men and women,
many of whom had been there for days, were sitting on
the hard-trodden earth floor. They received neither food
nor water from the guards, who simply collected people
in that building until the total number was sufficiently
large for them to be sent to the main prison in the town.
My guide, Konarenko, was well known. At one time he
had been a perfectly decent man. Indeed, until he was
caught he had carried out the duties of frontier guide
most conscientiously. When, however, his captors realized
that the peasant's profession was smuggling people over
the line, they had immediately separated him from the
group which he led, tortured him and then released him on
condition that henceforth he should work for them. A
refusal, they pointed out, would mean prison for him and
instant deportation of his wife and child to Siberia. On
the other hand, for every would-be refugee delivered up
they would pay him ten roubles. He had little choice.

At dawn, the sergeant unbarred the door and called

out several names, amongst them my own. We were
formed up in line and marched off under the supervision
of two soldiers, one in front and one behind. The latter
held his rifle and bayonet at the 'on guard' position, almost touching the back of the last prisoner who only
needed to slip in the snow to be effectively impaled. Such
was my return to the little town I had left that morning.
I no sooner found myself lodged in a crowded cell than I
was called to the office for questioning. There I found an
officer with a soldier standing beside him. The latter went
skilfully through my pockets, removing my wallet and
fountain-pen. I was asked for a few personal details, as
I had been at the frontier-post, and was then led back to
the cell. In the evening, I was again taken to the office.
The stove was red-hot and the air was stifling. The officer
was sitting without a coat. In the breast-pockets of his
tunic he had a dozen or so fountain-pens, as though they
were the cartridges of a Cossack in national dress. Having
read aloud the formal statement of my arrest and the
recommendation that I should be imprisoned, he ordered
me to sign it. I took the office pen and attempted to scrawl
my name on the document, but my efforts were in vain.
The nib was broken and did no more than scratch the
paper. Losing patience, the officer tore one of the confiscated pens from his pocket and handed it to me with a
flourish. I took it, knowing that it would function irre-
proachably; the pen, until quite recently, had been mine.
I had not suspected, however, that I should use it for
the last time to sign the order for my own imprisonment.

   The Soviet Union is a land wherein dwells the greatest respect for the liberty of the individual. No sentence
of imprisonment, deportation to the labour-camps of Siberia, or execution can be inflicted without the voluntary

consent of the accused. It is an interesting fact that never yet has such consent been withheld.

That is, indeed, the height of liberty.

*

I was taken to the prison and placed in a spacious, though very crowded, room from which every so often people were conducted to the adjoining office to be searched. This operation was performed by a soldier in a blue and white striped apron, tied at the back. He was a tall man, powerfully built, and in this garment resembled an attendant in the homicidal section of a lunatic asylum.

We went in two at a time, carrying all we possessed. In the room stood two tables placed against opposite walls. Behind one of these sat a sergeant who took down personal details on a dirty grey proforma. There we stood in the centre of the room, like star turns at a cabaret, while the soldier in the blue and white apron relieved us of our bundles, boxes or suitcases. He emptied the contents and sorted them carefully. Rags, papers, string, medicines and food were flung on a heap in the corner. Next came a more personal search. Money, watches, cigarette-cases and rings had to be tied up in a handkerchief and placed on the floor. The searcher turned out all the pockets of the hapless delinquent, took his braces or belt and then, with a large clasp-knife, removed all the buttons from his trousers and jacket. The prisoner had then to strip naked and throw his shoe-laces on the pile of rubbish in the corner. Crucifixes and medallions were ripped from around the owners' necks and joined the laces. When at last a man stood literally stripped of all he possessed, the soldier carefully inspected the palms of his hands, on the look-out for trifles, ordered him to raise both arms above his head, then to open his mouth so that the soldier could look at his teeth and underneath his tongue, holding the victim's head clasped in his hands. Finally, the prisoner was ordered to turn round, do a 'knees-bend' and, in that position, to hop forward, frog-like, for a couple of paces. The performance concluded with this item, the purpose of which I need hardly indicate. Before, however, an order was given to dress and march down the long corridor back to the cells, the prisoner had to present himself at the second table and deposit his valuables for safe keeping. Still mother-naked, he approached the table with his handkerchief bundle. Behind it sat a young woman, her thick dark hair pinned in a neat crown above her smooth forehead. In front of her, the naked man had to count out his money and spread the articles in his handkerchief before obtaining a receipt. The men approached her humbly, taking the receipts as though accepting their death-warrants.

It was a cold, bright morning. Outside the window, the black branches of leafless trees swung up and down. The woman gazed at the line of naked men, like a barbarian queen on her throne estimating the value of slaves brought before her. The silence in the room was heavy and stifling as that of some medieval mystery portraying the degradation of Man.

Only Ignatius, an athletic taxi-driver, felt quite at ease. He was more naked than the others since he had not even a handkerchief for his belongings. In his hand he held a few bank-notes and his wrist-watch. He sauntered up to the pitiless woman and, nodding pleasantly, presented her with his watch and money. Then, giving his hairy thigh a resounding slap and in no wise concealing his masculinity, he said with a broad and uninhibited laugh:

'Not bad, eh?'

The woman bit her lip and lowered her head.

The male had triumphed.

FOUR

Long Live the Jail!

'She's too old and scraggy. I won't buy a woman like that. I want value for my money—a young, pretty, full-bosomed girl. Her legs must be strong and thick,' said Balonis, the bandit, looking at the drawing.

For some time, I had been earning extra slices of bread by doing sketches for anyone wishing to be tattooed.

In prison, people tattooed themselves for pleasure, by way of a souvenir or out of boredom. Illiterates and intellectuals alike covered their skin with pictures, though the latter, as a rule, confined themselves to the date of their arrest, while the former carefully selected drawings for reproduction on the arms, chest or back—even on the stomach and less accessible places. The most popular designs comprised crosses, anchors, swords, serpents and Adam and Eve. Sailing-ships were also in great demand, though less so than the profile of a girl or the portrait of a nude woman with disordered hair.

The ink required to fix the design permanently on the skin was prepared from a solution of charred thread and the lead of an indelible pencil, ground to a fine powder. This compound was diluted in water, sugar added, and the mixture heated over a fire-place made from a piece of tin. Unfortunately, it was by no means easy to light a fire. If someone had managed to smuggle in a match, it could be split lengthwise into four, thus providing us with a quadruple chance of success. If, however, not even a quarter match was available, other means had to be used. There were two methods in vogue. The first required the sacrifice of a match in order to burn a piece of cloth. The charred material was reduced to powder and preserved in pots, specially modelled from dried bread. Despite the closest scrutiny, someone always managed to bring in a metal button. The latter would be threaded on to a string, and now the only other piece of equipment required was a porcelain shell. This was not hard to come by, for we had only to break the fitting which held the electric light bulb in each cell. Next in the process of bringing flame down to earth, the modern Prometheus and his assistant would take hold of the string at each end and spin the button as fast as possible, while a third man held the porcelain and the receptacle with the powdered thread. The metal would strike sparks from the porcelain and presently the powder would catch fire. It was then a simple matter to light a cigarette or a piece of straw.

There were amongst us experts whose cigarettes would glow after only two or three sparks had been struck.

The second method of producing fire consisted in taking a long wad of cotton wool and winding a second layer round it, then a third and so on until the stock was exhausted. The wool was then placed under a wooden board which was moved backwards and forwards on the floor using the wad as a roller. This was continued for some time—a back-breaking business. When eventually the wads of cotton wool were torn open, they would probably be alight at the very centre. This system, however, offered no guarantee of success and was only resorted to in the event of the materials needed for the first method not being available.

If a tattoo was required, the customer would lie down on the floor and the artist would place a piece of cloth with the design chosen, on his bare flesh. The design was then pricked out with three needles tied together and dipped in the solution of lead and ash. The next day, the punctures swelled alarmingly and had to be soothed with a cold-water compress. Cases of blood-poisoning, however, were extremely rare, thus proving the old adage that hygiene is no more than a bourgeois superstition and a clever stunt on the part of crafty chemists anxious to boost completely unnecessary disinfectants.

*

Years before, Yurko Warotnik, a young Ukrainian from the rolling uplands east of the Carpathians, had trained to become an assistant preacher of the Orthodox Church. Seduced by the Marxist credo, however, he had abandoned his studies and turned into an idealistic Communist. Stalin, for that matter, had begun his career in a similar fashion. Warotnik found himself in prison as a result of a drunken escapade. He richly deserved to be there and was the first to admit it. On his way to the prison he had rejoiced at the thought of those he would meet inside. As a good Communist, he knew the kind of people the Soviet authorities locked up—and why. When he entered the cell, he looked triumphantly at those present, much as a trainer might stand in a cage of wild animals tamed by himself. He no sooner beheld the assembly, however, than his face expressed boundless disillusion. A moment later, spying a vacant space on the floor, he asked quietly if he might occupy it and, permission having been granted, seated himself most humbly.

'I thought,' he later admitted, 'that I'd find the place full of generals, bishops and aristocrats, but they're all just like me—poor peasants and working men.'

'Maybe they've put you in the wrong cell,' somebody jokingly consoled him. 'But don't let it worry you, there's a few intellectuals here, too. Though only by accident, you know. Got in like yourself—drunkenness.'

It caused him no great delight to find that those present included a few school-teachers, a village scribe and other dignitaries of a small community. They were not princes or even millionaires. True, he could raise his spirits a little by regarding them as 'intellectuals,' a word which had come to mean something ultra-contemptible, used not only by the hardened criminals, who considered themselves lords of the cells, but also by the very judges who condemned them. It was scant consolation, however, to apply it to a village school-teacher or the secretary of a petty administrator. When one of the hundreds of roll-calls was in progress, Warotnik would push his way to the front and shout with pride:

'My hands are black with earth! I'm a working peasant!'

'What the hell are you shouting about,' the authority present would silence him. 'You're in the same boat as the rest of them! You're all equals in jail.'

This would subdue Warotnik slightly, but not for long. In no time at all he would subject us to a peroration in which he expresed his delight at the thought that those who had once found life pleasant would find it so no more. Besides that, he was deeply interested in the question of beds. There were twenty of them in the cell. They stood in two rows of ten, tightly pressed together against opposite walls. There were two beds between five men. Between the two rows was a narrow strip of floor on which the prisoners would stroll up and down in the day-time and on which those for whom there was no room in or under the beds would sleep at night. The part-owner of a bed was described as 'sleeping like a king,' while he who curled up underneath, where he was beyond the dazzle of the electric light bulbs, was rated a dormitory count. The possession of a place on or under a bed depended entirely upon seniority. The last arrival invariably occupied the corner by the door, beside the slop bucket which was not always hermetically sealed. As men were removed for transportation, trial or when they died, their places were taken by the next in line. The beds were occupied by those who flooded the prisons when the first wave of arrests struck the country: moderately wealthy owners of small property or medium-scale enterprises, arrested as capitalists. Picked up in their homes, they had been able to bring with them suits, overcoats, bed-linen, quilts and pillows.

Against these exploiters of the people, Warotnik directed his hatred of the nobility and the rich.

'Even here in jail,' he would shout, as we were settling down for the night, 'a poor worker and a peasant has to lie in the worst corner while people who did nothing but sleep in beds all their lives carry on enjoying the same comforts! But if *they* took the beds yesterday, *we* can do the same to-day!' he cried to the White Russian and Ukrainian peasants in his vicinity.

At first they listened to him in indifferent silence. Then, noting the lack of self-defence on the part of the bed-owners, they gave him their attention. Soon, several others joined in support of their self-appointed leader until, finally, the class-hatred of the poor devils sleeping on the floor grew so painfully vociferous as to portend revolution.

One evening, as the kings were making their beds and

the counts were crawling under them, Warotnik gave his rebels the signal which indicated that the hour had come. The revolutionaries hurled themselves on the privileged bed-sleepers and began to expel them. The coup, secretly prepared for several days, was sudden and unexpected. Encouraging each other with loud cries, the invaders struck out at their foes like a horde of Cossacks. The room shook with ferocious yells and the chaos of flying mattresses, clothes and blankets. The battle was so furious that the rattle of bolts went unnoticed, likewise the appearance on the threshold of the orderly and the guard. The sergeant had to shout several times before anyone paid attention.

'Citizen sergeant! We're being driven out of the places we've been in for the last six months!' cried one of the victims, sure that the guard would side with him.

'Them intellectuals are sleeping just like they was still at home! Now it's our turn to lie on the beds!' said Warotnik, stating his case. He was speaking his own Ruthenian dialect and speaking moreover in the name of the Ukrainian peasants, while his opponents were Poles and Jews, knowing little Russian—and besides that, intellectuals.

The verdict was a foregone conclusion.

'Well, if they've had the beds for so long, they can give them up for a bit, and you take them over,' the sergeant decreed.

This decision was final and not only irrevocable but requiring immediate implementation. At once, a migration took place. Old men, sick men or people who simply couldn't adapt themselves to the conditions of life in prison, removed their belongings and gave up their beds in dumb silence, as though surrendering a fallen city to a victorious enemy. Soon the beds were occupied by the conquerors, sated with victory, while the disinherited spent many long

minutes arranging their mattresses, coats, quilts and bed-
clothes on the floor. At midnight peace was restored till
next morning and all snored as soundly as usual.

Next day, Warotnik's forces savored total triumph,
sneering at the unfortunate bourgeois, deprived of their
beds not only by main force but by virtue of the authorities
who had sided with the victims of oppression.

Many of Warotnik's cohort confessed that they had
never before slept in a bed. The conquest was thus complete and even possessed a truly Marxist class-colouring,
in as much as those who had never had a bed before, had
now, under Soviet rule and albeit in a prison cell, finally
achieved this distinction.

Unfortunately, the revolutionaries did not foresee
that their defeated adversaries would strip the beds of all
their possessions and leave only the bare frames. In de-
fault of a blanket and pillow, it is far easier to sleep on a
floor, no matter how hard, than with steel springs biting
into one's flesh.

After a few nights, the unhappy conquerors rose
from their beds as though from the rack. Yet they were
ashamed to acknowledge defeat. With the stubborn ob-
stinacy of the peasant, they kept resolutely silent, lying
down each evening on their beds of torture, as though
suffering punishment, in the hope that they might get used
to them. But the iron bars and sharp springs grew more
unbearable with every hour that passed. The poor victors,
pale and wan through sleeplessness, could rest only in the
daytime and on the floor. It was not hard to guess that
they were striving to make up for the sleepless nights of
agony. Soon some of them began making overtures to the
erstwhile inhabitants of that devilish contraption known
as a bed. With cunning smiles, and in the most friendly
manner, they dropped broad hints that, in exchange for a

quarter-ration of bread per day, they would be willing to revert to the *status quo*. But the kings and counts, having swiftly adjusted themselves to the fresh conditions, were unwilling to forgo valuable bread in an attempt to regain beds from which they had been ejected by order of the prison guards. So the new aristocracy continued to suffer nocturnal tortures. The only one to do well for himself was their leader, Warotnik. For the price of one cigarette, he gave up his bed to a newcomer who had only recently joined our community. As a result of this transaction, although he had now to sleep by the door, he could not only stretch his aching limbs but smoke into the bargain.

This was too much even for the White Russian peasants, who now burned with resentment against their former leader. All that was now needed was a chance word to fire the swelling powder-hold of envy.

One day the long-suffering peasants threw themselves on Warotnik and beat him unconscious. It was not clear why. He might have received a larger bread-ration than the others one morning, or something of that sort.

*

Ivan Fiodorov was a poor White Russian peasant who came one day from his village by sledge to visit the market. By sheer bad luck he stopped to look at a drunken brawl and was arrested by mistake together with those taking part. He landed in jail where he chanced to occupy the space next to myself.

When he was questioned, he said he was only an accidental witness and was promised a speedy release, though he was told he would have to stay under lock and key until the whole matter was cleared up. So it came about that Ivan spent six months in prison with no idea how many more lay in store for him. It was apparently taking some time to establish his identity in the neighbouring village.

One morning, however, the guard came into the cell and shouted:

'Fiodorov!'

We all thought it strange that he hadn't called for all whose initial was 'F' to give their names, and then said, 'It's you,' when Fiodorov pronounced his, for this was the normal procedure in Soviet jails, the object being to avoid accidentally naming prisoners in some other cell.

'Here!' roared Fiodorov, elbowing his way through the crowd.

'Pick up your kit and get moving. You're to be let out,' the guard informed him, beaming in anticipation of some show of enthusiasm from the prisoner.

Ivan's peasant countenance betrayed not the slightest sign of elation. He received the news with complete indifference.

'It'll be time for dinner in an hour,' he said slowly, scratching behind his ear, 'so by right you owe me a ration of soup for to-day. I've got to build up my strength with a fourteen-kilometre walk ahead of me.'

The guard opened his eyes and mouth wide in amazement. It was not often that anyone was released from jail in the Soviet Union and never yet in the whole history of socialist incarceration had anyone failed to seize hold of the opportunity with the minimum delay.

'Yes, all right. You're entitled to it,' said the guard recovering his speech, 'and you will get it.'

So saying he shrugged and left the cell with head hanging and a look of utter depression on his face.

Ivan, with typical peasant thoroughness, set about quietly preparing for his departure. He packed his belongings and beat the dust out of his jacket. While he was doing so, a number of his fellow prisoners, far more excited by the unusual procedure than Ivan himself, were giving him the addresses of their families with instructions to get in touch with them and ask for parcels to be sent, which would prove conclusively whether or not Ivan was really a free man. Nobody believed what the guard had said, nobody, that is, except Ivan. (The parcels which began to arrive shortly afterwards put the matter beyond all doubt.)

An hour later, we heard the scrape of the soup-bin being dragged along the corridor. Carrying a full mess-tin of soup Ivan returned to his place with his usual unhurried steps, sat down on his blanket, undid his shirt so as not to be too hot while eating, and then systematically set about 'building up his strength' with mouthfuls of soup and bread. Finally he wiped the sweat from his face with his sleeve—for the soup was hot and the room very stuffy —dressed himself properly, shook hands all round and knocked on the door. The jailer's eye appeared at the peep-hole.

'You can tell the sergeant that I've finished eating and I'm ready to go,' Ivan announced in a toneless voice. 'You can set me free now, if you wish.'

The door opened and Ivan Fiodorov, the White Russian peasant who was not going to sacrifice food—albeit a meal of watery soup in jail—having had his dinner, walked out a free man, in gracious accordance with the desire of the Soviet prison authorities.

*

Someone was singing a popular Soviet song, 'Far Are the Boundaries of My Native Land!' When he came to the verse beginning, 'I know of no other land like ours where a man can breathe so freely . . .' the cell shook with jeering laughter while foul imprecations were hurled at the singer. The unfortunate songster was silent. This song, one of the best known in the Soviet Union, is transmitted by radio even to the condemned in the labour camps of Siberia. Once, even, the bitter frost failed to deter some miserable deportee who, tearing off one of his boots, flung it at the loud-speaker on its tall mast. The loud-speaker, struck full in its gaping mouth by the well-aimed missile, was silenced on that occasion as quickly as our singing prisoner on this.

The cell grew comparatively quiet, allowing one to reflect on freedom in a country where the labour-camps are filled with the innocent and where a man who dies in prison is spoken of as having been set free.

'You'll find real liberty in the Soviet Union only behind bars,' said Popov, a grey-haired Russian professor from the University of Leningrad. 'Because here we can all say what we think—about our government, our system, our politics and our justice. The fact that in every cell there's a spy and an informer doesn't matter; there's one here too. Let him inform. That's what he's paid for—to rot in prison and be eaten alive by lice. We have to suffer these conditions, but he does it for pleasure. Everyone to his taste. One man likes planting roses in his garden, another likes sitting in jail, listening to what other people say. Anyway, it does nobody much harm—the Soviet conception of justice is like a laboratory funnel; easy way in, no way out. So if they give you another ten years, it makes no difference. One way or another, you'll never leave this place or regain your freedom. On the other hand, you can say what you like in here and you're sure of to-morrow. If you go to the wash-house, you know you'll return. If they call you to the store, you can ask a comrade to look after your things till you get back and you know you'll be seeing them again in a little while. The same goes for trips to the steam baths or when they take you out for exercise. When you're outside and free, you may say to your wife: "Darling, will you wait ten minutes with lunch? I'll just hop out and get some matches." But if you happen to moan in the shop because the matches are no good and won't light, the chances are your wife will need a lot of patience because you probably won't be back for ten years. Similarly, you never know when your son will get back from the public baths or your daughter from her walk. You can never make an appointment and be sure of keeping it. Yes, in the Soviet Union, a prison is really the home of liberty and security. Long live the jail!'

And, parodying the recent vocal rendering, he sang:

'I know of no other land like ours where a man lives so free in jail. . . .'

FIVE

When the Sailor Ate the Black Queen

Serge was a squat, sturdy Russian, broader than he was long. He spoke so little as to appear almost dumb. He had a powerful chest, like a paving-stone, tattooed with blue profiles of Engels, Lenin and Stalin, circumscribed by a life-belt bearing the legend: 'Long live the Red Fleet.' His thick, muscular, pylon-like arms were covered with slogans no less topical. Everyone thought of him as a sailor, but no one knew for certain. It sufficed that he was neither a thug nor a thief and never assaulted anybody. He lived and slept under a bed like a mole in his hill, coming to the surface for food and crawling back to his lair once his mess-can was filled. He never even showed his head during the morning or evening roll-calls, assuring the guard of his continued existence merely by calling out his name. He took no part, of course, in our communal life, our games or discussions. Anyway, hunger and the painful questioning which some of us had undergone, had long since robbed us of the wish to joke, discuss or listen. Food became the only subject of our conversation—what we once used to eat and what we were eating nowadays. Many a poor peasant admitted that, on his farm, the pigs ate better than he did here and that he would now gladly eat what once he had given to his dog. More and more frequently men, like hungry wolves, would throw themselves on one another in impotent fury. Quarrels, fights and rows were constantly breaking out. The fights were always of short duration. The opponents, weak with hunger, had no strength for protracted combats but, after three or four mutually-delivered blows, would totter back to their belongings and rest on them, pale and trembling. The blood which flowed from noses and cut lips was the colour of weak tea. The bigger and stronger the man the sooner he was exhausted. It stands to reason that a big man needs more than a slice of bread. For that bread, men traded their clothes, boots and shirts, remaining clad only in grubby loin-cloths. But that was a short-term policy. Deprived of all their belongings, they were soon reeling round the cell as weak with hunger as the misers who, having denied themselves bread, were seated on sacks full of clothes.

Maddening apathy was induced by hunger, worry about the fate of relatives, recollections of home and the terrible boredom. Men tried to find an escape and to kill time by playing chess. The making of a chess-set, however, called for a great deal of work and self-denial, since the material used was more precious than gold. To manufacture a complete set, a whole loaf of bread was required. This constituted an immense sacrifice. The loaf was divided in two, half for the black pieces and half for the white. The soft parts were then carefully separated from the crust, which could be eaten. The bread was damp and greyish—too dark to make white chess-men and too light for black. When preparing the material for a white set, the sculptor would work the dough between his hands, and moisten it with spittle. After that, he dipped it in whitewash scraped off the wall. A black set required the burning of a rag and the inclusion of the charred remnants in the moistened dough. In the cell where I lived, the expert in the production of chess-men was Eric, a turner from Silesia. He executed orders for chess-men of many types, Indian, Chinese or Polish. His tools were the beautifully preserved nails of his two index-fingers. The production of the figures involved great ceremony. Eric begrudged his customers neither whitewash from the wall nor ash from the burnt rags, as he kneaded the bread long and thoroughly in hands which, probably for artistic reasons, he never washed. Certainly, the dough, when caressed by hands so long unsullied by soap and water, absorbed their dirt which helped to lend to the finished product the sable hue of incorruptible ebony. When all was prepared, Eric would set about his task with extreme seriousness. A Chinese set had beautifully turned dragons in place of knights, the Queen held a large umbrella, while the coolie-like pawns in their wide round hats wore neatly plaited pigtails. An Indian set had elephants, domed palaces instead of castles and a royal pair in the form of a Maharaja and his Ranee. A Polish set had galloping riders, a King with a crown on his head and soldiers in the uniforms of the early nineteenth century Duchy of Warsaw. When made, the chess-men were allowed to dry for several days, till they became hard as ivory. A chess-board, sketched out on cloth with an indelible pencil, and a bag made from the leg of an old pair of underpants and which could be drawn shut with a ribbon, were included by the artist to complete the set. All this cost two rations of bread, apart from that supplied by the customer as material for his order. The chess-men were so beautifully made that even the greatest misers and the most hungry among us ordered them, whether or not we knew the game. We played with them

in corners like small boys with lead soldiers. Everyone
wanted to keep a set as a souvenir to take home when
once he was set free, though the vision of release, home
and freedom became every day more misty, more unreal.
With everyone in possession of chess-men, however, interest in the game developed rapidly. Not only did veteran
players who knew the game from happier days now devote
their waking hours to the pastime, but there arose large
numbers of converts. Among the hundred or more inhabitants of the cell, blossomed much new talent. Pupils
who, but a short time before, could not distinguish the
moves of a knight from those of a castle, now defeated
their instructors.

Soon the magic of chess had us all in its power. There
were no more rows, fights or quarrels; pain and hunger
were forgotten as we all played chess—in the corners, on
the beds and under them. Down went the barriers which
had hitherto divided us into groups according to nationality, religion or social status. A murderer played with an
artist, a Russian with a Pole, a Jew with a priest. The ad-
vent of chess brought with it a period verging on bliss.

The days now flowed by, calm and peaceful and, had
it not been for our ever-sharpening hunger, our situation
would have been almost ideal. The soup we got for lunch
was simply hot water with a few grains of barley thrown
in. The soup for supper was again hot water with a few
fish-bones, while the bread was damp and only half baked.
The men began to look fat and swollen with unnaturally
rounded faces and deep folds under the eyes. They were
simply swelling with hunger. Weak gums bled at every bite
they took and the generous ration of salt caused running
sores to break out on their puffed legs. The prisoners lay
flat during the entire day, moving only at the sound of the
food-bins outside or when called to the wash-house.

One night a strange crunching noise was heard. Subdued and spasmodic at first, it persisted and grew in intensity. The men woke up and raised their heads to listen. In the yellow light, the rows of uplifted, waxen faces gave the impression of the dead awakening in a grave-yard from which the surface had suddenly been removed, like a metal lid.

'Mouse,' said someone. 'Rat,' another corrected.

A few took their boots from under their heads and began to hammer on the concrete floor. The crunching, however, continued, gaining strength and becoming quicker, louder and greedier. Shouting and hand-clapping was of no avail. At last, one man picked up the handle of the broom in the corner and crept in the general direction of the visiting rodent. Grasping the pole like a soldier with an out-thrust bayonet, he bent down and looked under the bed.

In his lair, curled up like a cave-man, sat Serge. In front of him lay an open bag of chess-men, while he himself was gnawing wildly at the stone-hard figures.

'My chess-men!' yelled Eric, failing to find at the bottom of his bundle his most beautiful creation: white Spanish colonists and an African village.

He leapt from his bed and with a single stride had reached Serge's cave. Thrusting a long lean arm under the bed, he pulled out a purple-checked handkerchief chess-board together with his collection. He was only just in time. All the pawns and other pieces were there, with the exception of a buxom, jet-black Queen who was fast disappearing between the cannibalistic jaws of the sailor.

*

My nearest neighbour not only understood nothing that was said to him, but also nothing that went on around him. The nightmare reality of a Soviet prison is not easily grasped by the mentality of a Briton. This man was English, born in Manchester, by trade a driver. His name was Edward Baldwin. As a sergeant in the B.E.F., he was captured by the Germans in France and taken to a P.O.W. camp in Poland. It was not easy to escape from a camp like that, but, somehow, Baldwin managed to slip through the barbed wire to freedom. By day he lay low in woods and barns. At night he marched East. Always East, making his way by the stars, the bark of the trees and finally with the help of a cheap compass which he bought in a village store. The peasants he came across did not understand him, but they gave him what they could. And so at last he reached the River Bug, meaning to cross into the Russian occupation zone, where he hoped to be given asylum by the Russians and eventually sent back to England. The naïve Baldwin did not know that the Russians have their own peculiar way of looking at these things. Caught while crossing the border, he was accused of espionage and thrown in prison.

They flung him into our cell during the night. The black and white room, filled with the bodies of sleeping men, looked like a wood-cut of Dante's 'Inferno.' The soldier's wide eyes gleamed with terror. He did not answer any of the questions thrown at him but simply stood there as though paralysed.

'Deaf . . .' said someone.

'. . . and dumb,' another voice added.

'English,' mumbled the Sergeant, taut with fear.

'What's that? English? Well, I'll be . . . How did you get here?'

I took him by the arm and led him to my corner. He sat down, smiling his gratitude.

Thereafter, we struck up a friendship and he became

my English-teacher. Lectures began in the morning after breakfast. The Sergeant used an entirely new version of the direct method, without text-book, pen or paper. We had just finished conjugating the verb 'to have,' when he took off his shoe.

'What is this?'

'This is a shoe,' I answered.

'Yes.'

The teacher then removed a fragrant sock and, waving it under my nose, asked:

'What is this?'

'This is a sock.'

'All right.'

He turned the sock inside out and began removing the troublesome little lice. Seeing my teacher thus engaged, I promptly pulled the shirt off my back and saying, 'What is this? This is a shirt,' followed his example.

We were working away like this when the door opened to admit the orderly with a piece of paper in his hand. He was at once surrounded by an uneasy crowd. It could only be one of two things—trial or transportation. The orderly would shoot a name like a bullet into the crowd and depart with the stricken victim. Like a hawk watching a flock of birds, he hovered above the prisoners waiting to sink a few words, talon-like, in the chosen creature and carry him off. The iron doors would no sooner shut than the usual questions and doubts would be voiced. What's he gone for? Release? Siberia? Death? Or maybe he's only been moved to another cell in the very same prison?

The guard drew his eyes over the tense assembly and shouted:

'Edward Edwardovitch Baldwin.'

I nudged my friend.

'Sir!' shouted the Sergeant in his English parade-ground voice.

'Pick up your stuff and follow me!'

Edward 'Edwardovitch' Baldwin, driver from Manchester and sergeant in the British Army, did not grasp the meaning of the particular Russian words, but he understood their portent. He fastened all his home-made tunic-buttons, sewn on by himself, and, thrusting his way to the door, threw us a final:

'Good-bye, boys!'

The door shut behind him. All this took place in March, 1941, in a building which, intended as a monastery, had been adapted by the Soviets for a purpose more in keeping with the times.

When, a few years later, I became editor of an Army periodical published by the British Ministry of Information, I wrote the above in memory of my first English-teacher. Unfortunately, the story was not published in the magazine and the manuscript was returned to me with the stamp: 'Stopped by Censor.'

'I am extremely sorry, but we couldn't possibly pass your excellent contribution,' said the excessively suave Intelligence Corps Captain in the British Censorship Department, where I went for an explanation. 'But, you know, war entails casualties,' he added mysteriously, as if making a revelation of some sort. 'Let us think that Sergeant Baldwin died at the front. Just at present we can't upset our great Ally. You do understand?'

I did not.

*

The prisoners whiled away their captivity with a varied selection of pastimes. One of the most innocent diversions was a sport known as 'cycling.' The game consisted of inserting long paper spills between the toes of a slumbering victim and then lighting them. The sleeper would lie quiet until the burning paper began to singe his feet, whereupon he would awake in terror and begin waving his legs in the air as though pedalling a bicycle.

If the light went out during the evening, as not infrequently occurred, for the electricity plant often broke down, some wit would be sure to dip a rag in the slop bucket and pass it over the faces of all he could reach. Panic-stricken yells would testify to the success of the joke. Or again, you could launch a heavy, hobnailed boot into the crowded darkness. The groans of the injured never failed to provoke gusts of laughter. When the lights went on again, the old hands found it hard to conceal triumphant grins at the sight of cut ears, split lips and bleeding temples.

Cards attracted many enthusiasts. However, cards were not always available. They were repeatedly being confiscated during frequent and unexpected searches. The latter were conducted by a number of soldiers at a time. They would rush into the cell, chase the inmates outside and lock them in the lavatory. Thus, the wash-house, meant to accommodate ten people at the most, was suddenly filled by over a hundred. How they could all fit inside, sitting on pipes and on the very walls, not even they themselves could understand. Certainly, the architect had never expected that.

Meanwhile the deserted cell was ransacked by the soldiers. Beds and palliasses were turned inside out and every nook and cranny probed. This would take roughly an hour, during which time quite a few of the men in the lavatory would weaken and faint. Then the prisoners would be brought back, three at a time, and searched just as thoroughly. The whole procedure took place in an atmosphere of frenzied haste as though for fear of the

prison authorities, the guards chasing the prisoners as as-
siduously as though they themselves were afraid of each
other. In the face of such odds, it was difficult to conceal a
pack of cards.

The cards were made either from the tops of match-
boxes or from cigarette tips, unravelled for the purpose.
Intellectuals played bridge, peasants silently submerged
themselves in sixty-six, while Jews haggled noisily over a
set of gin-rummy. The liveliest games were played in the
criminals' corner where baccarat and chemin de fer went
on from dawn till dark. Though the stakes were, in theory,
money, they consisted in practice of anything a player
possessed or could raise, such as clothes, tobacco and
bread, which were carefully priced and the appropriate
credit allowed. If a jacket was valued at a hundred roubles,
the owner of it would play on till he lost a hundred roubles,
then take off his jacket and hand it to the winner. I once
saw a player sitting bare-footed and half naked, wearing
only a pair of underpants. Nevertheless, he did not stop
playing but staked the ration of bread and the bowl of
soup he would receive the following day. Sometimes, men
even played for things which did not belong to them. At
the end of one game, a participant approached a certain
headmaster and informed him genially that he had lost
three hundred roubles.

'How sad,' the teacher commiserated, not for a moment suspecting that he bore a major share in the loss.

'Yes, but the point is, that's exactly the price of your
shoes.'

'I don't quite understand.'

'It's simple. My pals gave me three hundred roubles'
credit when I staked your shoes. If I'd won, you'd never
even have suspected the bank you were carrying about on
your feet. As it is, I've lost. It's just too bad.'

'But what's it got to do with me?'

'Only this much—you've got to hand over the stake. In other words—climb out of your shoes.'

Appeals made by friends were of no avail. In vain, the poor teacher explained that he couldn't be left without footwear. He finally had recourse to the jailer, asking to be placed in another cell. Unfortunately that did not lie within the scope of his powers, nor is it customary in Soviet prisons to transfer a prisoner anywhere at his own request. The helpless man insisted that on no account would he surrender his shoes.

'As you wish,' his tormentor agreed, 'but don't blame anyone if your life isn't exactly pleasant from now on.'

The result was that the old man spent the night sewing a pair of slippers made from a blanket and next day delivered his boots in person to the baccarat school.

If there had been a search and neither cards nor paper, to play the cycling game, were available, the prisoners took turns relating their adventures. In some prisons, shortened versions of books were popular. Unfortunately, where I was, there were few readers or students of literature. We listened with great interest, however, to the swaggering tales of the criminal element or the stories of how one or other of those present came to lose his freedom.

Two of these, a father and son with the strange name of Asparagus, who slept in prison in silk pyjamas and whose bags were stuffed with exquisite, monogrammed linen, would often recall the times when, as professional smugglers, they used to conduct rich refugees over the border. As they were crossing the plank bridge spanning the River Bug, which marked the boundary, they simply threw their patrons into the water.

Maciejko, a sixteen-year-old village lad, was inconsolable. He had been arrested after carelessly visiting a tailor who was to alter his father's trousers, to fit him for Christmas. On entering the establishment, he found the tailor engaged in demonstrating to some customer that Russian chemists wrapped pills in newspaper—which was not hygienic. Before trying on his trousers, the lad was obliged to wait till the tailor had finished his discussion. The next day, he was taken to the militia post. The tailor's opponent in the debate had denounced the craftsman for criticizing the economy measures of Soviet pharmaceutists and had named Maciejko as a witness.

'Did you hear him say that in the Soviet Union medicines are worse wrapped than in other countries?' he was asked.

'Yes, I heard him say so,' the lad admitted.

'Sign it.'

Maciejko signed.

'And why didn't you report it to the militia?' was the next question.

The lad shrugged his shoulders, not knowing what to answer. For not having reported counter-revolutionary opinions, he was arrested, though summoned as a witness.

One night, loud spasms of weeping were heard in the cell. It was Kaleta, a tall, handsome young man.

He had been employed as a driver for some time by the new authorities of his town. Once he found himself assigned to the political police for a nocturnal man-hunt. They drove round the town following a list of the names and addresses of the local manufacturers whom it was intended to arrest. Very few of them were found. The rich industrialists had known what to expect from the new rulers and had deemed it advisable to flee the country a long time before. As a punishment, their families were taken. That night, Kaleta made several journeys, his lorry filled to overflowing with old women torn from their beds, pregnant women or mothers with babes in arms. The memory of that nightmare was torturing the simple fellow in his sleep. He asked between sobs whether God would ever forgive him for lending a hand in the crime. His answer was a flood of obscenities from the criminals' corner. Someone, furious at having been roused from his peaceful slumbers, picked up a heavy boot, intending to throw it at Kaleta's head, but on second thoughts contented himself with imprecations. The thought of the gentle driver's iron muscles and his ability to break an opponent in two when angry, discouraged more than one from hostile action.

In contrast to Kaleta, the Jew, Parsley, would boast loudly of his achievements. As a rag and bone merchant of the highest order, he was the possessor of a few lorries in which he used to drive his co-religionists from the German occupation zone to the Soviet paradise, receiving generous payment in advance.

They travelled by night. Before day-break, the lorries would draw up in the square of some little town which, according to the river, was beyond the reach of the Germans. He would then take letters from his grateful flock for delivery to their families, announcing their safe arrival and recommending the services of the enterprising carrier to friends and acquaintances. After which he would turn his lorries and go back.

At first light, the refugees would be rounded up by a platoon of German soldiers, taken to a wood and shot. The towns, of course, lay deep within the German zone and the lorry-owner was a Gestapo agent.

Parsley was captured trying to cross the border with thousands of dollars gleaned from his victims.

Cyklis worked on the Soviet side. His hunting-ground

was any railway station packed with refugees. He would find a woman with a child, struggling along with a heavy bundle or a trunk, and would offer his assistance. No sooner would they come to an empty street, than he would make off with the luggage, leaving the woman without resources. He had been arrested for not reporting to the Refugees' Registration Office.

All those criminals who were in jail for minor offences, such as illegally crossing the demarcation line or failing to conform to the new security regulations, were not unduly worried at the thought of the sentences awaiting them, for they knew they would not be severe.

The tales so proudly told were listened to with admiration by all present, children included.

In our cell there were three boys, the eldest of whom was fourteen. The other two were aged twelve and ten respectively. They had been arrested for conspiring against the Soviets. During a lesson at school, they had been called out in the corridor, arrested and taken away without even being allowed to go home first.

The ten-year-old Johnny, so small and thin that he looked no more than seven, had been subjected under the new educational system to a cure for a disease known as belief in God, diagnosed by the Soviets as a drug employed by the capitalists to enslave the ignorant.

The treatment was as follows. For some days on end, the newly appointed teacher would order the children every morning to pray to God for sweets. She knelt down with the class and joined the children in reciting the prayer. No sweets were forthcoming. Obviously, God either rejected the children's prayers or He was unable to hear them. Again, it might be that He was evil and did not like children. Either that, or He was not omnipotent, or perhaps He did not even exist. After several days of fruitless supplication, the teacher suggested that, just for a change, they should ask dear Father Stalin.

She stood before the portrait of the head of the Soviet Government and, telling the children to repeat it together after her, she began:

'Beloved Father Stalin, you who love little children, send us some sweets.'

After that, she went on teaching the normal syllabus, and the next day she brought along a gigantic basket of confectionery.

Little Johnny belonged to a cub pack whose leader, a secondary schoolboy in his teens, wished to affiliate the members to the resistance movement against the invader. Unfortunately, he was arrested and, in the course of a painful questioning, he divulged the names of those under his command. The latter were immediately imprisoned. And so Johnny found himself in jail.

The two older boys adapted themselves to the new conditions more easily than did the more intelligent adult prisoners. They soon traded their school jackets for bread, learnt to smoke and played cards with the bandits. They stole at times. The youthful flush soon faded from their cheeks, giving way to a muddy pallor, and they began to look like the rest of us. But the boys started to cough before the others. Tuberculosis reaps a glorious harvest amongst children in such conditions.

Only the ten-year-old Johnny did not share his friends' ready acceptance of prison life. He did not smoke or play cards, and kept to himself. But he coughed more and more frequently, especially at night.

Not only children, however, were housed in the communal cell. There were several mental cases as well, and a man who was mortally ill.

One day the jailer came into the cell to see whether

this sufferer was still alive and then, for the first time, he saw Johnny.

'How did you get in here?' he asked the boy.

'He was liberated by the Soviet Union,' a few voices replied.

'Liberated? From whom?' asked the soldier who didn't sin by excessive brightness.

'From his mother,' someone explained.

Suddenly, the door, which was always open when a representative of authority stood amongst us, slammed shut. The soldier walked up to it and knocked on the Judas window, but the guard, some way along the passage by this time, didn't hear. The soldier knocked again, waiting patiently.

'Ha, ha! Now you're inside with us!' cried a voice in the crowd.

'What's so strange about that? In the Soviet Union, anyone can get anywhere. It's just as easy,' said the Sergeant, remembering his propaganda, 'to get into the Supreme Soviet as into jail.'

His words were greeted with a roar of laughter. A key grated in the lock, the guard opened the steel-plated door and the sergeant disappeared into the dim corridor.

SIX

Gentlemen

Outside the wooden shutters, which covered the barred windows, evening was falling, slowly and unnoticed even though it was spring. The air in the cell was hot and stifling, even more so than a month before in the prison at Gorki, where the room had been so crammed that we had had to stand on top of each other—unable to sit down. Worse than at Grodno even, where Warotnik had taken the beds by force. It was after supper and we had finished the washing-up. Half the inmates had been taken to the bathroom, and I was strolling up and down, making the most of the opportunity.

Backwards and forwards I went, with the Russian, Wolodzka, at my elbow. For the hundredth or maybe the thousandth time, he was telling me how he had murdered his wife, Katia.

The lock rattled open and the prisoners who had been to the bath-house came in, two at a time, hands clasped behind their backs. They brought with them noise, the damp chill of a concrete floor and mud on their soles and heels. The cell filled up again.

I sat down against the wall, on my bundle and coat, which was neatly folded in four. Wolodzka had wandered off somewhere, probably to join a card game. It was about

seven o'clock in the evening. I was gnawing a long piece
of straw, picking at it with my fingers while recalling that
exactly two years ago I had been swimming in the sea.
But the tropical heat and the constant uproar made thought
impossible. I felt sleepy and listless.

The jailer knocking at the Judas window was the
signal to get ready for the evening inspection. The men
got to their feet without undue haste and formed up in
fours. Again the lock rattled, announcing the entry of the
orderly N.C.O. accompanied by two soldiers. The prisoners made no attempt to stand to attention or to show
respect at sight of them. The Russian climbed up on a
bench and looked us over before starting to count. One of
the soldiers standing beside him counted independently.
The jailer lounged in the open door, an idiotic grin on
his face. The Russian on the bench held, in one hand, a
board with a sheet of paper tacked to it and, in the other,
a long pencil which he waved over our heads as though he
were conducting an inaudible orchestra. First, he checked
that we were all standing in fours, then the number of
ranks, lengthwise and across. Only then did he begin his
real task. There were more than a hundred men in a room
meant to accommodate a third of the number. No wonder
that the N.C.O. found it far from easy to arrive at such
an astronomical figure. The process of counting lasted
long enough but, despite that, the N.C.O. distrusted the
accuracy of his computation, for he asked:

'How many of you are there?'

'One hundred and thirteen,' said one or two of the
more obliging prisoners.

He compared the information on the paper in his
hand. ·

'Right. That's what it should be.'

He started to re-count but the numbers would not

agree. Shaking his head in extreme displeasure, he turned
to his assistant.

'What do you make it?'

The soldier shrugged his shoulders. Something was
wrong. One of them made it too many, the other too few.
The N.C.O. jumped off the bench, marched up to the
parade and prodding each prisoner with his pencil, made a
mark on the paper after every tenth one. After the counting came a laborious addition. At last he got it right. The
soldier, likewise, adopted the unusual method of his superior, but, having neither a board and paper nor a pencil,
he prodded each prisoner with his finger, counting them in
a whisper and bawling out the ordinals, ten, twenty, thirty,
until he worked through to the last man. Then he announced to his superior that the number for our cell was
correct.

The N.C.O. once more totted up the marks on his
sheet and nodded: 'Yes, all correct.'

This procedure, including all errors, was repeated
each evening with the inevitability of a cinema performance. At the end of it the N.C.O. heard petitions. One man
had lost his receipt for his money and wanted a duplicate.
Another asked to be brought before a judge for retrial,
while somebody else was without a shirt. The Russian
listened to all of them patiently, without so much as a
flicker of his narrow, Mongolian eyelids. After hearing
each case, he would solemnly promise to have it attended
to, and, asking the prisoner for his name, would move the
blunt end of his pencil over the page, pretending to write.
We all saw it, yet not one of us dared draw his attention
to the fact. Meanwhile other questions were being flung at
the Sergeant. When were we going to the baths next?
When would there be some tobacco in the prison shop?
When were they taking us out for exercise? The Sergeant

invariably replied that, in a Soviet prison, every con-
tingency was foreseen and things took place according
to a plan prepared at the highest level. Thus, when the
time came, we should have all three—baths, tobacco and
exercise. But prisoners of long-standing knew perfectly
well that, in accordance with the plan, of course, they sometimes took us to the baths four times in one week then not
for another six or seven months, till an epidemic of typhus
broke out. The same went for exercise. They would chase
us out every day for a week, then keep us in the foul air
of the cell for months at a time.

The Sergeant and the soldiers turned towards the
door and having said 'Go to sleep!' they went out.

The door slammed shut and night began, differing
only from day in that a dim bulb now threw a yellow
gleam in our eyes while during the day the gloom of the
cell was only relieved by the odd shafts of light creeping
through the holes in the wooden shutters. People settled
down for the night. For sleeping we adopted what we
called the 'Jack of Clubs' system, by far the most economi-
cal method of using the space in a cell devoid of bedding.
The first men lay down on the right, heads to the wall.
The second row thrust their legs between them so that one
man's feet were level with the other man's face. The third
row lay with their heads to those of the second while their
faces embraced the feet of the fourth row, and so on to
the opposite wall. There were in all eight rows, so clev-
erly arranged that the last like the first had their heads to
the wall. The formation was that of sardines in a tin. If
somebody wanted to turn over, he had to wait till the entire row was ready to do so. This was usually about midnight.

I lay on my coat with my head resting on my bundle.
Shielding my eyes from the stabbing light with a handker-

chief, I tried to sleep. Another day was behind me. I was one day nearer the end. But what end? Freedom or death?

I had been a long time asleep when I was awakened by a commotion in the cell. Raising my head from the bundle, I rubbed my eyes. It was still night but everyone had been awake for some time. They were all sitting on their meagre bedding, eyes turned towards the open doorway, on the iron threshold of which stood a soldier, studying a thin sheet of paper.

'No. It's not you. Somebody else whose name begins with "B," ' he said.

'Bobrov!' yelled a voice.

'No!'

'Baranowski,' shouted another.

'No.'

'Borodienko,' a third introduced himself.

'No!'

'Bogdanov.'

'No!' The soldier shook his head.

'Blumstein,' squeaked the owner of that name.

'No!'

He was very hard to please.

'Buryn,' growled a hoarse voice from over by the wall.

'What's that?' the soldier asked.

'Buryn.'

The soldier pondered awhile and, bringing the paper up close to his eyes, made an effort to decipher the name scrawled upon it.

'Bu—Buryn?' he asked.

'Buryn,' admitted the man with the deep voice, and rose to his feet, feeling that he was the one in question.

'Hm . . . Buryn. It could be Buryn at that. What's your first name?'

GENTLEMEN 87

'Boris.'

'And your father's name?'

'Terentiej.'

The soldier once more inspected the paper and Boris Buryn, son of Terentiej, stood on one foot while he pulled a long boot on to the other. He was a gigantic White Russian with a huge head on ox-like shoulders.

'No, it's not you,' decided the soldier. 'Anybody else?'

Silence. No answer.

'Come on there! Anybody else beginning with "B"?'

'There are no more!' shouted somebody.

The soldier went out.

'Son of a bitch won't even let you sleep,' came a growl from one corner.

The disturbed cell settled down to resume its slumber. Feet to head, head to head, head to feet, and so on. In less than a quarter of an hour the soldier appeared again and, smiling shamefacedly as though betraying a secret, and gazing straight in front of him, he shouted:

'What about Wittlin? Is there one here?'

'There is,' I answered.

'Then why didn't you say so?' roared the soldier, looking at me suspiciously.

'I've just said so.'

'But before?'

'You wanted the letter "B" before. My name begins with "W." '

'Capital B and capital W are the same thing.' He waved his hand, satisfied at having finally found the man he was looking for. 'First name?'

'Tadeusz.'

'Father's name?'

'Antonovich.'

'That's correct.' The soldier cheered up, grinned and wiped the sweat off the bridge of his nose with his index-finger.

'Come on!'

I began to dress. Slowly and thoroughly.

'Get a move on!' the soldier urged.

'Coming,' I shouted, tying my shoes with laces made from a bandage. I was an old experienced lag by this time. After one and a half years of prison with questionings, beatings and the 'hold,' nothing could surprise or upset me any more. At last I was ready.

'With my things?' I asked, just in case.

'No.'

'All right.'

Jumping over the heads, the legs and the bundles of the men around me, I finally stood in front of the soldier.

We went out into the dark corridor which smelt of decay. The jailer locked the door behind us. I put my arms behind my back in accordance with regulations and set off with my escort. We walked along a passage with big, studded doors on either side, each of which bore a chalked number. Behind each—men sound asleep. The passage came to an end with a huge iron grill, stretching from floor to ceiling. Here we stopped. The soldier whistled twice softly, obviously a pre-arranged signal. A door-keeper appeared and, with a very large key, opened a small gate in the grill. We went through. The crash of the gate being slammed behind us echoed loudly down the empty tunnel of the corridor. We turned into another passage and came to a second grill, barring our progress to a flight of stairs. Here the guard gave a different signal, this time hissing shrilly through his teeth. Another turn-key, another gate: we began to mount the stairs.

'What is it? Questioning?' I asked, wondering what

they could be wanting with me, for the official proceedings were long since at an end.

'You'll see.'

I tried to guess what I was in for this time. The soldier had given me the only answer I could expect from him. I had only asked in order to break the oppressive silence. What could they want now? Maybe they had come across something fresh. Perhaps somebody had reported me. But on what grounds? There would be more exhausting questions, more beating. What day was it? Wednesday. Always was my unlucky day.

We came to the end of the stairs. Ahead of us stretched another corridor. Much cleaner, well lit and lined with red carpet. Here were the governor's rooms and those of the judges and prosecutors. Also offices and apartments for the various dignitaries who came to visit the place. The sentry on duty there signalled to my escort that the prosecutor was busy with another case at the moment. The soldier then led me to the 'waiting-room,' a small cupboard of unplaned wood fixed to the wall of the corridor. This article of furniture is characteristic of Soviet prison equipment. It is used to prevent waiting prisoners from communicating with one another. The soldier opened the padlock, ordered me to get inside and locked the door behind me. He simply put me in the cupboard as though I were an umbrella.

I stood inside like a mummy in its coffin, resting my forehead against the rough boards. It was very stuffy but I consoled myself with the thought that, at least, should I faint, there was no room to fall down. After a while, I heard the footsteps of the last prisoner to be questioned and knew it would shortly be my turn. Nor was I mistaken. No sooner had the footsteps died away than the coffin was opened and I beheld the blue and red cap of my guardian, from under which there issued a laconic, 'Get out!'

As I walked ahead of the soldier to the prosecutor's office, it occurred to me what a nice thing to have a well-trained umbrella would be, always at the beck and call of its master.

*

The Prosecutor's study was a high, narrow room with brown painted walls. Opposite the door was a barred window, half hidden by heavy drapery. Against that background stood a desk, a lamp with a green shade, a telephone, a caraffe of water, together with a glass, the rim of which was slightly chipped, writing materials and a pile of documents. By the wall was a bookshelf, choked with papers; in the corner, a stand on which hung a military greatcoat. At the desk, in the uniform of a colonel, sat the prosecutor.

He nodded towards an empty chair and I sat down.

'Smoke?' he asked with a friendly smile.

'With pleasure . . . if I had something to smoke.'

He took out a leather cigarette-case, revealing a double row of white cigarettes with tips. He gave me a light from his own.

'Taste good?'

'Very good.'

Silence. The moments of waiting were uncomfortable, for it was quite likely that this pleasant interlude would turn into a painful inquisition, of the sort not infrequently followed by loss of consciousness.

'Are you hungry?'

'Of course.'

On the desk lay a parcel wrapped in a copy of *Izvestia*. He unpacked it and took out two slices of bread and sausage.

'Here, eat this.'

He did not have to ask me twice.

'All right?'

'Marvellous.'

'Listen,' he began, 'you've been in prison eighteen months now, and there's no knowing how much longer you'll stay there. But we know you're a quiet, sensible customer and, for that reason, you *could* be released quite soon.'

'Thank you.'

'Take out Soviet citizenship papers. When you're tried you'll get two years, so, counting the eighteen months you've done already, you would only have six months left. Then you'll settle in whatever Soviet town you may be directed to, and you'll be quite free. Well?'

'I don't quite know,' I said, swallowing a large piece of bread which smelt of dripping. 'In this place a man feels like a prisoner of war—a captured soldier; but once he takes out Soviet papers, it's the end. Besides, Comrade Colonel, if the Germans or the English had you in prison and promised you liberty on condition that you renounced your Soviet motherland, would you accept?'

'H'm, very nicely said,' he approved. 'Have some more.' He thrust the second slice of bread towards me.

'Do you know Kowalski?' He shot the question unexpectedly.

'Yes, I know him.'

'What is he?'

'A convict—same as myself.'

'I know that much, since he's here with you. But what do you know about him?'

There was not the slightest doubt now that we had a spy in our cell. Kowalski had been wounded, shot through the leg by a sentry when he was trying to cross the border.

The prison doctor wanted him to be taken to the infirmary but the political chief forbade it, so Kowalski had to lie in the filth and dust on the concrete floor of the cell. And since, at sick parade, the nurse only admitted the first ten in the queue each morning, Kowalski could never get to her. She usually saw only those who were fit enough to use their fists and feet to secure places among the lucky ten. They would be given cod-liver oil which they used for softening cracked boots, bandages for making sewing-thread and iodized cotton wool which, together with straw from the palliasse, they could twist in newspapers for a smoke. Those who were really ill or otherwise in need of medical attention could never get it.

The wound in Kowalski's leg suppurated, a wet rag being hardly sufficient to keep out infection, but the patient's good humour never deserted him. He sang songs and whistled merrily but never attempted to talk to anybody for very long at a time. They all knew he was a village schoolmaster, wounded while crossing the frontier. But an attempt to slip across the border was the most undistinguished of crimes and Jan Kowalski probably the commonest of Polish names. So it was whispered that the name and profession were false and served merely to conceal some important personality.

After a time, Kowalski and I became friends. It all began when I gave him my disinfectant gargle to bathe his wounded leg. I was the only person in the cell in whom Kowalski confided completely. One of the prisoners must have reported this new friendship to the authorities and, consequently, I had been called for questioning.

I sat on the edge of the chair, wondering what to say.

'Well, what about this Kowalski?' the prosecutor persisted.

'A village teacher, wounded in the leg . . . shot in the meanest way possible.'

'Why "the meanest way possible"?'

'Because, as he was running, the soldier shouted at him to stop, which he did. He was then ordered to lie down on the ground and the guard shot him.'

Since the wounded prisoner repeated the story frequently and to anybody it was safe to tell it.

'Yes, we know all about that,' said the officer, somewhat disappointed. 'What else?'

'Well, he is apparently a teacher.'

'Apparently! And in actual fact?'

'Who knows? He says he's a teacher.'

'Did he tell you that?'

'He did.'

'Why do you stick together?'

'He was wounded. I dressed his leg once, helped him.'

'Nothing else?'

'Nothing.'

'And what do you think about him?'

'I don't know. He's a gentleman.'

'What?'

'A gentleman.'

'English?'

'No, not English. Just a gentleman.'

'What do you mean by that?'

'You can describe anyone as such, regardless of nationality.'

'I know, but what do you understand by it?'

'Well, a gentleman could be, for example, someone like yourself, Colonel.'

'Like me? How come?'

'Well, you don't shout, or curse or beat people. You asked me to sit down, offered me a cigarette, bread and sausage. And you speak like a cultured man. In other words, you're a European or . . . a gentleman.'

'Hm, you really think so?'

'Of course, if I didn't I wouldn't say so. I've nothing to gain by lying. I've smoked the cigarette and eaten the food.'

'And you really know nothing about Kowalski? For example, that he's a general or a minister masquerading under a different name?'

'Certainly not! All I know is that he's quiet, well mannered and nicely spoken. A cultured man. A gentleman.'

'All right,' said the Colonel. 'Go back to your cell. Here, take these cigarettes with you. They're the last I've got.'

I smoked the cigarettes with Kowalski, and the next night I was called out again. This time I was taken to a different room, where a sergeant was waiting. Against the wall stood a chair, in front of a table on which was nailed a board, roughly the height of a seated man. The board stuck up in the air like the raised lid of a class-room desk or the ceiling of a doll's house: from it hung an electric light bulb. The whole affair looked like the retouching apparatus in a photographer's studio. The Sergeant ordered me to sit in the chair and clasp my hands behind the back-rest. My face was now right up against the bulb. The Sergeant pulled the switch and a blinding light of some three or four hundred candle-power hit me in the eyes. Instinctively, I closed them and immediately I felt a blow on the back of the neck, delivered by the Sergeant with the edge of his hand.

'Open your eyes!'

Another painful blow under the left ear forced me to look into the flaming white glare of the lamp. The soldier was standing over the desk, out of reach of the murderous rays.

'What's Kowalski's name?'

'Kowalski.'

My eyes closed again, but even through the tightly clenched lids that terrible light was clawing at my pupils. Another blow on the neck—sharp as though struck with the blunt edge of a knife.

'Don't close your eyes, you swine! What's Kowalski's name?'

'I don't know. Maybe it's Kowalski, maybe not. I don't know!'

The Sergeant switched out the light. I stood up and reeled across the room. I felt blinded. I could shut my eyes now, but under their lids fiery sword-blades crisscrossed, plunged up and down, down and across, while against an azure background golden rain poured into depths of blackness.

In the open door stood my escort. The Sergeant spat on the concrete floor, rubbed the spittle with the heel of his boot and swore horribly—thus proving that he was no gentleman.

SEVEN

The Court Is in Session

In the tropical heat, the men either lay prostrate on the floor, breathing heavily, or moved about slowly like drowsy flies on a sun-swept table top.

For some time now, the prison water-supply had ceased to function and the guard left no more than one bucket of water each day for the entire cell. The sick man who, until then, had been wont to relieve his fever with a rag dipped in cold water, was now denied that consolation by his fellow prisoners. The water, which arrived in barrels, was mainly used for cooking purposes, too little being set aside for drinking to permit the manufacture of a cold-water compress.

Nobody had washed for weeks. At first, when the prisoners were going to the lavatories, they had taken with them metal cups. These they filled with the grey dregs from the tanks which they reached by climbing amongst the pipes, like monkeys in the tree-tops. Later, however, they left the cups behind. The water was all gone.

As they filed along the corridors, the more enterprising would scan the spittoons in search of clean water. All in vain. They were filled with yellow sand.

For several days I lay ill and helpless with swollen legs. The cause of my sickness was hard to trace. It was probably hunger. My legs looked like tree-trunks and I could not walk. My condition deteriorated swiftly and, one day, I fainted.

The nurse, who was summoned at once, brought with her a hypodermic full of camphor. She arrived a good hour after being called, accompanied by a sergeant. By that time, I had long since recovered and was engaged in playing a return match of chess.

The nurse, however, had brought a syringe. She therefore had to use it, whether or not it was necessary. She injected the camphor into me and the N.C.O. beside her took my name. The next day I was removed to the prison hospital.

I was carried by two of my cell-mates who acted not so much out of kindness as in the hope of finding a few cigarette-ends in the corridor. In due course, I found myself in bed: for the first time in many months undressed, on a sheet, a pillow under my head and a blanket over me. On the table beside me was a glass of milk and a crisp white roll. In short, an idyll.

There were twelve beds in the ward. All of them occupied. Opposite mine, lay a youth of no more than seventeen. He was delirious and tossing with fever.

During the afternoon, another patient arrived. Looking around and not seeing a vacant bed, the newcomer sat down on a stool in the corner and waited uncomplainingly. Once having been sent to the ward, he could not leave without orders. The matron who looked in later in order to take the sick man's temperature, consoled him by saying that one bed would soon be free. The delirious boy was going to die.

She knew what she was talking about. Late in the evening, he began to die sure enough. He called for his mother, who, however, did not come. One of his neighbours hopped from his place and removed the milk and the bread from his table. After all, the dying man did not need it and it seemed a pity to let it go to waste.

A medical orderly was called to tie down the tossing, delirious boy. His groans soon grew weaker, changed to a quiet moan, a sob, a low, snoring murmur, then died away altogether.

The ward was silent except for the voracious gulping of the man who stole the bread.

The matron came in. She blew the flies off the dead boy's face, lifted his lids and looked at the staring, glassy eyes. Then she pulled a blanket over his face.

In a little while two muscular girl orderlies arrived, bringing with them a stretcher which was unfortunately too broad to spread out on the floor between the beds. They found it no easy matter to get the corpse off the bed on to the stretcher. Though they were strong girls, they were panting and sweating before they succeeded in arranging the boy's remains on the canvas, taut between the two poles. At last, they were ready and together lifted up their burden. As they were going through the door, one of them caught her elbow on the frame and the corpse fell to the ground with a crash. The proverbial malice of inanimate objects, no doubt. The girls picked up the body and went out.

The patient waiting in the corner lost no time. He leapt from his stool, tore off his clothes, jumped into bed and pulled the blanket over him.

Presently, we heard his measured breathing as he lay peacefully sleeping.

The next day, I had a high temperature. Despite that, two officers arrived bringing with them a paper for me to sign.

It was the charge-sheet presented to every prisoner before trial.

On the appointed day, the matron brought along my clothes and I was told to dress before going to court.

I dressed and left the hospital. The glasses of milk I had drunk during the past few days had strengthened me considerably. My legs were back to normal and I could walk quite steadily. Apart from a headache and a high temperature, I felt reasonably well.

The black prison van was waiting in the yard. I mounted the steep ladder-like steps and climbed in. It was very dark inside. Quite possibly, one could have looked out through the barred window but I had neither the strength nor the desire to do so. I was soon alighting in the yard of the court-house. As I entered the hall, I swayed and would have fallen had someone not supported me to a bench. I don't know who it was—maybe the escort who sat down beside me with his rifle on his knees and the tip of his bayonet in my ribs. We sat there like that for a very long time—a few hours at least—before it turned out that the Court was having a day off, and was not in session.

I was taken back to the prison in the same van and placed in a cell packed with more than two hundred people. That was the nethermost pit of hell. I was cheered by the thought of returning to the Court the next day. And so it came to pass. I was called out, given a piece of bread and a cup of hot liquid and again placed in that black metal coffin on wheels, which deposited me in due course outside the court-house. The Court was in session, and I had to wait in the passage for several hours before being summoned to the long hall with its raised table draped in red cloth. I sat down on a bench. Beside me stood a soldier with a rifle. I was no sooner seated than a woman in a faded green coat approached me. She was small as a dwarf and so fat that she seemed to roll rather than walk. Her hair was untidy and neglected. She looked fifty though she was younger, prematurely aged by hard living conditions. She reminded me of a fishwife. Smiling kindly, she asked me if I came from Warsaw and named a few streets in the northern sector where the poor Jewish families live. She hailed from that district. Having thus opened the conversation, my new acquaintance who, it transpired, was my solicitor and appointed defence counsel, began to comfort me with the assurance that I had nothing to worry about and would be best advised to confess everything. That would simplify the whole business and soften the judges' hearts.

I felt a throbbing in my temples and flakes of black snow fluttered past my eyes. I tried to look down on the floor at the toes of my boots, but I could not see them. If only the woman would stop jabbering and go away!

The official voice of the usher summoned all to stand. The Court was in session. The soldier presented arms, my counsel rose. I alone was too weak to get up. Behind the table sat the judges. The Prosecutor took his place on their right; opposite him, at the other end of the table, stood the young recorder.

The President of the Court ordered me to rise, then asked me if I had received the charge-sheet and whether I was familiar with its contents. I explained that I had been brought straight from hospital to the Court and that I had not read the papers which had been handed to me.

The Prosecutor then rose and pointed out to the Court that since I had signed the document I must of necessity have read it, for that was the procedure. I could therefore not claim ignorance of the case. As for my illness—well, I was standing there in the Court, was I not?

I must therefore be well enough, or the doctor would have kept me in hospital.

The Prosecutor's comments met with the general approval of the Bench, and the President stated that it made little difference anyhow whether or not I had read the charge since it was no more than a condensation of admissions I myself had made under questioning. The results of those investigations I knew well enough, having signed them a number of times already.

A judge spoke rapidly, using expressions which often eluded me. Anyway, I felt ill, hot and cold with fever and was shivering uncontrollably. I only wanted the whole thing to be over and done with and myself to be left in peace.

The President asked whether I admitted the truth of my signed statements. Before I could answer, I received a sharp nudge from my counsel, like the prompting of a class-mate, admonishing me to confess my guilt. I should have admitted it anyway, since, once signed, my statements could not be renounced, especially in my present feeble condition. The opposing sides were far from balanced. I could not keep my feet, did not understand what they were saying to me and could not be bothered to answer in a foreign tongue.

I pleaded guilty. The shortest, easiest and least wearisome solution. The Prosecutor rose to his feet and commenced his address.

He spoke with fluency and feeling. I could not grasp all he said, but I sensed that it was the speech of a clever and skilful lawyer.

My counsel spoke next. Smiling and puffing, she dwelt on my willingness to repent and my ill-health. She concluded by appealing for a mild sentence and promising, on my behalf, good behaviour in the future, even should I be

called upon to serve the maximum sentence. I was soon
to learn, however, that with the best of intentions, it is
hard to make amends once the maximum sentence has been
served. The President asked me if I had any special wish.
My counsel prompted me again, as though I were answer-
ing the teacher: 'A mild sentence . . .' 'A mild sentence'
I repeated after her.

The judges withdrew to confer. Everyone got up—
except me. Unable to stand any longer, I sat down.

The conference did not last long. Obviously, the
verdict had been prepared before the 'trial.' I, for one,
can hardly credit the existence of a typist capable of producing a couple of score of sheets in a matter of minutes.

The Court returned. Once again those present stood
up and this time I rose with them. The President read out
the findings by virtue of which Wittlin, Tadeusz, son of
Antoni, illegally remaining on the soil of the Soviet Republic of White Russia, accused of armed diversionary and
counter-revolutionary activities consisting therein that,
during the time of the German-Polish war, he did command a detachment of partisans fighting against the Red
Army and which destroyed two Soviet tanks, he being further accused of attempted flight from Soviet-occupied ter-
ritories with the intention of betaking himself to France,
there to make known information to a foreign power, and
furthermore having been before the war a journalist and
writer, a contributor to Fascist periodicals and a jurist in
the service of the capitalist order . . . was condemned
to be shot. He might appeal if he so wished for clemency
and a commuted sentence.

The case was closed. The judges, the Prosecutor and
the Public Recorder left the hall. The farce was over. My
counsel who had expected no other verdict began to console me officially with the assurance that my appeal would

be successful. The soldier pushed me towards the door. We left the building and climbed into the waiting van which took us back to the prison. I was shivering with cold and hunger.

That feeling of hunger led me to think I was on the road to recovery.

I got out of the van in the prison yard. The soldier led me past the kitchens, the baths and the mortuary, right round the main block which we entered by a small door. We climbed upstairs and came to three cells set in a narrow alcove—single cells. The jailer opened one of them and I noticed the number—10. The door shut behind me with a short, vicious snap. I was in the famous death-cell.

This cell was eight paces long and six wide. There was no window, and air from the corridor reached it only through small holes punched in the tin plating above the door. The floor was of black stone, while a refuse bucket and an electric light bulb constituted the only furniture in this primitive apartment. The walls were newly white-washed—to obliterate names and dates. That tight, dark box could not be more suitably called than by its Russian title, 'kamera.'

I spread out my coat in the corner, made my bundle into a pillow and sat down to eat the remains of my bread. I was neither afraid of death nor did I feel glad that the end of my troubles was in sight. I sank into total apathy but was nevertheless relieved to be alone. The silence and solitude, so long denied me, I found soothing, as though I had reached a calm anchorage after a stormy crossing. I felt quite happy. Nor did I find myself reflecting that this was indeed the finish of my excursion into crime. My head had stopped aching. I rolled a cigarette in a scrap of newspaper, lit it and stretched myself on my coat. I soon fell asleep with the half-smoked cigarette between my lips.

Awakened by a violent pounding on the door, I leapt to my feet in a panic. I felt completely rested.

'What is it?' I called in a frightened voice.

'Take your bread and tea.'

I stood by the door waiting for it to open, but it stayed shut. Only a small panel opened and a pair of hands with square black fingernails held out a tin of tea and a portion of bread.

'Drink up and give me back the tin.'

'Right. When can I go to the wash-house?'

'Why? Is your bucket full?'

'No, but I want to wash.'

'Like hell you do. Your number's up. Hurry up and eat your food, I'm coming back for that mess-can.' The panel snapped shut.

The bulb in the ceiling glowed day and night. Had it gone out the darkness would have been almost tangible. I only knew it was the following morning by virtue of the bread I got for breakfast.

Having eaten, I paced the floor, and aimlessly sorted out my belongings while humming a few tunes. I could not visualize the fact that I was about to be shot. I tried to remember things, but my thoughts drifted and it was hard to call anything to mind.

I lay down and slept till lunch arrived, or rather the tin of hot water with a handful of barley floating near the bottom of it. Somewhere around me, above me, below me, time flowed on. In the evening the square-nailed fingers passed me a bowl of hot barley soup once again and a couple of half-rotten potatoes. Had it not been for the meals, I would never have been able to distinguish between dawn and dusk. The hands which proffered the food were my only contact with the living. Clearly, I no longer belonged to the world of man. The condemned cell was an excellent preparation for death. There one ate, thought, moved but, at the same time, imperceptibly lost touch with life. When, after supper, the hands took away the mess-can and the wooden spoon, the voice said,

'Get to sleep.'

The panel shut. Lying there looking at the white ceiling, I reflected that, to all intents and purposes, I was already in the grave. The thought left me unmoved. Anyway, I was quite comfortable. I had eaten and had a cigarette, I felt much better than before my trial. As I drummed with my fingers on the wall, I scratched a long mark in the whitewash. One day in the death-cell was over. I took off my boots and clothes and fell asleep.

On the wall above me there were now four long scratches, side by side. It must be midday in the outer world for I had just returned my mess-can, having eaten lunch, which, for once, I had enjoyed. It had consisted of the usual hot water and barley plus a succulent piece of fish skin, that is to say, two courses. I took the chess-men and the rag board from my bag and set them up, meaning to play a game of draughts with myself. Suddenly, I heard the dry rattle of bolts. In a flash, I had the pieces rolled up and under my coat. My heart began to thud laboriously, quivering like the needle of a voltage indicator under the onslaught of high tension. They were going to take me out and shoot me. I felt cold as ice. The door opened and the guard told me to hand over my chess-men. That was all.

Nine marks on the wall. It was almost night, so I scratched a tenth mark and lay down to sleep. Well rested in the peace and solitude of the cell, I felt much happier in my mind. I even began to doubt whether they would ever take me out. Perhaps they would just keep me here for life. And even that thought didn't alarm me.

I fell asleep and dreamt of a green garden full of flowers. It was warm and sunny. In the distance I could see a red bus. All of a sudden it drove straight at me and hit me in the ribs so that I awoke in pain. I opened my eyes. Standing over me were a soldier and a sergeant. The latter had just kicked me. They both wore revolver holsters on their belts.

'Get up,' said the Sergeant, giving me another kick with the toe of his boot. I got up.

'You Wittlin?'

'Yes.'

'Your first name and father's name?'

'Tadeusz, Antonovitch.'

'Come along.'

'Shall I take my things?' I asked, knowing the answer I'd get.

It was as I expected.

'No. You won't need them.'

I went out in the passage with the Sergeant in front and the soldier behind. My brain was working slowly and with difficulty.

We went down a steep iron staircase which swayed like a suspension bridge. Only then did I realize where they were taking me. Little hammers began to pound in my temples. There was a roaring in my head like that of a furnace while an icy chill crept over my body.

I clattered noisily along a passage, my boots, which, in the hurry, I had neglected to tie properly, slipping off my feet. We traversed a labyrinth of corridors and stairs, now turning left, now right, up and down. It was taking us a very long time. Instead of breaking me, however, this via dolorosa had quite another effect. I simply ceased to care, thinking of our goal as no more than affording an earnestly desired rest. I tried to recall my mother and saw her as she was when she said good-bye to me for the last time. In Zofia's apartment. She was wearing a dark coat and a black hat.

'You've got to get away,' she was saying quietly. 'Terrible things will be happening here very shortly. Especially as far as you're concerned. They're looking for you already and how long could you stay hidden? Get away to-morrow at the latest. Afterwards may be too late. If you can't find a car, go by train or even on foot, but go!'

She hung a medallion round my neck and I kissed her hands for the last time. She smiled affectionately. Then she got up, saying, 'Look after yourself, Tadeusz,' and quickly left the room. I did not even ask her whether she had enough money to get home and she had such a long way to go—almost to the other end of the town. When I realized this, I ran out after her but she had already disappeared in the crowded street.

'Look after yourself, Tadeusz.'

There was no end to those corridors. Left turn, right turn, right, left, straight ahead then down and up and down again and straight ahead. Flights of stairs, long ones and short ones. Then single steps invisible in the dim twilight. I tripped continuously. My boots slipped off my heels, one of them in particular. So as not to lose it, I began to drag my foot along the ground. Our route stretched out hopelessly. We went down into a cellar, past a niche where stood a barrel falling apart with the damp, and across a mouldering wooden threshold beyond which was a dark vault. Instead of the usual stone under foot, this floor was of hard, dry clay, littered with fragments of broken bricks. The place was lit by an electric light bulb and looked vaguely like a disused kitchen.

In the corners under the ceiling hung great triangular, dusty cobwebs. On the walls were gas or water pipes. There were no traces of blood or brains. Perhaps because the walls were newly whitewashed. We had reached our goal. I stopped—without orders—seeing that we could go no further.

'Stand over there,' ordered the sergeant, tilting his chin at the opposite wall.

Obediently, I took a step forward. The Sergeant drew his revolver and slipped the safety-catch. The soldier took off his narrow belt. I was told to turn round, place my hands behind my back and put my forehead against the wall. The soldier then bound my arms, twisting the strap round my wrists in a figure of eight.

Pressing my burning forehead against the damp wall cooled it pleasantly. I made a tremendous effort to gather my thoughts together for the last time, to pray or something, but my brain refused to function. Between my shoulder-blades, I felt a strange sensation, like small quivering rings probing my skin.

A shot rang out. I hunched my back, burying my head in my shoulders like a man sheltering from a storm under a tree which is struck by lightning. But I did not fall. The bullet had struck the wall above my head. A second shot! A third!

'What? Still alive?' asked the sergeant. 'Then get out of here,' he added, putting away his revolver while the soldier undid my wrists.

The strange execution was over. As we left the cellar —that place of abortive doom—I was swaying like a drunken man. Soon we reached one of the upper floors.

It was obvious that I had been led to the 'execution' not only by a roundabout route, but that we had passed through the same corridors many times. A torture quite beyond comprehension. We stopped outside the judge's study and the sergeant went in. After a while he came out, led me in and then left the room.

Behind a desk with a green-shaded lamp sat the judge.

'Sit down,' he said. I sat down. If I hadn't I would have fallen.

'We have received an answer to your appeal,' he went on. 'Comrade Kalinin was kindly disposed to your petition and has commuted the death-sentence to twelve years' hard labour in a closed camp. You will go to Sucha Bezwodna,' he said and his voice seemed to come from very far away, from the top of a high mountain. 'You won't be too badly off there. Right, sign here.'

Holding the pen with difficulty, I appended my signature.

'Very well, you can go,' he said, putting away the paper in his brief-case.

I got up and went out. In the corridor the soldier who had tied my hands in the cellar was waiting for me. The sergeant's job was apparently done. He had vanished.

'What did you get?' asked the soldier. 'Fifteen?'

'Twelve.'

We walked towards the gate leading to the court-yard. Bolts rattled and we were out.

The night sky spread above our heads—a May sky, star-spangled. The shimmering light of the pale moon lit the dried-up prison gardens where the clumps of untrimmed shrubs looked like forgotten graves.

A grey sack was lying on one of the stone steps.

'Yours?' asked the soldier, touching it with the toe of his boot. 'Right, pick it up.'

I bent down and did so. It was my kit-bag.

'Get going!'

He strode along quickly and I had trouble keeping up with him. Ahead of us, clouds of grey steam were curling upwards and I knew I was bound for the bath-house.

EIGHT

Kind-hearted

I mounted the stone steps to the bath-house entrance. The scent of steam, damp and carbolic filled my nostrils. The hall was packed full of men I did not know, faces I had never seen—the prisoners from the other cells. They were all due for transportation and they filled the air with a noisy, joyous uproar. Sometime acquaintances bumped into one another again, loudly recalling their previous meetings in other towns, prisons or cells. Separated brothers, fathers, sons and friends were here reunited. After greeting each other warmly they would indulge in a carefree exchange of information regarding their respective sentences, and the names of the localities to which they were to be sent. They bandied such phrases as, 'Sucha Bezwodna —fifteen years,' 'Twelve years—Archangelsk district,' or, 'Ten years—Novosibirsk,' as thoughtlessly as though they were saying, 'I'm off to the Riviera for the summer,' 'Switzerland for six weeks,' or 'A month in Paris.'

They were as merry as guests at a reunion dinner-party. Those who were under the impression that certain persons held high positions in the outside world as like as not encountered the supposed dignitaries here in the prison bath. Frequently, someone would notice the person who had denounced him or the man who had testified against him in court, only to suffer the same fate as himself. In such cases, they made a mutual pretence of not seeing one another. But the rest of them were nothing but a bunch of happy schoolboys who had gone up a form and were now about to set off for the holidays. And, indeed, every man jack had been graded and issued with a free ticket. But there was yet another reason for all this merry-making. The sight of another man's misfortune is the best of all consolations. The men talked about anything and everything and the entire prison system of scrupulous isolation foundered completely. It was hard to see why the authorities could not have managed this business of transportation some other way, but perhaps they thought that convicted men who would shortly be packed in cattle trucks were no longer dangerous.

The carefree conversations, however, in no way interfered with the process of undressing. The convicts pulled off their clothes—patched with rags and burnt by disinfectants—tied them in bundles on the benches, placing their shoes underneath. Then they moved round happily, naked and grimy.

'Attention!' roared an official voice. All heads were turned towards the door, by which stood a soldier.

'Hand in your receipts,' said the soldier. 'You're going to get back your personal belongings.'

These words caused another paroxysm of happy emotion. People began to fumble in their shoes or to undo small handsewn amulets hung round their necks and in which were hidden the precious receipts. They crowded round the soldier, terrified of being too late. The moment it was a question of getting something friends became cool or even hostile towards each other, even though all that had to be done was to hand in a receipt. The soldier waited patiently till he had all the receipts in his possession, then

away he went. He was no sooner gone than two more
soldiers came in, wearing blue and white striped aprons.
They were carrying wooden stools and hair-clippers. The
stools were placed under the dusty windows and the barbers summoned their clientele to a free but compulsory
haircut. The men walked up in line, like sheep for shear-
ing, and this operation, likewise, was performed with
lightning rapidity. The very same pair of clippers which
a moment previous was shaving the arm-pits and abdomen
of a fellow prisoner was now in close contact with your
own face, neck and scalp. A rampart of grey, white, black,
brown and yellow hair rose round the stools, till at last
the barbers had finished.

'Anyone else?' they asked, glancing round at the living skeletons which, deprived of their growth, now looked
even skinnier, but younger—unrecognizably so. Rejuve-
nated skeletons!

'Nobody else,' a few voices replied.

The shorn sheep began to file out of the room and on
to the baths. There a hunchback in an apron handed each
man a piece of soap, reeking of fish-oil and no larger than
his index-finger. The bathroom was a large stone-paved
hall, from the walls of which jutted small partitions, like
stalls in a stable, with wooden footboards and showers
overhead.

Several men crowded into each of these stalls at the
same time and stood waiting. The first few sprinklers began to drip. Large single drops merged to a thin trickle
which in turn became a grey torrent of scalding water. It
was impossible to stand under the downpour, let alone
wash in it. The other showers were not working at all and
the naked men crowded under them in vain. But all obstacles can be overcome. There was another way of taking
a bath in the circumstances, besides dashing in and out of

the showers which were working, and being thoroughly scalded. A few men had pieces of rag which they soaked in the boiling stream, then smeared with soap. With these they lathered themselves from head to foot in the hope that the water would cool down a little and enable them to wash the soap from their bodies. Unfortunately, no sooner had the prisoners smothered themselves in dirty grey lather than the water stopped running. In an effort to coax a last few drops so as to wash the soap out of their smarting eyes, the bathers, grey-streaked with foam, hammered on the pipes. No luck. The scanty supply of water was exhausted.

A soldier came in and drove out the dripping prisoners with a volley of curses. They looked even more grimy now than before their baths. We all thronged into the hall where, amid violent imprecations, the prisoners attempted to rid their bodies of the dirt and soap. They could not dress since their clothes were being disinfected. After a while, the hunchback who had distributed the soap came in and flung a single bundle, containing everyone's clothes, into the middle of the crowd. Everyone thrust forward, eager to recover his own rags, but the clothing was scalding hot, wet and stank of carbolic. Many of the articles, stained brown with patches of acid, tore like tissue-paper as they were opened out.

The soldier in charge of us appeared in the doorway.

'Attention!' he yelled. 'All those who gave up their receipts!'

Silence descended on the crowd. The soldier called out a name.

'Here!' came a voice from the throng.

Half-dressed and holding the remainder of his rags in one hand, the man in question left the room. After a while, the soldier came back and fetched another, then a third . . . a seventh . . . an eightieth . . . and, at last, myself.

On a bench in the corridor leading to the yard lay a heap of little bundles. The first of these was mine. The soldier untied it.

'This strap yours?' he asked, picking up a belt.

'Yes.'

'Cigarette-case yours?'

'Yes.'

I took my things.

'The watch yours?'

'Yes, it's mine.'

'Take it.'

I picked up all my treasures, as happy at having recovered them as a child with its Christmas presents.

'Shaving tackle, brush, neck-tie, suspenders,' the soldier enumerated. 'All yours?'

'Yes, they're all mine.'

'Sign for them.'

I laid my things on the bench and took the proffered pencil.

'Sign here, where it says "Received by . . ." ' He pointed to the place with his finger.

I signed.

'Right,' he said, scooping my property towards him with a sweep of his hand which left me in no doubt as to his intentions.

'What are you doing?' I shouted. 'Those are mine!'

'Nothing's yours,' he answered phlegmatically. 'A prisoner's not allowed to have things like that. Even if I gave them back to you, they'd only be taken from you before the convoy leaves. Oh hell, take these and clear off!'

He picked my tie and suspenders from the heap of stolen objects and flung them at me.

I went out in the yard where all those who had preceded me in enacting the foregoing comedy were standing
in a long line. We waited there till everyone was out of the
baths. Then we were sent to a so-called transit-cell where
we made ourselves as comfortable as possible on the floor.
We had no idea how long we were to be there. The would-
be prophets amongst us and those who claimed to be experts on prison routine maintained that they would have
us out of it in under an hour, although it was just as likely
we would be there for the next few months.

*

Two sergeants were calling the roll. As each man
answered his name, he received the stereotyped order,
    'Get your things and clear out!'
Laden with his possessions, he would go out to the
passage where the N.C.O. in charge was forming the prisoners up in ranks. The cell emptied quickly. Only a few
were left behind—those whose papers were not in order
and those who were too ill to move. The latter were beyond caring what became of them, and the authorities, for
once, were in full agreement.

Out of the passage into the yard. It was a beautiful
May morning smelling of grass and spring. One of the
prisoners began to hum a popular tango, 'Look at the
lovely world around you. . . .' We all knew we were
about to embark on a long train journey and that from
that day onwards we would have all the sunshine and air
we could wish for.

The yard was swarming. The draft being prepared
for transportation was gigantic and would almost empty
the prison entirely.

As he strolled about the yard, the prison governor
smoked one cigarette after another, which he selected from

a variety of silver and gold cases. Against the wall stood
a table littered with heaps of documents. Close by, two
soldiers were carrying out a final search of the prisoners.
A pile of confiscated objects, such as tin spoons, aluminium
cups and wire-framed spectacles lay at their feet. Anything
made of, or containing, metal was taken.

Beside another group, which had already been
through the search, there stood, like a modern slave-
trader, a young lieutenant—the draft-conducting officer.
Guards and escorts surrounded the prisoners, holding in
check on their long leads half-tamed sheep-dogs and giant
Alsatians which lay with their heads on their fore-paws.

The hours dragged past. Sprawled on the grass, the
men waited to be taken to the train. I took off my cap,
closed my eyes and turned my face to the sun.

'How're you feeling? All right?' asked someone in
Russian, nudging my arm.

I opened my eyes. A sergeant with a merry smile was
standing over me.

'I'm quite well, thank you,' I answered.

'Why are you sitting with your head bare?'

'I like it that way.'

'I dare say, chum, but it won't do you any good. I'd
advise you to put your cap on. You've been sitting in a cell
for months and now you come straight out and expose
yourself to the sun like this. You shouldn't do it, really,'
he said with genuine concern. 'The sun is high—it's past
midday, you know, and there you sit bare-headed and your
hair cropped at that. You might get a headache, a touch
of sunstroke or even inflammation of the brain. Be a good
fellow and put your cap on.'

He spoke in all seriousness and with sincerity. It
would have been difficult not to comply with his request.
So as not to offend the kindly soul, I put my cap back on.

'Now that's much better,' he said with satisfaction. 'And if you want the sun on your face, just put the peak of your cap over a little to one side.' Having given me this kind advice, he went about his business with an easy mind.

A pleasant, decent sort of chap. Only how did he come to know me? I could not remember where I had seen that honest face before.

Sitting there idly, I tried to reconstruct in my mind the circumstances of my previous encounter with that soldier. And at last it all came back to me.

It was he, and no other, who had once stood behind my chair in the Prosecutor's office—he who had beaten me, beaten me thoroughly over the neck and head—in no way concerned, moreover, at the possibility of my contracting inflammation of the brain. He had hammered me systematically and with conviction, until I had lost consciousness. But obviously, apart from his honourable profession, the Sergeant was a decent man at heart: he had been worried in case I should get a touch of the sun as I sat there on the grass in the soothing warmth of that May morning!

A kind-hearted, compassionate fellow.

After a final search, we were all ready for loading. The draft was divided into battalions, surrounded by guards. In the ranks, we were required to kneel or to sit on our heels—this was extremely uncomfortable over a period of time. One's legs soon began to ache. The only method of obtaining relief was to address a complaint or petition to the officer in charge of the draft—which entailed standing up. A schoolteacher in front of me took advantage of this privilege.

'Citizen Commander,' he began piteously, as the officer drew near, 'during the search I was deprived of my spectacles and I'm almost blind without them.'

'Were the rims metal?' asked the commander.

'Yes, wire frames.'

'Regulations forbid the possession of sharp instruments and metal objects by prisoners on draft.'

'But without them I'll be falling over all the time and
I'll be quite useless for work.'

This argument convinced the officer. Nevertheless, he
hesitated.

'Is that true? It's as bad as that?' he asked.

'Certainly. Without my glasses, I'm a helpless cripple.'

The seemingly merciless officer was touched by the
sad plight of the prisoner whose dim, red-rimmed eyes
bore witness to the truth of his statement. The commander
walked over to the pile of confiscated articles and brought
back the vital pair of glasses.

'There you are, take them and wear them!' he said
graciously.

The poor man was delighted. He took hold of them
eagerly, wiped them on his sleeve and adjusted them on his
nose. Very shortly afterwards, however, he was once again
on his feet.

'What is it now?' asked the commander impatiently.

'Citizen Commander,' stammered the prisoner plain-
tively, 'these aren't my glasses.'

'What about it? If I give them to you, they're yours.
Don't worry, nobody's going to take them away from
you.'

He could not see what the prisoner was getting at.

'Thank you, I know,' assented the poor man, 'but
they're no use to me. You see, I'm short-sighted and these
are for long-sight.'

'Stop bothering me! Glasses are glasses—short-
sighted or long-sighted, it's all the same! You wanted

spectacles—you got them. What more do you want?'

The young officer, who had evidently never needed a pair of spectacles, was very annoyed by the discontented recipient of his favours.

'But I can't see through them,' groaned the man.

'Can you see me?'

'Yes, I can see you, Comrade Commander.'

'Well then, if you can see me—that's all you need to worry about. You've got eyes like a hawk! And stop making a damned nuisance of yourself!'

Thus having spoken, the officer turned round and walked away briskly.

The sun moved slowly down the sky till it was hidden by pink clouds. The whole live cargo of over two thousand men had been thoroughly checked and was due to leave at any moment. A grey-haired old man rose to his feet in order to attract the attention of the young lieutenant in command of the draft.

'Citizen Commander,' he asked, 'my son is in the other group over there. I am old and ill and my son could look after me during the journey. Please have me transferred to the other group or have my son sent over here.'

'No. It's not allowed!' replied the officer to whom the separation of father from son meant less than nothing. 'Once you're in this group, you stay there.'

'But the governor promised me that my son and I would travel in the same truck,' the old man despairingly protested, and taking advantage of the approach of the prison governor he turned to address him.

'Citizen Governor! Isn't it true that you promised to send me and my son away together?'

'I'm your commander!' the lieutenant interrupted. 'You're not in prison now but on draft; and I'm the draft-conducting officer! As for him . . .' he pointed to the prison governor, a major with many decorations, 'as far as you're concerned, he's a mere nothing—old rags and ribbons. He doesn't count. I'm the only one who counts now. And I don't approve. Understand?'

From the pocket of his tunic he took a whistle and blew it. That was the signal to get ready.

The leading detachment picked up its kit and the first hundred men, myself included, moved off.

We marched surrounded by almost twice our number of soldiers armed with submachine-guns. In addition, there were dogs on the leash and plain-clothes men with drawn revolvers. The gate-keeper opened one set of gates and then another in the outer wall, beyond which lay freedom. In a swirl of dust, scooped from the sandy road by our shuffling feet, we marched out of the prison.

Behind us came the second detachment, then the third . . . fifth . . . tenth, and so on, till the yard was completely deserted. There remained in the prison only N.C.O.s, jailers, guards, orderlies and—the governor, 'old rags and ribbons'—a mere nothing.

It was a long march to the train. Surrounded by guards, the weary prisoners trudged through the small suburban street, while passers-by stood on the pavements and watched. Their faces betrayed neither sympathy nor surprise but complete indifference; it was as though they were watching a herd of cattle. The reaction of the prisoners at the sight of free people was totally different. They looked around them with unfeigned wonder, for during their many months in prison they had had time to forget the existence of men who moved without restriction and of women in colourful, flimsy dresses.

Although the clothes worn by the poor people of the

provinces were anything but elegant—simple, cheap and very ordinary, in fact—to the convicts who were beginning to forget that there was any other existence except the drab, grey life of a prisoner, they appeared as the raiment of wondrous beings from another planet.

The town, which consisted of ugly detached one- or two-story houses, once white but now dirty grey, co-operative shops with shelves yawning and little apparent excuse for remaining open, rough streets and broken pavements, innocent of all greenery except for a modest strip of grass or a stunted tree—where the only attempts at beautification, if one could call it that, were scarlet banners with propaganda slogans or portraits of Lenin and Stalin —this inexpressibly doleful town, representing the world 'outside,' sent the straggling herd of deportees into raptures.

Unfortunately, they were not long allowed to enjoy their first sight of the town. The procession turned down an empty street, under a bridge and into a vaulted sewer where the prisoners had to wade up to their ankles in mud and excrement. The dogs kept up a noisy barking and the sound echoed dully through the tunnel. When we re-emerged above ground, we were halted and ordered to squat down. It is always thus: at any halt you must at once squat down, not because those in charge wished you to rest, but to stop you thinking of trying to escape. To get up from the sitting position and leap away to one side before dog or bullet reached you was an impossibility.

On this occasion, the prisoners had scarcely obeyed the order before a stout officer in the uniform of a colonel of the Security Police appeared on the bridge above their heads, and began to address them. It was not a speech, just a flood of the most vulgar abuse. The prisoners, sitting in the damp cloying drain, oblivious of the filth adhering to their rags, just sought to recover their breath after the exertions of the march, and looked with utter indifference at the stout officer hurling insults at those who were being, to him, rightly, deported to Siberia. As his fury increased, he became almost blue in the face, and soon we were watching him and wondering whether he would first have a fit, or choke on the foam that was appearing on his lips.

Eventually the speaker tired, panted and stopped. The prisoners were ordered to their feet and urged into a run that soon brought us out on to the highway, where, in the distance, we could see the station buildings and the long red snake of a goods train.

Thirty-six prisoners were pushed into each truck and the doors barred. In each truck were two tiers of wooden bunks fixed to either wall and, in the corner, a tin trumpet having egress through the floor and intended to serve as a lavatory. Day and night, light was admitted by a small, barred window, for it never gets dark in Siberia during the summer. The purple twilight lingers all night.

The journey lasted a month. It took us through towns as similar as identical twins, through villages, past fields of corn, fields of evenly ploughed fallow, about which was a striking lack of life. There were seldom people to be seen, sometimes none at all. At the points some old country crone, her head wrapped in a shawl, would be standing like a statue, clasping a flag, a yellow rag tied to a gnarled stick picked out of the wood, which she held aloft as a signal to the engine-driver, not merely while the train was approaching, but until the whole several score of trucks had disappeared over the horizon. Then we came to a world of strange sad settlements without names—only numbers. The inhabitants of these places, who were working in wooden powerhouses or locomotive sheds, wore quilted coats and trousers, while fur-coated guards with rifles surveyed them constantly from the tops of wooden towers. By night, the settlements were lit by the beams of searchlights, sweeping the mesh of barbed wire entanglements which surrounded them.

Further on still, not even these punishment camps were in evidence. The train chugged slowly along a single track laid by the hands of condemned men through the silent tundra. In whatever direction one looked, there was nothing to be seen but the mournful birch trees, tall and white, reaching skywards or leaning at an angle in the soggy red moss. Utter silence and not even a bird in sight to show that man was there.

At night, when the train stopped at its secret halts, the guards would tap the carriages with mallets, rousing the sleeping prisoners to make sure that none had attempted to escape. Occasionally, the body of a man who had died would be slung into a wayside ditch, or somebody who was giving trouble would be transferred to the punishment coach—the prison within a prison.

The food consisted of hard broken biscuits, sugar and small fish which were swallowed whole. Water was scarce and some days there was none.

Once during the journey the doors were flung open and we were ordered to get out for searching. The train stopped on a high mound, at the foot of which those in command of the draft stationed themselves. We all had to leap from the open trucks and roll down the slope to the feet of our guards. Anyone frightened of jumping was urged on by one of the dogs. How they enjoyed seeing a grey-haired old man flop from the train and bounce down the bank like a rubber ball, with his cap fluttering behind him and his bag rolling in front. At the foot of the slope we had to squat on the ground, as we had when we emerged from the sewer, and for the same reason. Then we had to

crawl back up the bank on all fours. Eyes, nose, nails and
mouth were all full of black grit by the end of it.

Every morning at dawn, when the doors were unbarred so that a bag of biscuits could be thrown in while
the guards covered us with their rifles, a young corporal
would climb into the truck. He was tall and fair, pretty
as a girl, with fresh rosy cheeks untouched by razor. His
tunic bore several decorations for sport. He was filled
with an honest, sincere enthusiasm for everything going
on in his country which, of course, surpassed all others in
culture and civilization. He was glad to answer the questions put to him by the prisoners surrounding him, and
always with a smile. He would have been prepared to chat
freely for much longer at a time had it not been for his
duties and the presence of the guards.

'What's it like in these camps?' he was always being
asked.

'Don't you worry about the camps,' he would console
his listeners. 'It's true they'll make you work but there'll
be plenty of food, a bed for everyone, and once a week
they'll take you to the baths, give you clean linen and in
winter you'll be issued with caps, coats and boots. There's
also a library, a gramophone with records, a radio and
newspaper. There's a shop where you can spend the money
you earn on whatever you like—same as a market. Then
there's an infirmary and a rest-house. On your free day,
you can go to the cinema; but the greatest attraction of
all is something you won't find in any capitalist country—
that's a telephone. And you'll be allowed to talk through
it.'

He spoke in all sincerity and with deep feeling. But
the childish youth offered no suggestion as to whom one
could ring up, with whom one might hold a conversation
and what matters one might discuss. He merely wished to

dazzle the foreigners with this evidence of Soviet civilization by which he himself was so obviously enthralled.
When some of the prisoners mentioned that they had already had a few opportunities of using a telephone, he only
shrugged his shoulders condescendingly, dismissing their
claim as no more than an idle boast. To all questions regarding the labour camps of Siberia, he answered with a
care-free smile,

'Don't worry your heads about it! They'll let you talk
on the telephone to your heart's content.'

'It's all right for him,' they would say as soon as he'd
left the truck. 'He's only got to see us as far as our hard
labour, then away with him back to Moscow, Odessa or
some other place.'

But the corporal did not get back. He stayed with his
charges in the camp. Having been too gentle with the
prisoners during the journey, he was found to be unfit to
perform the duties of an escort. An escort should never
attempt to console his slaves with the prospect of using
that product of Soviet genius, of which the decadent West
knows nothing, the telephone.

NINE

The Vision

After four weeks in our prison on wheels, the doors were opened and the journey, we were told, was at an end.

Not far from us was a green copse in which, like reddish mushrooms, there sprouted neat little wooden houses. It looked cosy and inviting, much like a country health resort. The stillness which enveloped the place was only disturbed by the ceaseless rustle of the trees, and the air was full of the scent of resin. This hamlet was called Kozva.

The prisoners got out of the trucks in silence, and marched off with their kit in a solemn procession. The engine of the deserted train gave a hoot and set off on the return journey, towing the empty red wagons behind it as easily as a child hauling a string of match-boxes. Our last link with freedom dissolved before our eyes.

Our way led through the copse with its quiet dwellings and into a dark forest of pines, which echoed with the noise of invisible axes. Then the path grew broader and opened into a spacious clearing, a soft damp meadow of yellow grass. The further we marched, the more our feet sank. Water spurted up from under our boots, transforming the meadow into a morass. A single false step was enough to plunge a man up to his waist in mud. Un-

able to extricate himself, if his companions failed to come
to his aid in time, he was lost.

Happily, we soon saw in the distance a pale gleaming road made of felled branches, stripped of their bark
and secured with stout pine logs. This led to the camp.
Here, unfortunately, there was no sign of neat little houses
with electric lighting, glass window-panes and shutters
with cut-out heart-shapes. In a space cleared of trees stood
a few score of huge canvas tents, each capable of accommodating two hundred men.

Once inside, we found ourselves under a flapping roof
supported by a number of poles. The tiered rows of bunks
were spread with fern and pine-fronds, while the floor
was of sand sprinkled with pine-needles. In the middle of
it was a stove with a high chimney-pipe, red with the heat
of the roaring fire. There were men sitting round the stove
on heaps of fire-wood, each man holding a jam-tin of
snow which he was engaged in thawing. It was the month of
June and a warm summer at that.

In the intervals, while bread and hot soup were being
handed round, the new arrivals strolled through the clearing, visiting friends in other tents, walking in the fresh
air, talking and resting after the journey, as they watched
the steel-grey River Pietchora flowing steadily below
them.

Only prisoners allocated to this particular camp were
required to work. Those of us who were merely in transit
and bound for other destinations were not burdened with
duties.

This glorious idleness resulted from no feeling of
compassion on the part of the authorities. It was just not
worth while setting in motion the immense administrative
machinery required to form fresh labour battalions, when
the drafts in transit were shortly to be embarked in galleys.

and dispersed throughout the many and varied camps of Siberia.

Kozva, a locality situated in the so-called 'autonomous' Soviet republic of Komi, was a grass-grown waste, a dumb wilderness sparsely populated by deported prisoners whose tents and huts were surrounded by barbed wire. There were many such compounds. At the entrance to each, on the heavy log gate guarded by a sentry, was a vivid poster exhorting the wretched prisoners to engage in joyous, devoted labours for the greater glory of their beloved Soviet Union.

These camps, which stretched for miles, were so extensive that even inside them a prisoner had the illusion of freedom. Only the wooden watch-towers, with sentries perched in their crows' nest, dispelled such a fantasy. However, surveillance was less strict here than elsewhere, for Kozva lies in an area so forsaken by God and man that escape is impossible. Although, at first sight, the place seemed no more than an ordinary forced labour camp, similar to thousands scattered throughout Russia, it was, in fact, of particular importance, being the main distribution centre for all convicts deported to Siberia.

Here, the prisoners were dispatched by trades according to the demand in particular camps for carpenters, joiners, drivers or mechanics. Industrial workers and professional men alike were treated as general labour and divided up into the strong who were fit for heavy work in the mines, the weak who could be employed in the forest, and those who were so worn out as to be unfit for work of any description.

Selection was made by a medical commission, consisting of a nursing orderly with a Red Cross armband and the rank of corporal, whose inspection amounted to no more than a cursory glance at each prisoner. Nor was his verdict of any practical value, for as soon as the prisoners came to their final destination, they were employed as the authorities on the spot saw fit.

Walking aimlessly by myself through the surrounding countryside, I came upon a strange colony. I saw village women wearing white blouses embroidered with multi-coloured crosses. They had flowered kerchiefs on their heads. Some were carrying children in their arms. The men wore white linen trousers, black waistcoats and wide straw hats with a blue ribbon. There were also boys in homespun pants and blouses caught in at the waist with a cord. They were all bare-footed. Peasants from Bessarabia! When the Soviets had occupied that part of Rumania, to which they had for years been laying claim on the grounds that it was inhabited solely by Russian nationals, in order to prove to the world that those areas contained no Rumanians, they had deported entire villages.

Any attempt at lengthy conversation with these unfortunates would have aroused the suspicion of the nearby sentries and would undoubtedly have led to reprisals. So I preferred to make a hasty withdrawal.

On my way back from this educational excursion I was confronted by an odd sight. Walking light-footed over the thin carpet of snow, which covered the path trodden between the tents, was a beautiful young woman. Her chestnut hair, set in European fashion above a clear, white forehead, framed delicate, subtle features. Her graceful figure was clothed in a dark evening frock, silk stockings shone on her slender legs and on her feet were lizard-skin shoes with high heels. She had a grey squirrel coat thrown over her shoulders.

She was walking slowly, giving the impression of a lady deep in thought, strolling home from dining with friends or from a visit to the theatre. Even the bucket she was carrying in her hand did not dispel the illusion. The ragged men who passed her—half-savage Turkomans, Uzbecks, Tadjicks and Chinese—stared at her as though she were some strange creature from another planet. They stopped in their tracks, craning their necks as she went by, like country bumpkins at their first sight of a gazelle in a zoo.

With her eyes fixed on the ground she moved on slowly, to vanish at last behind the canvas walls of the women's tent.

Not for a moment imagining that I should soon see her again, I wondered whether she had really been there at all or whether, perhaps, it was only a trick of tired eyes, dazzled by the distant white shimmer of the snow-capped Urals.

*

Far below us flowed the broad river. We marched down the steep slope of our hillside clearing to the river bank, where some way from the shore and linked to it by a gangway, three barges lay rocking at anchor.

As we drew nearer, it was obvious that the barges, which from high up on the hillside had appeared small and slim, were, in reality, of colossal dimensions, but the gangway proved to be no more than a narrow plank, pliant as a spring-board. This plank rose almost vertically from the low beach to the towering gunwale and it gave under our feet like the string of some giant bow, aimed at the sky. It was a wonder it did not snap under our weight, as we embarked, and plunge us into the water.

The prisoners held on to each other, each man fixing his eyes on the shoulders of the man in front of him so as not to look down at the swirling, brown tide below. In an

unbroken line, like rats on a hawser, we boarded the old
craft and were glad to settle down in the hold. It was
amazing to see just how many galley-slaves such an ark
could accommodate. It took all day and night to load the
three barges. Once aboard, the men lay down in the bunks
below decks but the guards detailed to look after them
were so busy that they forgot we needed food. Under
battened hatches, we waited in vain for bread till the
anchor was weighed. Parched with thirst, we listened to
the noise of the waves lapping against the sides of the
barge.

At daybreak, a long blast on the fog-horn preceded
a sharp tug at the hawser. Then we heard the loud monotonous plash-plash of the waves, stroked by the bottom of our boat. Once the barge was in mid-stream, we
were allowed on deck where water was being brought to
the boil on iron stoves.

The three enormous barges, roped firmly together,
crawled on their way like huge black tortoises. They were
hauled by a small, squat tug with the icy name of *Polar
Ranger*. All round us the surface of the water looked flat
and motionless—only the steep banks on either side seemed
to slide swiftly behind us.

A soldier watched over us as we thronged round the
stoves on deck. He stood on the roof of the wheel-house,
looking down on us. His ragged coat was held at the waist
by a string like that which was fixed to his rifle in place
of a sling. The prisoners assembled at the feet of the soldier looming above them, like tourists in front of a me-
morial. They lifted their heads to jeer at him.

'Hell of a fine belt you've got there! Where I come
from, the peasants lead their cattle to market on a rope
like that!'

'And where did you buy that sack on your back? And those old galoshes you've got for boots?'

At first, the soldier tried to ignore the barrage of mockery. He remained stoically silent, glowering at the mob like a chained bulldog tormented by urchins. He waited patiently for us to finish drinking our hot water and clear off, but the prisoners had no intention of dispersing. All too seldom was there a chance to jeer at a representative of the oppressors responsible for bringing them so far north. The laughter which had at first been timid and intermittent now grew louder as the taunts were multiplied. It became challenging and spiteful, with every guffaw sharp as a wasp sting. There was no escaping this mockery.

'Silence!' roared the soldier at last. 'Remember you're convicts bound for Siberia!'

'And where are you off to? America?'

'Ah, but I'm free.'

'What do you mean, free? Who's free in your country? Fine sort of freedom to fight for!'

'Shut your face!' snarled the soldier.

'Tell me, does your gun really fire? Looks as if it's made out of an old poker.'

'Mind it doesn't fire at you!' threatened the guard.

'Try it out. And is it true your army 'planes are French?'

Suspecting nothing, the soldier eagerly assented.

'Of course they're French. They're all French.'

'You're right enough there—the same bloody 'planes Napoleon left behind at Moscow!'

A wild roar of laughter shook the barge and the steep riverbanks threw back the echo of it.

Then something incredible happened. Two bright

heavy tears rolled down the soldier's cheeks and the great hulking peasant started to weep like a child.

The cold of those white Siberian nights with a pale, sickly gleam by which you could read, pierced us through and through. The prisoners, inadequately nourished by hot water, went below decks to sleep off the hunger which was becoming ever more acute.

A draft of women convicts was separated from us only by a thin wooden wall made of planks. Behind it were a few score of thieves, prostitutes and other assorted criminals: Russian, Ukrainian, Cossack, Tartar and Azerbaijan. Locked up in such close proximity to the men prisoners, they were yet more restless than the latter. Their long sojourn in captivity had affected them quite differently: more than food and sleep, they desired men.

One of the planks dividing us was soon prised free and a woman crawled through the opening, to find herself amid rows of men, lying one beside the other, like brown loaves on a baker's shelf. We heard no affectionate exchanges, but a few heavy sighs, quickened breathing and a hasty struggle followed by a moment of silence while one lover changed places with the next. This scene caused no undue commotion. The barge was wrapped in darkness, many of the men were sound asleep, totally unaware of the amorous delights available, and the woman, moreover, was dressed no differently from the men. This daring escapade might well have passed unnoticed by the authorities had it not been for the malice of man. Someone whose moral susceptibilities were above average or who, perhaps, was himself incapable of such amorous pursuits, ran off to report. We heard the rapid tread of army boots and in rushed the soldiers who, obviously well directed, made straight for the scene of the crime. They caught hold of a

man by the neck and flung him on the floor thus revealing
the girl. She betrayed no fear. She was a street-walker.
That was what had brought her to prison, to trial, and
now to Siberia. Nothing worse could befall her.

A soldier grabbed hold of her legs and started to
pull her, but she was perfectly willing to go of her own
accord, which she did with an impudent smile of triumph.
What could they do to her? But the authorities were well
able to deal with the case.

With the soldier as escort the girl set off in the direction of the ladder, parading between the rows of men who
surveyed her with regretful longing—sorry to see her
leave so soon. She was taken up on deck and there ordered
by the soldier to remove her padded jacket, her blouse, a
sweater in shreds and her vest. Thus stripped, she was
placed in the bow and made to face up-river. She was going
to freeze, so that she might cool down a little.

In the grey, misty silence of the Arctic, the half-naked
woman with her shameless smile and hair streaming in the
wind, the full, white flagons of her breasts thrust proudly
forward, seemed to challenge the forest deities lurking in
the tundra, slowly gliding towards her.

Behind the girl stood a soldier, silent, sullen and indifferent. He was not a man, not even a male with whom
she could go. With bayonet levelled at the girl's bare back,
he stood there motionless as though carved out of wood.
The punishment lasted one hour, and the frozen girl had
hardly gathered up her clothing to go below when another
woman was sent up to take her place on that unusual
pillory.

Days and nights passed. Each morning we were given
dry biscuits, herrings, sugar and herbal butter together
with boiling water. Several times a day the lavatory on

deck was open and we were furthermore permitted to lounge, walk about the deck, sing, play cards or smoke and even shave with a piece of smuggled glass.

At the end of ten days, the barges drew inshore and we could see creatures in amazing purple hats with veils. They looked like revellers at a fancy-dress ball wearing women's hats of a bygone era. These hats, consisting of a wire frame covered by a thick veil which was tucked into the collar of the shirt, were a protective measure against mosquitoes and were worn not only by the soldiers and their superiors but also by the slaves. Work was impossible without them, for the hovering swarms of mosquitoes were ever ready to strike at eyes, mouth and nose.

The barges slowly made fast to the shore where guards were waiting with dogs, restless on the leash. The old men and cripples as well as the women and children were to land here, for this locality was given over to lighter agricultural work.

As the guards shouted their names, the prisoners filed down the planks and formed groups on shore under the eyes of the sentries. In a broad meadow stood a band of children, young lads and girls—adolescent criminals— while some distance away were gathered the old and infirm and behind them a close-packed throng of women— old hags and young girls together.

They were ragged and dirty but strong and masculine in appearance, wearing trousers, army jackboots, padded jackets and caps. On their backs they carried bags and bundles containing their belongings. Only one particular girl kept well clear of the rest. She sat all alone, at a distance, on her suitcases which were colourfully spangled with hotel labels from Paris, London, Moscow and New York. A light fur cape hung from her shoulders. With her chin in her hand, she sat there staring silently at the river.

That was the woman I had first beheld, like a vision, on my way back to the tent.

No sooner had the draft allocated to this area been disembarked than the tug gave a sullen hoot and chugged onwards, pulling behind it the three barges—like a grimy child with three kites on a string, all too unwieldy to take the air.

A young man stood beside me on deck, leaning over the rail. He was handsome, clean-shaven, with hair neatly combed and he wore a military uniform which still bore traces of the insignia taken from him at the same time as his freedom. The young man kept his anguished eyes firmly fixed on the lovely girl drifting ever further in our wake with the fast vanishing shore. Lounging at his side was Shevchenko, a squat, tousle-haired Ukrainian in a torn coat—a professional bandit, agent provocateur and informer.

'You, Yermulayev!' he said, and his lips twisted into a cynical grin. 'You were in love with her.' He nodded towards the woman. 'You wrote her letters and love poems and you got nothing for it. Me, I went to her one night, took her and had her.'

'You're lying!' shouted the youth almost in terror. 'She would never go with you. She's so fine, so beautiful.'

'So fine, so beautiful,' mimicked Shevchenko, wilfully tormenting Yermulayev. 'Maybe she would go with me, maybe she wouldn't, but I didn't ask her. I just went up to her while she was asleep, my lad, shoved my fist over her mouth and that was that. She could hardly breathe. As for talking love to her or writing poems, I didn't try, since I don't know how to write and I can't talk American.'

'Shut your filthy mouth!'

'If you want me to, I will.' Shevchenko shrugged. 'But it was I who had a real American, not you. Tell me, is it true she worked in the American Embassy and the militia took her off the train at night, when she was on her way to Leningrad from Moscow? Quiet like, so no one would know what'd become of her? That's what I was told anyway. Neat work, eh? You should know all about it. You were talking to her in German or American. Did she ask you to let her American king know where she'd been taken? Come on now, own up!' He laughed.

Yermulayev wiped the tears out of his eyes with the palm of his hand, glanced coldly at the criminal and then, with a sigh, he whispered gently, even amicably:

'Ah, you swine! But why didn't I think of treating her the same way myself? Hell, what a fool I am . . . what a fool!'

TEN

Ingratitude

As we ploughed northwards up the Pietchora we met the rivers Usa and Katiu, then, climbing into the Arctic circle, we followed the Inta through to the Great Inta, which river is so broad that one can hardly see from one side of it to the other. After three weeks' sailing we at last put in to land, at a harbour called the 'Twenty-seventh kilometre.' This meant that the punishment camp for which we were destined was some twenty-seven kilometres distant.

Twenty-seven kilometres through a wood did not seem very much at first. It was hard, therefore, to understand the sudden solicitude of our escorts who decided to take the sick and the feeble a roundabout way by boat and to divide the remainder into small groups to be sent in daily batches. This considerate treatment was fully comprehensible, however, when it transpired that on our twenty-seven kilometres through the forest we would have to negotiate a treacherous swamp by way of a path fit for three men abreast but along which the guards drove us in files of six. They did so intentionally so as to dispel all thoughts of escape. The men, as they marched close packed along the narrow path, knew well that a single false step meant total immersion in that quaking bog of yellow-black mud. From time to time, a man would fall exhausted, only to struggle up again, kicked by the soldiers, take a few faltering steps, fall again and once more be kicked to his feet. Many flung their bundles with all they possessed into the black abyss of the bog—lacking the strength to carry them any further. Then their boots would follow, as they tore them from their sorely aching feet.

The column, which had at first marched in close order, spread out into a long line which gradually changed to a broken chain of weary loiterers, kept together in the rear by the lowered bayonets of the guards. At last the road came to an end. The escorts, anxious to reach our goal as quickly as possible, whipped up the pace of the marchers. The proximity of the camp which was hidden from us by the intervening tree-studded morass was at last revealed by the barking of the dogs guarding the labour battalions, the clatter of axes, the screech of saws and the sight of treeless areas through which wood-cutters were carrying the newly felled timber.

The column mounted a wooden highway which brought us to a clearing. There, behind coils of barbed wire, stood a collection of huts. Unspeakably weary, the prisoners were taken in to be fed.

In the large dining-hall, decorated with propaganda slogans, were long rows of tables and benches. Waitresses brought round bowls of hot soup, fish cutlets and potatoes. Stone mugs of hot tea with sugar and raisin buns constituted dessert: a veritable home-coming party, a feast such as the prisoners were never again to see.

While we were eating, the commandant of the camp walked into the hall and scanned the faces of the new arrivals in the hope of observing their wonderment at the sight of such a magnificent repast. But their ashen faces and feverish eyes betrayed only a bestial hunger and a deadly weariness. The commandant strolled up and down the hall a few times, then, turning to the prisoner nearest him, he asked,

'Taste good?'

'Yes.'

'Do you like all this?' The eyes of the commandant indicated the plate, cup, spoon and fork.

The convict shrugged his shoulders. This was not the wildly enthusiastic answer expected of him. The bewildered commandant gazed at the assembled prisoners who, with heads bent low over their bowls, appeared quite unmoved by the wonders of culture and civilization surrounding them. Then, as he walked towards the exit, he said with pronounced disappointment,

'That's what you get for giving them a restaurant, real plates, service and treating them kindly. They don't even appreciate it. What an ungrateful bunch!'

*

The mine in which I was working had a shaft over two hundred feet deep. It was a damp, black well. This pit produced no coal as yet for we had first to cut through layers of wet clay, earth and gravel before reaching the coal face. The rubble was hauled to the surface in a huge tub, let down from above on a massive chain, the upper end of which was attached to a roller made from a tree-trunk. The tub was pulled up by two malaria-stricken horses plodding round in circles. When the tub was full, one of the miners struck an iron bar with a hammer. This was the signal to haul away. When the container had been emptied by the surface-workers, the man in charge of the horses gave a similar signal and the tub was again lowered. One had to be on the look-out while this was going on so as to avoid being crushed, for the bucket was heavy.

The miners used to descend by means of ladders fixed to the slippery walls of the pit. Although it was quicker and less exhausting to go down in the bucket, dangling on its chain, than by ladder, the former method, being considered dangerous, was strictly forbidden. How strictly could be seen from the signboard at the entrance to the pit on which was written: 'Warning! The tub is to be used only for carrying soil, and workers are forbidden on pain of punishment to ride in it. One ring above ground is the signal for lowering, two rings below signifies "tub full," and three rings—"men riding in the bucket." '

The mine was equipped in the most primitive fashion, the gallery floors often consisting of no more than a narrow plank thrown down on the wet, slippery mud, or of a log stripped of its bark, on which it was necessary to tread as warily as a tightrope-walker. Quite a few of the many and apparently shallow patches of water were really so deep that a false step could prove fatal. Once, a sentry was murdered by the miners and his body thrown into one of these puddles. No trace of it was ever found.

Not far from the main workings there was, true enough, a shed that trembled with the reverberations of an engine of some sort. That shed housed a generator which supplied only the searchlights on the sentry-towers; even the camp commandant's office was lit by paraffin lamp. As the power-house was surrounded by two fences of barbed wire, those who worked there were strictly isolated from the remainder of the convicts, and the many guard-posts, perched like dovecots on their tall poles, kept unauthorized persons at a distance.

Once, at dawn, as the night shift was finishing and the bucket was returning to the surface, Bobrov fainted.

He was helpless for so long that we thought he was dead.

His workmates took him up and laid him on the grass, hastily built a rough stretcher and carried him back to camp. The doctor was called and diagnosed a heart attack, promising to have the sick man taken to hospital. Instead of the ambulance arriving, however, the doctor reappeared shortly afterwards accompanied by two of the camp officers. It would be more accurate to say that they appeared with him rather than he with them, for the look on the doctor's face was that of a schoolboy who has just had a telling-off. The officers gazed sympathetically at the patient, then approached his bunk with all the compassion of nursing sisters.

'Hm . . . yes . . . weak heart,' said one of them, looking at the sick man. He turned to the doctor and continued, 'It's not so very terrible. It'll pass off. This climate's to blame and the food. You've got to admit it's not quite what you'd get in a Moscow restaurant—and the work's a bit on the heavy side. No doubt about that. But, after all, this isn't a health resort or a hotel, just a labour camp and a coal-mine where people have got to work to speed the development and to increase the growth and the power of the Soviet Union. I've got a weak heart myself for that matter, but I don't try to get myself taken to hospital, because I'm working for the good of my country. So don't you be too generous with your hospital, doctor. Keep it for the people who really need it, or you might find yourself down the mine. Give that man three days off duty. Let him lie down and rest—there's no need for him to go to the sick bay. Now don't you worry, old man,' he said to the patient giving him an encouraging smile, 'everything'll be all right. You just lie here for three days, have a good rest and by the end of that time, you'll be begging to go back to work out of sheer boredom.'

With that, all three of them went out. The sick man was my closest neighbour. I looked after him and took him his bread, soup and water. Bobrov, an engineer by profession, had also been a colonel in the Red Army. He was an intelligent, quiet chap who didn't say much and rarely joined in a conversation. It took his illness and my nursing to bring us together.

'It's true this place is no health resort,' I said as we lay resting beside one another. 'They told me that in prison during an interrogation and they gave me a thing or two to remember it by. Look.'

I took the sick man's hand and laid it on my head so as to let him feel the marks on my scalp where I had been struck with the butt of a revolver. But when I looked at my neighbour's face to see his reaction, he seemed to be smiling indulgently, as though he were a grown-up and I a small boy presenting his knee, scratched by a fall.

'What a babe you are,' he said, with sympathy and understanding. 'Take a look at this.'

He lifted up his hand and showed me two small parallel scratches on his wrist, about a finger's breadth away from each other. The marks looked like needle scratches and were hardly noticeable in the half-light of the hut. There were similar traces on his other wrist.

'You see,' he explained, 'those are also souvenirs of an interrogation. They cut the skin and drew the sinews with hooks. I've got the same marks on my back. Of course, I confessed everything. Later, in court, they gave me fifteen years. I've done seven, though I've not been in this camp a year yet. I was on the White Sea first and then in the Solovieckian Islands. You've heard of them, I suppose? They were the worst of all at one time. If a man hadn't the strength to work full out during the day, they didn't admit him into the camp at night; so he could not get to the cook-house for his meal, but had to wait till the gang came out to work again the next day. He then rejoined them and carried on if he wasn't found frozen to death or had been eaten by wolves. It's all very well to punish a schoolboy by making him stand in the corridor, but it won't do in Siberia. Before they sent me there, I was in solitary confinement in Lubianka prison, where there wasn't a sound to be heard. The prisoners were not allowed to talk to themselves, nor even allowed to cough. It used to make me happy just to hear one of the guards cursing outside in the corridor.

'My crime wasn't so very awful,' he went on. 'As a married man, an engineer and a colonel living in Moscow, I was entitled to a three-roomed flat. I had one in the centre of the city in a modern house and with a good view of the Kremlin and the river. One day Vorobiej dropped in. He was the regimental education officer. He made out he'd just called by chance as he was in the neighbour-hood and felt like saying hello. Actually he'd come for a purpose, namely to see what way I was living—what books I had on my shelves; in short, to carry out an inspection. It was quite understandable as the education officer was also the political watchdog of the regiment. He was charmed with my home, but expressed doubts as to whether it wasn't perhaps on the small side for me. Especially, he said, as he presumed my family would eventually increase. Children would arrive in due course and it might be hard to find a larger set of rooms later on. Fortunately enough, he happened to know of a set which were more com-modious and suitable in every way—not actually in the centre of the town or even in a modern house, but to com-pensate for that there were five rooms in the set. He was prepared to fix up the whole thing on my behalf and he himself would take over my old rooms which he thought quite adequate for a single man. I told him not to bother as I was perfectly satisfied where I was and had no intention of moving. I was a bit sharp and Vorobiej understood that he'd do well to leave. He excused himself, advised me to think it over and let him know when I'd like to have a look at those five rooms. After which, he went. But that wasn't the end of it. Vorobiej not only took a liking to my home but also to my young wife, Maryla. My wife was of Polish extraction, the daughter of a Kiev doctor. She was really exceptionally beautiful and might well appeal to anyone. One day she told me that Vorobiej was running after her and that she often found him waiting for her outside the house. On a few occasions, while I was in the office, he had telephoned and asked to speak to her. Once, when my wife was not at home, Vorobiej showed up again. We started talking about something quite trivial, then he asked where my wife had gone and finally proposed —no more nor less—that I should divorce her and move into those five rooms so that he could marry Maryla and take over my home. As he was smiling all the time he was saying this and was up to his eyes in vodka besides, I thought he was joking. Finally, however, as he insisted on having an answer, I let him know my ideas on the subject. I stood up, punched him on the jaw and threw him out. He was drunk—but not so drunk that he didn't know what he was saying or what he'd come about. He didn't resist when I grabbed hold of his collar, but he did assure me that I'd have cause to remember him and that I'd pay dearly for my pleasant attitude towards him. He kept his word. I used to go along to the Institute of Physical Culture, where I practised gymnastics, fencing and ju-jitsu, which was taught by a Japanese. The instructor was arrested shortly afterwards and I followed. It was a funny thing that nobody else taking the course was interfered with; at least, if they were, their names were never mentioned during the enquiry or later at the trial. I was accused of spying for Japan and for being an accomplice of the instructor to whom I was alleged to have given information. Just what information they didn't specify. The chief witness was Vorobiej, the political watchdog of the regiment—and he was quite sufficient. You know the rest of the story.'

A medical orderly approached the bunk with two small bottles, sent by the doctor—tincture *convalariæ* and *adonis vernalis*—to be taken by the patient every three hours with a spoonful of hot water.

The orderly put down the medicine and went out.

*

The prisoners, exhausted after the day's work, lay sleeping soundly. The hut was lit only by two tallow candles suspended from the ceiling by a thin wire and by the red glow from the stove falling on the pile of white firewood in the centre of the room. The sound of heavy breathing mingled with the rumble of snores. Now and again a man would sigh deeply, cry out in his sleep, murmur drowsily or scratch himself in a subconscious effort to ward off the bugs.

Apostolidis, a small, puny Greek with black eyes like those of a bear cub, awoke, sat up in his bunk, pulled on his boots and wandered outside, still half asleep. When he came back after a minute or two, the warmth of the crackling stove embraced him agreeably. Apostolidis paused, picked up a couple of sticks from the heap on the floor and, lifting the lid of the stove with a stump of wood, threw them into the fire. He wiped his hands and sat down on the nearest bench.

The cheerful glow caressed his aching feet, narrow chest and wasted face. Then his eyes closed and he fell asleep, despite himself. Alas, he was not long undisturbed.

Lichatchov, who was a professional brigand, got down from his bunk without a sound and in stockinged feet tip-toed across to the little Greek. He crouched by the bench and, slowly inserting two fingers into the pocket of Apostolidis' trousers, brought out a small rag purse on a long tape which was sewed into the pocket. Delicately, he undid the string round the neck of the purse and drew out a card about the size of a postage stamp. In replacing the empty purse in the sleeper's pocket, Lichatchov awakened the Greek and, realizing that he had been robbed, the horrified Apostolidis set up a hue and cry.

'Stop! Give it back to me!' he yelled in a frenzy of terror, seizing Lichatchov by the sleeve of his shirt. But the brigand was tall, strong and broad-shouldered and the feeble Greek had no hope of regaining his property. Nevertheless, he would not let go.

'Hand it over! Thief!' he screamed. 'Thief, thief, thief!'

The shouting and the noise of the tussle woke up the rest of the hut.

'Help!' cried Apostolidis. 'Help me! He's stolen my bread card!'

The theft of bread was tantamount to sacrilege. Had Lichatchov been trying to murder the Greek out of hatred or by way of revenge, probably few would have to run to the victim's aid. The principle of life in camp was 'every man for himself.' The theft of a bread card, however, was a crime capable of driving the starving prisoners into a frenzy. The hut shook with the drumming of feet as the prisoners leapt from their bunks. In the twinkling of an eye, Lichatchov was set upon by a furious mob, a few dozen strong. They laid hold of his head, hands and feet, threw him to the floor, beating the breath out of him and tearing at him ferociously. The huge wooden structure shuddered with the grim commotion of a man being lynched. Whether or not the uproar was heard all over the camp or somebody went and informed the authorities, a posse of guards suddenly invaded the hut armed with truncheons, and the prisoners, under a rain of blows that fell indiscriminately on heads and shoulders, fled back to the shadowy security of their bunks. On the floor by the stove lay the remains of Lichatchov—literally torn to shreds. Beside them stood Apostolidis, trembling in every limb, wide-eyed with horror.

'What's going on here?' asked one of the guards.

'He stole my bread card and I called out for help,' Apostolidis explained. 'My card must be still on the floor if it hasn't been trampled to pieces or stolen by somebody else.'

The guard made no reply, his very silence exonerating the murderers from blame. While the administration of the camp was in the hands of officials and minor functionaries, the guards—being sentence-expired criminals themselves—had the same mentality as the prisoners, who were often their fellow countrymen or even fellow villagers. To commit murder as a reprisal for the theft of a bread card was, in their eyes, a perfectly normal reaction, the only right thing to do. No sooner was peace restored than the guards left the hut.

Not long afterwards a two-wheeled cart, drawn by a mule, pulled up outside and in came a couple of men who took hold of Lichatchov's corpse by the feet and dragged it away. It was thrown on the cart like a sack of oakum.

When dawn came, the prisoners went to work as

usual. The authorities had no intention whatever of holding an enquiry into the death of Lichatchov, the murder being adequately justified by the alleged theft of a bread card.

Brawls and fighting were comparatively rare in camp. Hard work in the mines or the forest under the eye of an armed guard resulted in such exhaustion that the prisoners were left with neither the strength nor desire to quarrel. Only a question of food could possibly lead to an outbreak of violence.

Men who subsisted on starvation rations were loath to sacrifice a crumb of black bread or a spoonful of watery soup. When, at the end of a shift, the prisoners, mess-tins in hand, stood waiting for food in a queue several hundred yards long, their happiness was tinged with exasperation. The tickling of anticipation in throats and nostrils at the delicious aroma of cooked barley or potato meal was almost unbearable and those behind became temporarily the implacable enemies of those in front.

As one after another the prisoners appeared at the cook-house window, the cook filled each mess-tin with soup and slapped down a portion of salted fish on the lid. Even then, you dared not rush back to the hut for fear you might slip or fall over a root and, in falling, go hungry.

One day, as he was walking along carrying his peasoup, Djulgashin, a powerfully built and half-civilized Uzbek, accidentally collided with a Kirgiz called Minyeyev who was likewise returning. Minyeyev's mess-tin swung on its handle and some of his soup was spilt. Djulgashin suffered similarly. The mutual loss was of too serious a nature to go unpunished and Minyeyev, catching Djulgashin by the arm, stood pointing in speechless fury at the wet patch on the ground. His look was most eloquent. The two men laid down their tins and heedless of

the fact that what remained of their soup would soon be
cold, and quite forgetting their hunger, faced one another
squarely. Their small, slant eyes, half buried under their
narrow foreheads blazed angrily; the nostrils of their
short, square noses were flaired like those of wild beasts
and their lips, compressed in blind rage, were merciless
and cruel. There they stood in threatening silence, for all
the world like a couple of wolves about to bark and snarl
before launching themselves at each other's throats. And
that was what they did.

The first insult came from the ominously pursed lips
of the Kirgiz:

'Scum!'

His voice was a slow menacingly quiet murmur.

'Refuse!' came the reply. The frozen anger which
so possessed them that they were unable to move was not,
however, sufficiently thawed by this initial exchange for
the real fight to begin. It needed the stimulating flood of
abuse which followed to free them from the curse of immobility, to loosen their muscles and set their hands flail-
ing. The first insults, like the first drops of rain, unleashed
a torrent of oaths and abuse which became increasingly
vulgar, elaborate and obscene, as the protagonists exploited the ample resources of the Russian language. Sisters, wives and children alike were referred to in the
most reprehensible terms, then came the graves of their
fathers and mothers, who, if not dead already, were bid-
den make haste.

The exchange of abuse was somewhat protracted.
Djulgashin and Minyeyev were taking their time. Each
one allowed the other to finish his sally. Each granted the
other time and opportunity for a primitive mind to devise
a retort no less disgusting. Their words came slowly and
carefully, not loud, but quiet like the wary steps of two

bulls circling each other before charging with horns lowered. The pair of them had the mentality of savages. They
were like a couple of centaurs, incarnate half man, half
beast, with little more intellect than a pair of buffalos.

At last when the supply of curses, degrading similes
and vile abuse with which each had favoured the other's
relatives was exhausted, they turned their attention once
more to themselves. There was hardly an animal to which
each did not in his turn liken his opponent, though not one
of the animals mentioned could possibly have taken offence
at the comparison.

With every alternate sally, fists were more tightly
clenched, arms raised as if to do battle and heads thrust
belligerently forward. It was obvious, however, that the
moment of greatest tension had not yet arrived for they
drew apart once again, their grip relaxed, and they ground
out a series of fresh insults:

'Son of a dog.'

'Son of a mangy bitch.'

'Tail of a pig.'

'Misbegotten son of a she-ass.'

'You heap of cow-dung!'

'Swine!'

'Filthy beast!'

'You . . . you . . . you bloody intellectual!'

And that was the culminating thrust, the most offen-
sive piece of abuse imaginable, defiling the subject to such
an extent that naught save blood could atone. He who
had been so basely dubbed 'intellectual' flung himself on
his adversary in a blind fury. Like a couple of mastiffs
they struggled and rolled on the ground, locked together
in a fatal embrace. So incensed were they that it was obvious this was no ordinary 'scrap,' but a fight to the death.
Over and over they rolled, clamped tightly together—a

two-headed monster in convulsions, four legs kicking, four threshing arms on a single trunk, inseparably linked.

Their caps flew off, and wherever they rolled, they left a brown trail of blood from split lips and battered noses. Happily, the combat was of short duration. Up came the guards at the double and using their rifle butts indiscriminately and kicking where they could soon render both men unconscious, picked up the bodies like a couple of rag-bags and carted them off to 'solitary.' On the ground where they had fought lay their padded caps, soaked with pea-soup, and the two empty mess-tins.

That fight, which was watched from a distance by the other prisoners, was something quite out of the ordinary. It was talked about until late in the night.

'Strange the way they went on insulting their mothers and fathers but never laid a hand on each other until somebody mentioned the word "intellectual." All the more strange because neither of them can read or write,' I said, settling down beside Baklanov.

'Nothing strange about that,' he replied gravely. 'If I use a rude word about somebody's mother, it doesn't mean much. It doesn't really mean anything and isn't an insult because, not knowing the woman personally, I'm in no position to say whether or not, for example, she walks the streets. But if it's a man I can see, a fellow I know personally, and I call him an intellectual, I'm insulting him to his face, because the word "intellectual" stinks of capitalism. Clear?'

'As a crystal,' said I, drawing my tattered blanket about me.

ELEVEN

The Incomparable Physician

Outside, suspended in the pale brilliance of the polar night, was a grey mist like that of an early morning in autumn. There was still an hour to go before our day began, but the prisoners were prematurely roused from their heavy sleep by a noise and bustle unusual at that hour, as a hundred or so men crowded into the hut. It was a fresh draft for which insufficient accommodation had been prepared, and which was now being distributed among the already overcrowded huts. The men were all young, dark-haired and well built. Their choice of dress was extremely odd for an arctic expedition, ranging as it did from summer hats, light suits, sports shirts and elegant walking shoes to shirt-sleeves and military uniforms with Soviet insignia. A few were carrying guitars and mandolins. They were speaking some incomprehensible language which, at first, sounded like German but which, when one listened more carefully, was akin to no European tongue. Latvian! Chased in out of the cold, they thronged the hut, shouting and pushing, finding room where they could.

Each of the permanent residents promptly removed his shoes from under his head and put them on, since in a commotion like this things—and especially shoes—were apt to disappear. It was also wise to keep an eye on one's blanket, bundle of spare clothes and the iron pot and wooden spoon—all one's goods and chattels in fact, for once lost they were irretrievable.

That day the Latvians received a double ration of bread and fish and were exempt from work. The lightly-clad civilians were young men picked up in the streets of their native Riga while they were out walking. As for the soldiers, that was another story.

The Soviet authorities, in forcing Latvia to become another voluntary republic of the Union, also formed an independent Latvian Red Army with compulsory conscription from the age of eighteen. The young warriors received arms and uniforms, similar to those of the old Latvian Army, except for the red facings on the sleeves, collars and caps. After a few weeks' intensive training, the Free and Independent Latvian Red Army took part in large-scale manœuvres culminating in all sorts of athletic contests for which valuable prizes were awarded. After which they were ordered to hand in their rifles and uniforms. The Free and Independent Latvian Red Army was then covered with machine-guns and finally wound up in Siberia. In that way the entire youthful element, alone capable of armed opposition, was dispatched in one gulp. To the Latvians revolution was an acquired taste; the Russians remembered how at the time of the Bolshevik revolution the older inhabitants of this most recent Soviet Republic had become adept at the spilling of blood in the interests of the new order.

Thanks to the large rations of bread, fish, sugar and margarine, the Latvians soon brightened up. No wonder: the journey was over, they had food and bedding. They became almost merry and the air was full of their laughter and lively discussions. The strains of a mandolin could be heard and a clear, young voice raised in song. A few of them started to shave in front of a triangular scrap of broken mirror. From one corner came the pleasant chirping of a mouth-organ.

The following day the Latvians continued their rest. They were even issued with a ration of tobacco. On the third day, however, they were split into labour battalions and sent out to the river where, standing knee-deep in icy water, they had to fish out the logs as they floated downstream. They were still clothed in summer suits, sports shirts with ties and had only their brown walking shoes on their feet—or else they were wearing light field-service uniforms. When the young men began to demand more appropriate clothing, they received the answer that the stores were empty at the moment, but that as soon as supplies arrived from Moscow they would get plenty of everything. Unfortunately, no one had any idea when the supplies would arrive, so they would just have to put up with things for the time being and carry on with their work—since that was the purpose of a labour camp. Moreover, there'd be no food for people who did not work.

After a week under such conditions, the Latvians mutinied. One frosty dawn while Siberian logs were being efficiently dealt with by Latvian hands, somebody gave a long, shrill whistle. The guards were immediately disarmed. The savage Alsatian was caught by the hind legs and had its brains dashed out against the nearest tree.

The rebels, now in possession of the guards' rifles, had no sooner dug themselves in on a hill than the ground shook under the feet of an approaching detachment of soldiers. The insurrection, however, was only a final despairing gesture. No means of escape existed and the outcome of the battle was obvious from the start. There was a rapid exchange of shots and on both sides dead and wounded lay stretched in the snow.

By that evening all Latvians were locked up in the isolation hut—even such as had had nothing to do with the uprising, even those who had been working in the camp for years. Latvian? Lock him up! In accordance with this principle, Dr. Zeunis, the camp doctor, some time professor in medicine at the University of Riga was likewise incarcerated and his infirmary closed and padlocked. The camp had now no doctor. There being no doctor, there could also be no sick, for there was no one to examine them, to enter their names in the book, release them from duty and send them to hospital. So men went out to work with high temperatures, sprained hands and swollen legs. If you did not work, you got no bread ticket and you starved to death. Such a state of affairs, however, could not last long, Soviet labour camps being primarily intended to produce the maximum possible.

One night, the group leader entered the hut, holding aloft a carbide lamp.

'Hey, there! Any of you a doctor?' he shouted. Nobody answered.

'Is there a doctor amongst you?' he repeated.

All of a sudden I glimpsed a spark of hope. I had been felling trees for several months and had just about reached the limits of my endurance. A few more months and I should probably die of exhaustion, but here was an opportunity not to be missed.

'Who's making all that row?' I enquired from my high bunk in a drowsy voice, as though I had only just woken up.

'Is there a doctor?' came another shout from below.

'Why? Somebody ill?' I asked, speaking slowly, without undue concern and in a rather superior manner.

'We need a doctor!'

'Then I can help you,' I consented magnanimously. 'Where's the patient?'

'To hell with the patient! Are you a doctor or not? Speak up!'

'Yes, I am,' I admitted reluctantly. 'But if there's no patient, why are you shouting your head off in the middle of the night? Can't a man even sleep?'

'What's your name?'

I gave him my name and he wrote it down on a smooth board which served him as a sheet of paper.

'Don't you go to work to-morrow. Wait here till they call you,' he said, and he left the hut, bearing with him his bright sphere of lamplight.

'Whether or not I get caught out to-morrow,' I thought to myself, 'at any rate, I've got one day off.' I straightened my cap, turned over and, for the first time in many months, slept soundly and well.

At dawn, when the men marched out to the forest as usual, I ate an unhurried breakfast, then went to the barber's to have my hair cut. Out of sheer boredom I spent some time in the kitchen peeling potatoes—for which they gave me a bowl of pea-soup. It was like being on holiday. They came to fetch me round about midday.

'You're to go to the commandant at once. He said to call you.'

The commandant's office was in a small house with a veranda. As I walked towards it, I tried to collect my thoughts, but I had no idea what I was going to say. 'I'll cook up something on the spot,' I decided. 'First see how the wind lies.' I bore one piece of advice well in mind. This was a hint given me by the murderer Wolodzka, one of my cell-mates at Minsk. 'If you're ever talking to one of our commandants,' said Wolodzka, 'never be polite. They don't like well-bred intellectuals. When he starts cursing you, just let drop a word or two about his mother. He'll respect you then when he sees you've a tongue in your head and that you're not a milksop.' Whenever I had occasion to act on this advice, it stood me in good stead.

I mounted the veranda, knocked on the door and went in. Behind the desk sat a middle-aged man with fine, regular features. I said good-day and gave him my name. I kept my cap on since it was not one of the local customs to uncover when greeting someone. The officer returned my salutation and pointed to a chair. I sat down confidently, placing myself well back on the seat, not perched on the edge.

The commandant studied my face for some time before asking,

'You a doctor?'

'Yes.'

'Hm, maybe you're only a quack?'

'No, I'm a doctor, a physician.'

'Sure?' He didn't believe me. 'A doctor or only a doctor's assistant?'

He called it 'doc-as,' one of the innumerable short-cuts favored by current Soviet usage.

'I'm no "doc-as"!' I bristled, wounded in my professional dignity. 'I said I was a doctor and I meant doctor.'

He narrowed his eyes, puffed out his lips and, shaking his head doubtfully, he said,

'Hm. Something still makes me think you're lying.'

'Then I'll go straight back to the hut. I didn't come here to see you of my own accord. You sent for me. That's right, isn't it?'

'Yes, that's true enough,' he admitted.

'Am I asking you for anything?' I went on heatedly. 'I've been hacking down trees for so long now I can go back and hack some more. If you hadn't woken me up last night, I wouldn't be here.'

This seemed to convince him. Nevertheless, he tried once more.

'And you're sure you're not a "med-brother"?'

Med-brother was what they called a male nurse.

'Med-brother,' I replied, 'is practically the same as an orderly, and I'm a physician.'

'I see. And where did you learn to be a physician?'

'Well, obviously, at a university.'

'At a university! Well, well, aren't you clever! What university?'

'Warsaw.'

'Warsaw, you say.' He bent low over his desk then, trying to catch me off my guard, he suddenly snapped,

'Do you know anything about medicines?'

'Of course. A fine doctor I'd be if I knew nothing about medicines.'

'We'll see about that. Wait outside.'

I went out on the veranda and shortly afterwards the commandant appeared and nodded to me to follow him. We went towards the hospital. Once there, the officer called the dispenser and told him to test me. The terrified old man who had been deported ten years previously, solely because he was the son of a manufacturer and had studied chemistry in Germany, opened the medicine-chest.

The shelves were covered with flasks and bottles standing in neat rows and each bearing a label with a Latin inscription. I had no difficulty in reading them— Valerian drops, bromide, iodine, zinc ointment, opium, Dover's powders, Rivanol, protargol, boric acid, salts, ether—the normal requisites of any household medicine-chest.

Taking the bottles, boxes and packets in turn from

the shelves, looking as wise as I could and sniffing the contents, I explained the uses of each. The fact that I could read Latin was, to the commandant who only knew the Russian alphabet, ample proof of my qualifications. I passed the examination with distinction, received the keys of the infirmary, and the very same day installed my belongings in a private apartment beside the consulting-room. I was now the doctor; I could go no higher.

I was given Romancev as an assistant. He was a young Ukrainian from Kiev who, before having been deported for five years for returning to barracks late, had served with the Red Cross on the Finnish front. As a trained medical orderly his knowledge of medicine was far superior to my own. I therefore decided to live in peace with the man.

The next day I began receiving patients. As I was putting on my white smock, I observed a look of horror on Romancev's face. It seemed I was putting the smock on back to front. After all, not everyone knows that a doctor's coat is tied at the back. Outside the door stood a long queue of sufferers waiting impatiently for my salutary aid. I told them to come in one at a time. One man had a sore throat, one had cut himself, another had something in his eye, somebody else's nose was bleeding, while yet another had diarrhœa. I spent half the day bandaging, smearing on ointment and taking temperatures. The sick register filled rapidly with the names of the doctor's delighted patients. Equally delighted was the doctor himself, who had had no idea what a wonderful doctor he was.

Stiopkin, a giant of a White Russian, came in towards evening. He sat down on a stool and began complaining. He had a cough, he said, catarrh and a temperature; his ears were ringing, his head ached and his chest was wheezing.

'Do you want to get off work to-morrow?'

'Yes, but I want you to stick some cupping-glasses on me.'

'Right you are. Lie down.'

The giant stretched out on the wooden settle and dragged his shirt up over his neck, exposing a back like the top of a table. I took the glasses out of their box, twisted the cotton wool on to the copper rod, dipped it in the methylated spirits, lit it and began cupping for the first time in my life. I held the glass in my left hand, the fire-tipped rod in my right; flame into glass, glass on to back, and so it went, one after another, until, unfortunately, at the seventh glass, I got my hands mixed and, instead of the cupping-glass, I applied the rod with its blazing wick.

With a wild roar the roasted giant leapt from his couch, and, still half naked, with the cupping-glasses clinging to his back, dashed out in the open.

'Wait!' I yelled after him. 'You'll smash all my glasses.'

The poor man, however, threw himself on the ground, writhing as though possessed.

Romancev had a lot of trouble the next day finding those glasses.

I filled the days which followed with a similar devotion to duty, always displaying an amazing degree of competence and a wide range of medical knowledge. There were no accidents and few mishaps. My injections were apt to be clumsy, and on one occasion I poured into a patient's eye drops intended for the nose. On another occasion, while I was painting a patient's throat, the cotton-wool swab, soaked in iodine, slipped off the stick and was swallowed by the unfortunate man. I explained that iodine was very healthy and possessed strengthening properties.

One day I had a visit from the Tartar, Araslanov,

who was a section leader in the camp and who used to give me a hard time of it when I was working in the forest. He came for help. He had pains in his back and couldn't bend down. I laid him on the table and massaged him so energetically, not forgetting to pummel him with my fists, that Araslanov not only found it impossible to bend down but also to straighten up.

Every week the cook would drop in and ask for a few crystals of potassium permanganate. I used to give him what he wanted without ever knowing what he did with it. One day, however, I asked him out of curiosity. The cook explained that those workers who achieved one hundred and fifty per cent. of their prescribed task received a bonus in the form of a cutlet. This was indeed a valuable award, for no other deportees ever saw meat. Since, however, this dish was prepared from the flesh of horses which had succumbed to malaria, the cutlets were first treated with disinfectant in order to kill the germs. After hearing about this, I understood why the best workers so often complained of sickness.

One night, I was awakened by a violent knocking at my door.

'Doctor, get up!'

I opened the door. On the threshold stood a soldier with a lamp and a rifle.

'Get your clothes on and come with me,' he said.

I dressed quickly and followed him outside.

'Where are we going?' I asked as we left the barbed wire entanglements behind us and struck off along a path leading to a well-lit colony of small bungalows.

'To a woman voluntary worker.'

'What's the matter with her? Sick?'

'Sick my eye! She's having a kid.'

A cold sweat broke out on my forehead. God Almighty! What was I going to do? I had no idea how to set about it.

'Why didn't you tell me before?' I cried in the depths of despair. 'I'd have brought my instruments with me!'

'Instruments! What the hell do you want with instruments? You a musician or something? Going to give her a tune?'

'What am I to use then? My bare hands?'

'The woman's got scissors, rags and hot water. What more do you want?'

'How do you know so much about it?'

'Because my woman had six and I never called anybody. Did it all myself.'

'You're a clever chap. Do you like spirits?'

'Course I like spirits. Why?'

'Because if you help me I'll give you a glass to-morrow.'

It was a wild promise, since there wasn't a drop of spirits in the camp. We halted, rolled a cigarette, lit up, inhaled the strong, bitter smoke, spat on the ground and ambled on our way, not hurrying in the slightest.

When, half an hour later, we arrived at our destination, the process of labour had already begun. The soldier stood his rifle in the corner while I threw off my jacket, rolled up my sleeves and then, calling loudly to one another, by way of mutual encouragement, we went to work. Our ghastly performance is better left to the imagination. Suffice it to say that I lost more sweat than had I been carrying bricks. In the end, however, complete success crowned our efforts and between us we had increased the population of the Soviet Union by yet another screaming Bolshevik.

The days continued to drift past amid the eternal cupping-glasses, enemas, drops, powders, sticking-plaster and bandages. My patients developed a genuine affection for their doctor. Foremost among them was old Allardan, a Turkoman. I made such a mess of setting his broken index-finger that the bone grew at an angle, as a result of which Allardan was released for good from the back-breaking labour in the forest, given light duties in the kitchens and was ready to sing my praises on every occasion.

One morning they brought in Kozakov. His foot was badly gashed. I stopped the flow of blood and dressed the wound. When I had finished, the patient was taken to the isolation hut. It seemed that Kozakov had split his foot on purpose with an axe, with the object of being admitted to hospital where they would feed him better and not send him out to work. Instead of being placed in hospital, however, he was lodged in solitary confinement—on a diet of water with forty grammes of bread per day.

That afternoon an inspection took place. The inspectors commented upon the evidence of tidiness, cleanliness, and industry, as well as the good treatment accorded the patients; they looked approvingly through the sick register and examined the contents of the medicine-chest.

'And what's this here?' asked the chief inspector, just before leaving, and he pointed at a large tin box standing on top of the cupboard.

I took it down and opened it.

'Grey ointment,' I said.

'No, it's not grey ointment. It's Dr. Wilkinson's ointment. What do you use it for?'

'I don't use it at all.'

'Is that so? Very interesting. And what should Wilkinson's ointment be used for?'

I looked rather sheepish, having no idea what to say.

'You're a fine doctor if you don't even know that!'

he proclaimed. 'In the Soviet Union every child knows that Wilkinson's ointment is used for treating scabies.'

He smiled grimly and walked out with the others, slamming the door ominously.

Group-leader Titov woke me up at five in the morning.

'Hey, you—doctor! Get up for roll-call and clear your things out of here. From to-day you're back on general duties. You'll be digging coal.'

The idyllic existence was at an end. I put on my padded trousers, jacket and boots, took my little iron mess-can to the cook-house window where I was given my breakfast—sticky dollops of dough made from grey flour. Then I went and stood in the ranks of my detachment as the guards counted us interminably. At last the escort slipped the safety-catches of their rifles, declaimed the usual formula about people trying to escape being shot without warning and the detachments set off, in silence, with dragging feet.

Through the grey mists of dawn the mine workings loomed ahead of us in the distance. We marched on through the dead, frozen stillness, deep in thought and clutching our scraps of black bread. Only the dog on his lead barked loudly.

'Dr. Wilkinson,' I thought. 'You and your balm for the treatment of scabies, to hell with you both!'

*

Although in Siberia during the summer, there is no such thing as night, nevertheless night-blindness is common enough. It afflicts every inhabitant of Siberia and is due in equal measure to the local climate and the lack of vitamins. The symptoms of avitaminosis—otherwise known as scurvy—include wounds which will not heal, suppurating boils, bleeding gums, loss of teeth and, in the advanced stages, lameness, loss of control over arms and legs, stiffening of the joints and 'night-blindness.' Those who fell victim to this last affliction used to set off for work in the morning, perfectly normal and healthy, and at night return—sightless, tapping their way with heavy sticks. The symptoms develop at dusk and disappear at break of day. During the Siberian summer when, to all intents and purposes, there is no darkness, the victims lose their sight about the time evening should fall and retrieve it when, according to clock and calendar, it is once more dawn.

Once contracted, this disease rapidly worsens, but a small dose of vitamins can sometimes cure it completely. A spoonful of cod-liver oil poured into a gaping wound would cause it to heal, while a few spoonfuls, taken as medicine, were sufficient to relieve the blindness. Unfortunately, that excellent medicine was in short supply.

At dusk, as one procession of blind men wound its way slowly out of the woods, another sightless crocodile set out from camp to work. The men walked slowly, one behind the other, hands resting on the shoulders of the man in front. Even so, unable to find the way out through the narrow gate, they invariably walked into the barbed wire fence, cutting themselves and bumping against one another. In such a condition they were obviously of no value as a labour force.

The camp authorities, fearing for their own skins, had to think of some means of improving the health of the workers. If the output of the camp were to fall below the prescribed minimum those in charge would lose their posts, and change from dignitaries to deportees in the process.

One morning, the second-in-command of the camp climbed into a motor-boat and set off downstream. Experts maintained he was off on a four-day trip, since at two days' distance lay the base where oils and vitamins were readily available. A week passed and the emissary failed to return. In the camp, the rumour spread round that he had fled to America, to Alaska. There were even those who stated they had heard the officer declare that intention before setting out. But ten days having elapsed, the officer returned. Though he brought with him neither vitamins nor a barrel of oil, he had solved the problem no less efficiently. He had, in fact, arranged for a barrel of milk to be delivered daily at the camp from the nearest peasant settlement in the locality. It was well known that a few glasses of milk would suffice to relieve the most persistent night-blindness. This milk, regarded as a medicine, was placed at the disposal of the doctor, who had to decide who was going to drink it. At that time I, myself, was performing the worthy function of doctor.

The next day, a bearded water carrier arrived with a barrel of milk on a two-wheeled cart. He put down the barrel in the hall of the infirmary. It contained reindeer milk—thick and yellow, with an indefinable odour. Milk was hardly the word for it, but, like the miraculous waters of Lourdes, it was to restore sight to the blind. I called the storekeeper who, at that time, had nothing to sell but cigarette papers and tin spoons, and told him, on orders from above, to take the precious barrel and issue the milk to the men when they returned at night. I gave him a list of the names.

From that day onwards a new life began in the camp. I went on prescribing the milk to the worst cases amongst those who reported to the shop at the end of their day's work, and the throng of blind men daily stumbled along the half-rotten duckboards, each man holding a container of some sort, whether mess-can cup or rusty preserve tin.

They hurried towards the wooden kiosk and lined up in front of the window where the milk awaited them.

That reindeer milk really did possess miraculous properties. Only three days—that is to say, three rations scrupulously measured out—were needed to cure the blindness and the men could go back to work with their sight as good as ever. I made sure of a fair share for all by striking the names of the cured from the list and substituting those of the more needy sufferers. There would soon have been general rejoicing in the camp, not only on the part of the cured deportees but also among the camp officials who'd been spared disgrace. It was not to be.

After a certain time, Volkov, the shopkeeper, stout and red faced, a clever professional thief and a prisoner of many years' standing, appeared clad in a new, warmly padded jacket. Day by day he began to grow fatter. With comparable rapidity, the yellow reindeer milk, drained of its fat, took on a white and watery appearance. In addition, Volkov suddenly began to smoke cigarettes; not those made from coarse tobacco twisted in scraps of newspaper but real, factory-produced cigarettes—a brand called 'Rocket'; several times, too, he smelt of vodka. Moreover, Nina Pavlovna, a young student from Odessa convicted of political offences, a delicate girl with large wistful eyes, clean and quiet, who had hitherto preferred to slave away painfully rather than submit to the attentions of the group leader, now paid frequent visits to the shop and could be seen at evening making her way to Volkov's quarters. It really was wonderful what that reindeer milk would do.

Sad to say, however, it grew ever more watery and entirely lost its beneficial effect. It had become nothing more than a foul, malodorous liquid which did anything but restore sight.

Furtively at first, and singly, then openly, boldly and

in unison, the sick began to complain. But complaints and grievances aired to me could in no way affect the existing conditions. I was just a convict, like a shopkeeper himself—with this difference, I was new, without connections, an intellectual and a foreigner whose knowledge of Russian was faulty. I could not attempt to combat the influence of Volkov, a wily criminal who was more than at home in the camp. It was equally unthinkable to deprive Volkov of his right to distribute the milk. Such a step would invite the hatred of Volkov and his associates and might even lead to my murder. Besides, the eyesight of the camp officials, who had no right whatever to the milk, had likewise shown a sudden improvement; they were not going to see their milkman changed. In reply I said,

'What can I do, old man? I only put your name on the list and prescribe the milk. I don't dish it out. I can't tell Volkov how he's to behave—I'm only a convict myself, same as Volkov and you.'

After waiting in vain for some change, the unfortunate sufferers lost patience, and the half-blind victims of the deception decided to take matters into their own hands and teach the shopkeeper a lesson. It happened one evening. The men were making their way to the shop window with their flasks and flagons and, as usual, carrying sticks. Only the latter were not ordinary walking-sticks but heavy, gnarled branches that would have helped nobody to find his way, but that made excellent cudgels. That they were intended for use as such was made quite clear by the way they were waved in the air.

The little kiosk stood on the morass itself and was linked to terra firma by four planks leading away from it. Volkov in his wooden hut, like a large owl in the hollow of a giant tree, was hemmed in on all sides by a scowling mob of criminals who, all in all, were no weaker or worse than himself and who had decided to deal with him once and for all.

I stood by the window of the infirmary and watched the gathering with some interest. The low growling of the men soon gave way to the thunder of curses accompanied by the lightning flicker of falling cudgels, bent upon wiping the rickety hut and its crooked guardian off the face of the earth.

'Come out of it, you swine,' they yelled. 'We've got an account to settle!'

'You bastard! Drink our milk, would you? Grow fat on our medicine, eh?'

'Trade our milk for cigarettes, would you?'

'Swap it for vodka, eh?'

'Treats himself to a woman—a prostitute at that— and pays for it with our health!'

'Come out of there, you bastard, or we'll smash you and that brothel of your to smithereens!'

The plight of Volkov, completely surrounded and with no hope of escape, seemed bound to end in tragedy. If he came out, they would tear him to shreds, and if he did not, they would batter him to pieces as well as his puny shelter. If he denied ever having touched the milk they would not believe him, and if he admitted his guilt they would kill him without any compunction—and rightly.

But Volkov knew how to handle the situation. He threw open the door of his hut which was raised above the ground on heavy poles, like a lighthouse rearing above a sea of swamp. Standing upon the topmost step, as on a rostrum, he lifted his bushy eyebrows in amazement and addressed the crowd in a calm, steady voice.

'Comrades! What's all the fuss about? What do you want?'

'What do we want? You ask that, you swine? You

drink our milk, trade it for smokes and vodka, feast your woman on it, water down what's left of it for us and then you have the face to ask us what we want!'

'Comrades! Wait a minute, please! Not so loud! Not all at once! I can't understand you if you all talk at the same time!' he replied, stretching out his hand in front of him, like an actor politely quieting an audience clamouring for an encore. 'I'll give you my answer right away! Do I dish out the milk, or do you?'

'You do, you son of a bitch!' roared one man, waving a knotty stick above his head. 'And you drown it in water!'

'Hm. I drown it in water, you say. And what else? That I have vodka, new boots, cigarettes and a girl? Is that the trouble? Hm. And would any of you act differently in my place? You'd never touch the milk, I suppose—give it all to the others and not taste a drop of it? Which one of you'd do any different to what I did, I ask you? Who'd deny himself cigarettes, vodka and a girl if he had the chance of 'em? There's an old Russian proverb which says, "You can't sit in water without getting wet." '

Volkov's words had the same effect on the seething temper of the crowd as cold water on red-hot iron. Raised fists and cudgels sank slowly as though the men's arms were drained of strength. Their voices died and violently gesticulating hands, heads and bodies froze into immobility. A long deep silence settled over the noisy gathering. It was broken at last by the ringleader who spoke in a gentle voice:

'Well, comrades, there's no more to be said. Volkov is quite right. It's too bad, but that's how it is. So let's just form a line as usual and you, Volkov, call out the names on the list and dish out the milk you've got ready for us and— damn your eyes!'

TWELVE

The Kiss

The polar dawn struck the black sky like the mordant lash of a fiery stock-whip. The band of light coiled and twined like a monstrous thong—one could almost hear it swish through the frosty air. Then the light changed from purple to gold, gold to yellow, yellow to silver and then to a flood of milky-white brilliance which, with colours swirling like the reflections in a waterfall, raced finally in a white river across the awestruck heavens.

'You won't be seeing that much longer,' came a cheerful voice close behind me.

I looked round. Grisha, young and handsome with blond hair was standing behind me smiling.

'You Poles will soon be out of it,' he went on.

'You may be yourself,' I said encouragingly.

'Me? What do you mean?' he asked in amazement. 'I'm not a Pole, just a Russian and, besides, I've got fifteen years—you know what for.'

I knew Grisha's story. He was an aircraft fitter and at one time had been working in an aircraft factory. The engineers at that factory had been imported from Germany. Having exploited the knowledge of these foreign technicians, the Soviet authorities had then imprisoned them on charges of espionage. Almost the entire personnel of the factory had been transported on the same pretext. It was a wise move, for the engineers, as directors of the factory, did, in fact, know its secrets, even if only those concerning output which was their own responsibility. That information might endanger the régime were the Soviet Government to permit them to return to their own country.

Grisha was my friend, if one could call anybody a friend in a labour camp. The powers that be in such institutions took care to render such intimacy impossible, for friendships might breed the danger of mutiny, conspiracy and escape. All deportees in general, and political offenders in particular, were prevented from staying long in any one camp. Indeed, most of them spent half their sentence in transit from one camp to another.

This constant re-shuffling of prisoners—in addition to the informers, spies and agents provocateurs disguised as prisoners—conspired to evoke a perpetual spirit of distrust inimical to the growth of friendship. A second and equally effective method of combating any thought of mutual assistance amongst the prisoners was the system of separate cook-houses and a variety of bins containing graded food according to the output of the workers. Thus, there were fifteen bins of which the first, and worst, contained, apart from a tiny piece of bread, only watery soup and a mouthful of fish, constituting the so-called 'punishment dinner.' Little more was forthcoming from the second bin, which was intended for the weakest workers who had only the strength to carry bricks or collect firewood. They were given a slightly larger ration of bread and their soup was less transparent. Woodcutters, road-builders and miners ate food prepared in the better bins. Besides bread, soup and a ration of fish, they received either cooked black potatoes, or soya, or barley, or peas, and a kind of paste made of dark meal.

The fifteenth and best bin was reserved for the sick and for nursing and expectant mothers. It was for that reason that prisoners wilfully contracted pneumonia and many of the women got themselves with child solely in order to be admitted to hospital where as well as having no work to do they were well fed.

Those workers who exceeded the prescribed daily output were rewarded with a sweet cake or a horse-meat cutlet. Whereas in the past a worker of more than average physique, whose output was consequently in excess of the required minimum, could easily assist a less well endowed comrade by crediting the latter with his surplus, the new system of edible rewards precluded such charitable behaviour. Friendship in camp restricted itself therefore to a mutual liking, pure and simple, involving no responsibilities or, at the very most, the performance of insignificant actions.

The polar dawn poured white amongst the clouds as Grisha and I stood side by side with raised heads watching the phenomenon.

'Just look at the way the light's twisting about!' he said, then, harking back to our interrupted conversation, 'No, my friend, I won't be leaving this place. My position's different from yours.'

'I know,' I admitted, 'but I heard that if you write out an application to volunteer for the front, they'll release you, the same as us.'

'Yes, that's right.'

'Well, then.'

'They'll only release common criminals and not those convicted of political offences,' he explained. 'And, anyway, why should I volunteer? What for? To defend them?' He tilted his chin in the direction of the armed guard standing on the watchtower. 'Am I going to shed my blood for those swine? Like hell! Here, at least, I've got a safe job. And as for them, I hope they cop it and the sooner the better. No, pal, you don't catch me volunteering. Your case is different and you'll be going out in the world—but not me. So long.'

We shook hands and he went off to the hut with his blue airman's jacket and his round pilot's helmet. Its dangling ear-flaps danced to the rhythm of his light, youthful steps.

*

Lonka sighed, hunched his shoulders and buried his chin in the upturned collar of his greatcoat.

'To be an agricultural engineer, you've got to take a course at a so-called Higher School, a university to all intents and purposes.'

'Same with us,' I chipped in.

'Is that so? I studied at one of those places. I used to work very hard and I was mad about my future profession from the word go.' He stubbed a piece of charred wood which had fallen from the stove with the toe of his boot. 'I didn't have much to do with my fellow students and spent most of my time doing private study. I lived with my old mother of whom I was very fond. You know how it is. My elder brother who's a major in the tanks used to help my mother a bit. Then there was my married sister living in the same house, but she didn't get on well with my mother. You know, children aren't always keen to help their parents. Well, it was hard on the old lady. I used to console her by telling her that as soon as I'd finished my studies and got a job she could come and live with me. I had only a few months to go to my finals when I met Tania, a fellow student at the school but one term my junior. I won't describe her as it doesn't matter. Enough that she was twenty and very beautiful. She really was— I'm not exaggerating, a brunette and such a—oh, well, never mind, it makes no difference. Besides that, she was really the first girl I'd seen very much of. It wasn't surprising then that I fell madly in love with her. I never thought she cared for me. You see, on the whole, I'm very shy, and then Tania was tall, while I'm rather a titch. Even at school, the boys used to call me "sparrow." It hurt me a lot. But sometimes our most secret wishes come true. Tania loved me too, and when one night at the pictures I told her I'd like her to be my wife, she agreed very gladly. Shortly afterwards we were married. Tania came to live with us and my mother took to her like her own daughter. I got my diploma and started work in a planning office. In the evenings I used to help Tania with her studies, as she was still getting ready for her examinations. Tania's cousin and a friend of his used to come and visit us. They were taking the same course as my wife and I taught all three of them at the same time. I was very happy. I had work which I liked, a wife whom I loved and a mother who could share my happiness. We lived like this for five months till one night two militiamen came to the house with a plain-clothes man and took me away. I was in prison for six months before I found out why I'd been locked up. It was only while I was being interrogated that I learnt I was an enemy of the people because I'd criticized the institution of collective farming, Article 58 of the Criminal Code, Paras. A and B. Back in my cell, I remembered having said in the family circle that a farmer on his own land would work his fingers to the bone, but on a collective farm where everything's common property he's hardly likely to bother so much. And so if there's a storm during the night or a cloud-burst and his potatoes are lying out in the field or the freshly mown hay is in stooks—none of it being his own property—he'd sooner stay in bed with his wife in the warmth of their cottage than chase about in the cold to rescue what's not his. And for that reason—because of the peasant character—collective farming is not the best thing for production. But I was at a loss to know who could have reported all this. Only the family had been present at the time I'd said it. I couldn't think who it could have been. It was in court I learnt that while, in fact, only members of the family had been present, it was they who had done the reporting. The chief witness against me was my beloved wife, Tania, a professional agent who had even had her suspicions about me at the university and had only married me the better to keep an eye on me. The two fellow students, her cousin and his friend, were likewise officials of the Security Police. At the trial all three of them swamped me with their evidence. Tania, having given her testimony, asked for a divorce as she no longer wished to remain the wife of a criminal, and, in addition, she had now done her job. She was given an immediate divorce without my consent even being asked for—I just ceased to count when they gave me ten years. Well, that's it. I'm now in my fifth year. I'm not really too badly off," he added contemplatively. "I've got a job in the office; I'm not in the forest or the mine. My only worry is my mother. The poor woman has had no idea what's been happening to me since the moment I was taken from home. I didn't see her in court the day my case was heard, and from here, as you know, you can't send letters or let anybody know anything. Now that you're going to be let out fairly soon, and you'll be going to Buzuluk, you'll be passing through Orenburg, or Chkalov as it's called now. Please drop in on her and tell her I'm still alive. The address is, Number 7, First of May Street. You'll remember my name—Shapochkin.'

Outside, silent darkness settled down around the hut.

'Well, I'm off,' he concluded. 'All the best to you and when you're in Chkalov, please don't forget to do me that favour.'

He repeated the name of the street and the number, got up, twisted a strip of blanket round his thin stalk-like neck, squeezed my hand and walked out slowly in his high cap and the overlong black coat with its sheep-skin collar.

Out of the hut he went, into the snow and the darkness, into the blue-white Siberian winter—a small, sad man who looked like a kindly but ill-treated goblin.

Amnesty. Such a thing was unheard of in Siberian labour camps. Nothing of the sort had ever occurred since those institutions for the seclusion of man had come into existence. Rumours and unfounded hopes of premature release had been cherished on the occasion of May Day, the anniversary of the November Revolution and Stalin's birthday, year after year, but when, year after year, they had proved utterly vain, prisoners ceased to console themselves with such fancies. In the same way, from the moment Poles first found themselves in the ranks of the deportees, they one and all said they would soon be back in their own country. The old, experienced convicts laughed at this. In the early days of their sojourn in Siberia they, too, had entertained similar hopes. Soon, however, the rumour concerning the liberation of the Poles began to reveal some basis of fact. The news was quietly whispered around that the first drafts had already been let out of neighbouring camps. It seemed this had been mentioned on the wireless, though no one had actually heard it. A deputation, consisting of five of the Poles most highly thought of by their fellow countrymen in the camp, went to the commandant who received them politely and declared that he, also, had heard the news but had been given no definite instructions as yet. As soon as he received clear orders he would free all concerned. He took the opportunity of confiding that he, himself, although the commandant and subject to different conditions, had also had more than enough of this camp and would gladly get out of it, the sooner the better. The more so because his wife had written to him saying that she was in difficulties and having to work in a factory as an ordinary hand in order to support herself and their child.

The delegates returned from their interview with the commandant, beaming with delight. The commandant had also heard about the releases; it was therefore not just a rumour. The next day they were all locked up in the isolation hut on bread and water—for all meetings and deputations with the exception of those previously approved by the authorities are forbidden in the camps, as indeed they are throughout the Soviet Union.

The behaviour of the guards varied according to the nationality of the prisoners they were dealing with. Towards the Russians, their own people, they were completely callous, treating them like beasts of burden. On the other hand, they showed such respect for the German colonists, who had been born and bred in Russia for generations without, however, becoming in the least russified, that they did not even swear at them. They were afraid of the hot-blooded and vengeful Latvians, ever ready to throw themselves at the sentries. They joked about the Jews, for a bespectacled book-keeper struggling to carry a tree trunk or an old merchant falling exhausted by the labour of digging trenches was a comical sight in the eyes of men blessed with their sense of humour. They hated the Poles who, to their own detriment, worked quickly and competently. However, from the moment that it became obvious the rumoured amnesty was assuming the vivid hues of actuality, they began to flirt with the Poles as with rich relations paying a visit. The Poles were no longer driven at their work; they were allowed to go more frequently to the baths and to the barber, while during a conversation the guards would often honour one with a paternal slap on the back. As a result the whole discipline of the camp relaxed. The older convicts, seeing all this, consoled themselves with the thought that the Poles, once released from this camp, would find themselves not at liberty but quickly and unexpectedly transferred to another. The same thing had happened to themselves in the past. Those who survived the construction of the White Sea Canal had been brought back to Moscow and thence dispatched to fresh camps, where they were given new sentences.

But at last the day came and the camp was in a turmoil. A commission arrived and began making releases. One after another the group leaders would shout out the name of a man asleep in his hut, or sick in hospital or locked in the isolation cells—or even run out to the forest or the mine and fetch the prisoner in question back from work.

The first draft consisting of over three hundred men was made up of prisoners serving so-called 'children's' sentences—three to five years for paltry crimes such as crossing the frontier or not being in possession of a passport.

I therefore nursed no hopes. However, they came to fetch me at dawn. If mistakes occur anywhere, they certainly do in the Soviet Union. At the same time as I was

released they set free a Russian who had been ten years
in the camp for attempting to escape into Persia. His release was obviously a mistake due to his name being Wis-
niewski, which was Polish. Fortune is blind and treads
strange paths. There were a lot of other Russians in the
camp with Polish names and who were even of Polish
descent, but they were not set free.

I was summoned to the office and opened a door
marked 'Security Police.' Freedom was at hand. Behind
the desk sat a young, dark-haired man with laughing eyes,
Captain Chapygin, as well as two female clerks, one of
whom was wearing that acme of elegance—a hat. The
Captain, having checked my particulars, asked which I
chose—to join the Red Army, the newly formed Polish
Army, or to stay on in the camp as a free and well-paid
worker. The last course, which may appear strange, was by
no means inconceivable. The proposal was readily accepted
by many who had previously served the authorities as informers and who now preferred not to leave the camp for
fear that beyond its confines their erstwhile fellow workers
might string them up on the nearest tree. When I expressed
my wish to join the Polish Army, I was asked, 'Why?'

'Somebody's got to join it,' I said. 'If everybody joins
the Soviet Army there won't *be* any Polish Army and
Comrade Stalin has ordered its formation.'

The Captain did not quarrel with that answer, but
smiled and handed me a document with which I was to
report within two months to the Polish staff in the Buzuluk
locality. He then wished me good luck and held out his
hand—a signal honour and proof that the prisoner was
now unconditionally recognized as a free man.

I left the office and went to the cashier who paid me
the money I had earned first as a woodcutter, then as a
doctor and finally as a miner. I was supplied with rations

for the journey from the store close by, then promised an issue of fresh clothing and new boots before I left, for the liberated prisoners as they travelled across Russia were to be living advertisements for the excellent clothing issued to deportees in the Siberian labour camps. It was an empty promise. Nobody got any new clothes, but, for all that, everyone was happy enough to be going, even in the rags they had been wearing for months.

All formalities having been completed, nothing remained save to take leave of one's friends.

I went to see Sturm, the engineer. We talked Russian, as he did not acknowledge his Polish origins. He was known, however, to have been born in Warsaw whence, as a student at the Polytechnic and an active communist full of enthusiasm for the new order, he had gone to Russia. He was arrested as he was crossing the frontier and accused of espionage. When he defended himself in court by declaring that he was an idealistic communist and for that reason had fled from a capitalistic country, he was told that if such were the case he should have stayed in his own country and helped prepare the revolution and not have come to the Soviet Union where everything had already been done and where they had got on nicely without him in the past and would continue to do so in the future. He was sentenced to be deported for ten years. Having served his term, and being certain that he would now be released, he was told that whereas he would cease to be regarded as a prisoner he was nevertheless not at liberty to leave the camp. This time he was there for life. From then onwards he worked as an engineer and was well paid, though he had nothing to spend the money on.

While I was having lunch in the cook-house, Natasha Stepanova came in and asked to have a word with me in private. Natasha, who had been condemned years before for a political offence, worked in the camp as a store assistant, issuing food to the cooks. In a small hut separated by a wall from the storeroom itself, where it would have been risky to talk within sight and earshot of everyone at large, she gave me a bag of sugar and a sweet-cake which she had baked herself, after which she asked me to let her brother know about her when I got out.

'Write down the address,' she whispered imploringly. 'Chelabinsk, Wasienko Street, No. 74, Siemion Stepanovitch Dzerzavin—and I'm his sister, Natalia.'

'I'll remember.'

'Wouldn't it be better to write it down, though?'

'All right,' I consented.

'Only, what if there's a search?' she whispered. 'They'll find it.'

'If I hide it well, they won't,' I reassured her. 'Don't you know how letters are smuggled out of prison?'

She didn't know, having been sent straight to the camp after her trial.

'You write with an indelible pencil on a piece of damp cloth which you sew into the lining of a garment,' I explained. 'No searcher will ever feel that. I'll write down the address and sew it in my cap.'

'Thank you.' She smiled prettily. 'Have you a needle and thread?'

'I think so. If not, I'll borrow them.'

'Wait. I'll give them to you.'

She took a spool of thread from a wooden box and broke off a length of it which she wrapped round a sliver of wood and handed to me together with a needle. I shook hands with Natasha and went out.

I spent the night in a hut reserved for those who were leaving. Nobody slept. We repaired our clothes, sang songs and kept the stove blazing, to do which we all but demolished the building. Oh, what a delight it was—with the lack of fuel as an excuse—to smash the bunks and tear up the flooring, and, in the morning, batter the now useless iron stove, dig out its brick foundations and send its tin pipe crashing to the floor with a kick.

I used up all the thread Natasha gave me, sewing my tattered trousers through which my underwear, in no less ragged a condition, was clearly visible. While I was hunting for some thread of my own, I lost the needle. As a result, I could not make a note of her brother's address to sew in my cap as promised. To quieten my pangs of conscience, I resolved to memorize the information.

At dawn, just before we set off, they held a roll-call. There was no search, except by one sergeant who came up to me calling 'Wittlin?' snatched the cap from my head and tore out the lining. Thank goodness he found nothing suspicious inside. He wrenched it again, more violently still, and ripped out the wool and rag padding. Still he was unlucky. Disappointed, he flung the cap, now in shreds, at my feet in the snow.

There was no doubt that Natasha was employed as an informer and that she it was who had denounced me. Certainly, no one could possibly have overheard our conversation in the deserted store.

As our names were read off the list we were formed up in fours and, led by two soldiers, who were unarmed and unaccompanied by dogs—their only purpose being to show us the way—we started on the return journey, that twenty-seven kilometre stretch which had once seemed so utterly devoid of hope.

As the detachment was marching through the camp for the last time, Natasha ran out of the store. No sooner did she catch sight of me marching happily in the ranks, than a bright smile lit her gentle, swarthy face. She ran

along beside us, picking up the step like a girl seeing her
fiancé off to the front, and whispered,

'You're going, my dear. Look after yourself and safe
journey!'

'Thanks! All the best!'

'You haven't got a cap,' she said, more disappointed
than surprised.

'Doesn't matter. I don't suppose I'll freeze. I'll buy
another on the journey with some bread.'

'You haven't forgotten what I asked you to do, have
you?' she reminded me shyly.

'I haven't forgotten—Siemion Stepanovitch Dzerzavin, Chelabinsk, Wasienko Street, 74. His sister Natalia
is well.'

'Yes, that's it. Thank you,' she said with a sob. 'Do
you think I'm a swine and that I reported you?'

Not knowing what to say, I shrugged my shoulders.
Anxious not to appear as stupid as she had thought me,
I replied:

'I'm too old a bird to be caught that way. I didn't
write it down.'

The pace of the detachment increased. Soon we would
be through the wooden stockade gates and beyond the
barbed wire entanglements. Natasha quickened her steps
and, running beside me, flung her arms round my neck.

Our lips met. We might have been lovers.

THIRTEEN

The Road to Freedom

When we had been travelling a week, the train steamed into the station at a place called Kotlas. It was early one dull morning and the houses on either side of the tracks gaped at us soullessly from the black sockets of their shuttered windows. Dozens of men in tattered clothes poured from the train on to the station which was embellished with a few wretched trees. Nothing remained to grace the abandoned red trucks save empty tins, cigarette packets, a few boards from the broken bunks, the well-trodden straw, damp with slush, and the stove overturned on the floor.

At first the men stood around helplessly, each grasping his bag of personal belongings and the inevitable messcan, surprised that no one was taking any notice of them. After a while, they began to disperse, in groups or singly. Some went away, just as they were, dirty and unkempt, in search of a photographer, so as to have a souvenir to take home to the family—as a present, perhaps, for Christmas was not far off. Others went to buy things in the market, or to a restaurant, the baths or the barber's. Those who had gone to find out about the next train for Buzuluk, came back with the news that the booking-office was closed till the following day and the station-master had heard of no train going there.

The grey town of Kotlas is a port on the northern reaches of the River Dzhvina. It was the first settlement of free people encountered by the deportee returning from the Urals; for those proceeding under arrest to the labour camps, it was the last glimpse of freedom. From Kotlas onwards there was only a single line going north, and that was exclusively reserved for the transportation of prisoners. The trains set off full and returned empty. But from Kotlas, which is in the region of Archangel, southwards, numerous rail routes give access to the free world. Even at Kotlas, however, on the very threshold of liberty, one could easily be given a fresh sentence on some pretext or other—hence, many of the new arrivals, panic stricken at the very thought of it, were solely intent upon getting as far away as possible. The sooner the better.

I left the barber's shop and went into the town. Passing the railway bridge, I crossed the market square— a silent wilderness of deserted booths—and entered a restaurant in the station down by the river. It was on the first floor of a wooden building. Heavily made-up waitresses were serving bowls of soup in the large dining-hall, the walls of which were decorated with nymphs and fauns at their ablutions. You could order as much soup as you liked, only you had to be quick about it before the supply was exhausted. Accordingly, I surrounded myself with six plates of soup and began my meal. I had my own bread with me and for a few roubles I was able to purchase a glass of red wine. The only difficulty was to deny oneself the pleasure of ordering several. As I sat there drinking, I congratulated myself on having emerged from my tribulations with a whole skin. I wished myself a similar run of good luck in the future. The wine which

was a deep purple and strongly alcoholic went quickly
to my head. Feeling that I had triumphed over the Soviet
conception of justice, I found the world not a bad place
after all. I sat there till evening, when they began to turn
people out in order to tidy up before dinner. There was
no help for it. Once more out into the frost-bound streets.
I picked up my bag and mess-can and staggered back
through the town. The cold air hit me like a hammer. My
only conscious thought as I stumbled light-headedly in
the direction of the station was for the safety of my kit-
bag. I knew I would meet some of my friends there and
hear what chances there were of continuing the journey.
It was a straight road and there was no risk of going
astray. It led through the market to the snow-covered
park, on the far side of which lay the railway station.

As I expected, several of my travelling companions
were there, either standing about, uneasy and helpless, or
else stamping up and down the platform. They resembled
a herd of cattle terrified by a premonition of unknown
danger. What was the matter? It appeared that during
our absence in town our more far-seeing companions who
had remained in the station had witnessed the arrival of
a luxurious passenger train, and had bought tickets and
left straight away for Buzuluk. And that, by all accounts,
was to be the last train going there direct. The general
dismay of those left behind was therefore quite understandable.

Meanwhile, groups of friends from the camp were arriving every minute—clean shaven, bathed, fed and photo-
graphed. Every one of them listened to the tragic news
in undisguised terror. As the crowd grew, however, our
spirits rose. So many men all bound for the army would
certainly not be left long in such conditions. They would
have to run an extra train.

The station-master, surrounded by the protesting multitude, declared his own standing to be insufficiently high to enable him to take independent action, but assured us that if the authorities provided the trucks, he would make the necessary arrangements. Without specific instructions, however, it was hard to do anything. He spread his hands despairingly.

It was dusk. Once more hunger began to gnaw and it was time to think about supper. Just then, as though to spite us, a steamer with Soviet recruits put in at the pier and the harbour restaurant was entirely reserved for the young soldiers. There was only one other restaurant open in the whole town and that was a tenth-rate soup-kitchen. It was a long way off, through unlit streets of dirty hovels, on the edge of a wide vacant patch of ground in the middle of which stood a primitive shelter over a ditch dug in the earth, for the people of Kotlas knew nothing of sewers.

A large signboard inscribed 'Soup-kitchen No. 2' marked the entrance to a low, single-story house in front of which stood a long queue of people waiting patiently. As he entered each man was presented with a tin spoon, on surrendering his cap as deposit. Anyone failing to return the spoon as he left forfeited his cap. Soon a number of customers were leaving bare-headed. That didn't worry them much, for most of them had a spare cap in their kit and they were glad to come by a spoon—such an indispensable article on a long journey. The staff of the soup-kitchen, seeing what the game was, had recourse to another method. Anyone failing to return his spoon had to pay a fine of ten roubles, which provided the staff with an additional source of income. If you happened to turn your head away before you had finished your meal, the waitress would swoop on your plate and remove it, together with the spoon. You could kick up a fuss and complain loudly that your food had been taken away before you had finished, but nobody believed you. You paid your fine at the door and if you went on being awkward, the militiamen took charge of you. Thus, it cost two roubles to eat in the restaurant and ten to get out of it.

I left the soup-kitchen and returned to the station where, every few hours, fresh drafts of freed prisoners were arriving from different camps. The little station was thronged. Amid the constant uproar and bustle, relations, friends and acquaintances, reunited as by a miracle, joyfully embraced one another.

Night fell and, crowded together in the stuffy waiting-room, the men settled down to sleep on the floor in front of the closed ticket-office, forming a queue in anticipation of to-morrow's sale. An icy wind blew in from the platform. As the night wore on, the cold grew more intense. Somebody slammed the door. Those who were thereby prevented from forcing their way inside could be heard shouting and cursing out in the street. They had now to sleep in the park, in the cold. The air in the crowded waiting-room was so foul, the windows being tightly shut, that it was better to get out of it, even though one knew the door would only be opened to let one leave and there was no chance of being re-admitted.

Unfortunately, it was not safe to walk about the streets. There were numerous patrols on the look-out for tramps and if you were once picked up you could say good-bye to your freedom for a long time to come—perhaps for ever. Nor was there any place to sit down. Every niche, every arch, every street bench was occupied by civilian refugees or evacuees. Surrounded by bags and boxes, crates and furniture, they slept amid red quilts and palliasses on which old men and groaning women with their children swathed in kerchiefs were reclining in state.

The door of the sky-blue harbour restaurant was still open. They might still be selling wine or plates of soup. In the darkened dining-hall the tables had been pushed together and the chairs piled in a pyramid on top. Only two or three tables near the service counter were still gleaming with cloths and cutlery. I could see bottles of vodka, plates, knives, forks, tomatoes, cucumbers, fish and a fragrant dish of scrambled eggs as well as bread and butter. There were soldiers sitting at the tables. They were still wearing their caps, but their sheep-skin coats were unbuttoned. On their knees and clinging drunkenly round their necks were the waitresses. From the shadowy walls, satyrs, fauns, nymphs and shepherdesses gazed down upon them. There was obviously nothing to be gained by intruding. Besides, such situations are best left alone, whatever the latitude or longitude.

At dawn the travellers began to string out in front of the ticket-office. The queue stretched out of the building, along the broken fence round the station garden and so into the town. After a few hours, the office finally opened and the official began selling tickets, as slowly as possible in order to enhance his own prestige. It took him an hour to dispose of a few dozen. He then announced that all the seats were sold, closed the hatch and covered it with a stout board which he secured on the inside by means of an iron bar. Outraged hammering, accompanied by curses and abuse, was of no avail. The cashier did not even hear it, for he had left the building by another exit. Notwithstanding, no one vacated his place in the queue. For all we knew the cashier might well return, having been ordered to sell some more tickets. Then, to have lost one's place would be nothing short of catastrophe. So we all stood there waiting, without knowing for certain why. Then a train drew in. The crowd rushed it from all sides before the engine had even come to a halt. But the coaches, which were packed with refugees, were surrounded by conductors, railway staff and militia. No one could get on without a ticket. It transpired, however, that apart from the few dozen lucky people who had got to the ticket-office that morning more than two hundred others also had tickets, though no one knew how they had come by them. After a short halt, the conductors helped to thrust the passengers inside by placing a knee in the small of their backs, squeezed in themselves, slammed the doors shut, and the train pulled out. Those who tried to ride on the steps were hit over the head by the conductors, leaning out through the half-open windows. Their caps were snatched off and tossed as far as the station building, while the militia caught hold of their legs and tugged.

I stood and watched the train disappearing round the bend, amongst the black silhouettes of sheds, ramps, water-tower, the low thicket of the points switches and beneath the raised arms of the signals as they bestowed a last blessing upon it, wishing god-speed as it went on its way, taking with it our last faint gleam of hope. The station, which so recently had been the scene of commotion, was once more silent and deserted.

'Well, how go's it? Still alive and kicking?'

Somebody slapped me on the shoulder and I looked into a pair of roguish eyes, twinkling with genuine delight at this meeting. I recognized that shrewd, young, ever-smiling countenance at once. It was Fonka. We had known each other in the camp.

Fonka, a professional thief, had had rough luck on his last outing. Fortunately for him, he found a good lawyer whom he lavishly rewarded with stolen money and thanks to whom he was given a 'child's sentence'—three years in Siberia. That was where we had met and Fonka, at the time, was already a convict of some standing. He had, in fact, completed his sentence a few weeks previous and being a common, not a political, criminal he was now free to go home. As usual, he was smiling as he stood there stamping his feet in the snow.

After spending the day together roaming through the town we stamped our way through the night, round and round the snow-covered park which was thronged with homeless wanderers. Fresh goods trains had been arriving, loaded with thousand of freed prisoners.

At dawn I went to the military stores to draw bread, while Fonka who, not being a soldier, was not entitled to a ration, agreed to hold our place in the ticket queue— for which service he was to receive half the bread. When I got back with the loaf, I saw him wedged in the crowd not far from the office which, however, stubbornly refused to open.

'Open your knife and cut yourself off a bit,' I said, handing him the loaf.

He took out a knife, cut off a slice which was much less than half or even a quarter and began to eat in a leisurely fashion, as though he had just had a good breakfast.

'Where did you get it?' he asked.

'In the barracks. Second street on the left behind the square.'

Away went Fonka. I doubted whether he was following my directions. He could scarcely hope to be given bread at the barracks. It was issued by two soldiers under the supervision of an officer who carefully scrutinized the papers of all applicants, and during the day the queue had grown to immense proportions so that, however quickly it might be issued, Fonka would never be able to squeeze into the line before dawn the following day.

A sudden ripple of excitement ran through the crowd around the booking-office. The window opened and business began. Standing no distance away, with my mind full of pleasant thoughts, I fingered my money-bag in anticipation. The first contented customers were already wandering away, tickets clasped between their teeth, buttoning up their padded jackets from under which they had previously extracted rag wallets. But they were not putting away those large, close-printed travel forms. They would be read from end to end and due delight taken in their possession.

In a little while I, myself, would be starting to unravel the contents of a similar document, I reflected. Now I was only ten away from that most desirable little window, nine . . . eight . . . seven . . . then the window closed relentlessly and up went the board and the bar. All tickets were sold out and the waiting-room had to be vacated, for, in accordance with the new sanitary regulations, no one was allowed to sleep there.

I was no sooner outside in the icy embrace of the frost, than I spotted Fonka. He was walking along with a smile on his face and two whole rations of bread under each arm. It was no use asking how he had got hold of it all. Anyway, his methods were inimitable.

'We're going to sleep like kings to-night,' he gaily announced.

'Did you get a room in exchange for bread?' I asked.

'Room be damned,' he replied, shaking his head contemptuously. 'We'll be sleeping with women.'

'Have they somewhere to live?'

'Oh, you intellectuals are just like kids. You don't understand anything,' he snorted, like an impatient schoolmaster whose pupil has been grappling in vain for an hour with the multiplication tables.

'We're not going to sleep with girls—the way you think. Just with women—like I told you. They're coming down to the kiosk as soon as it's dark. Then you'll see what a night we'll have.'

In the park stood an old dilapidated bandstand, just a circular roof on eight poles covering a decayed wooden floor, two steps above ground level. During the summer, on public holidays, a band used to play in this stand which had now been crammed with people for days on end. It was here that Fonka had fixed a rendezvous with the ladies.

They appeared at dusk. Three of them. Their collective ages must have totalled some hundred and seventy years, for each of them was well over fifty, while together they would have turned the scales at several hundred-weights. They were as big as boilers and fat, too, though it was hard to say how they managed to keep so. It may have been a residue from the good old days. They had huge scarves and peasant kerchiefs wound round their heads and they were carrying a large brown quilt. Catching sight of Fonka, they came up and addressed us.

'Well, my lads, how's it to be?' asked one of them.

'See here, mothers, you'll get one and a half rations of bread between you—that is, half a ration per face— all right?'

'Right. Let's lie down and get to sleep.'

We scooped the snow from the steps of the band-stand by a communal effort, then one of the women pulled out several old copies of *Pravda* from under her skirts and laid them on the damp earth. We spread out the quilt on the papers and the largest of the female boilers lay down in the middle. To either side of her, or rather to the shawls and kerchiefs in which she was swathed, Fonka and I clung like leeches, while the two other ladies lay down at either edge of the quilt, sheltering our backs from the cold by the application of their huge stomachs and enormous breasts. So there we lay, Fonka and myself, for all the world like a couple of currants in a bun. It was as warm as a feather-bed and we had not been so comfortable in years. Soon our eyes closed and we were overcome by a sleep which was peaceful, rosy and joyous.

It was broad daylight when we awoke and the others were already queueing—either at the ticket-office or at the army bread stores. When I got back to the station with my daily ration, instead of dashing straight to the ticket-office, where Fonka was standing guard, I went along the platform to find out when the next train was due to arrive. No one knew anything about a train, but in front of the station-master's office there was a swirling crowd of men, women and children. One did not need to be a detective to deduce that the station-master was disposing of tickets at more than the official price. That accounted for those hundreds of passengers in possession of tickets for which they had never queued and who were always first aboard whenever a train arrived.

I squeezed in amongst the crowd and soon learnt that anyone could get a ticket by slipping the station-master a hundred roubles. The fee was not excessive and well worth paying. The travellers stood, waiting for the station-master's office to open, jammed together like flies glued to a paper. Suddenly, framed in the open doorway through which wafted frosty clouds of grey moisture, there appeared a militiaman in his blue unform. The representative of authority looked at the crowd and, as though suspecting some underhand dealings, went away without a word. That was more intimidating than any attempt to clear the corridor and drive the people away with kicks

or the butt of a revolver. Shortly afterwards he returned
to confirm his suspicions. He stood on the threshold, carefully observing the assembly through narrowed eyelids—
after which he went away again. There was no doubt that
the gathering clouds would soon release a thunderbolt
equally fatal to the station-master for accepting and to
the passengers for offering bribes. The dense crowd instinctively scented danger. In a deathly silence they began
to leak out into the street, as it were secretly, one after
another, so as not to risk walking en masse right into the
cordon of militia which might be waiting for them outside.
It appeared that the station-master, who was in comparable danger, had observed the attendant enemy through
the garden of frosty flowers on the frozen window-panes
of his office, and, sensing the impending aggression, had
decided to defend himself. He opened the door of his
office and, standing on the threshold, surveyed the assembly with a look of surprise.

'What do you want here, my friends?' he asked in
astonishment.

'We want tickets, Citizen Station-master,' came a
few humble voices from the crowd.

'You've come to the wrong place then, my friends.
There's a ticket-office in the station. Right over on the
other side. You have to go round this building and come
in from the street, not from the station,' he explained
benevolently, as though nobody knew the whereabouts or
the purpose of the booking-office. 'You'll have to go over
there and stand in the queue.'

'But people were buying tickets from you yesterday,'
cried one of the bolder spirits.

'Certainly people were buying from me,' the station-
master admitted. 'Mothers with babes in arms and fathers
carrying their children. Obviously, they can't stand out in

the cold all night or suffocate in the crowd outside the ticket-office. Why, their young ones, the very future of the Soviet people, might die in their arms. I helped these people by selling them tickets myself and I'll do the same to-day. If you can help people, why not? If anybody's travelling with a small child, he's only got to wait here, write down where he wants to go and get his money ready. But the money's got to be dead right according to the controlled fares because I can't give any change. If anybody's thinking of waiting for change, I can't fix him up. Just remember, I'm doing the same to-day as I did before. Not a kopeck more than you pay at the booking-office. All clear? Right then, people with children line up along the wall on the left!'

After these few words he retired to his room, closing the door behind him. It was a cunning move and would undoubtedly get the station-master out of the fix he was in. There was no one to check up on what he had done the previous day and, anyway, who would punish a man for devoting himself to the service of others?

The crowd put two and two together, the words they had just heard and the militiaman hovering suspiciously. They knew what the station-master meant and realized that his decision would stand in the face of any bribe, no matter how generous. Disappointed, they slowly left the hall, only a few women with infants and a couple of men with children muffled in scarves remaining behind. I was amongst those who left.

I raced out of the station building into the town, looking right and left as though searching for a victim to pounce upon. In a side-street, near the railway line, between two rows of wooden cottages, I perceived the object of my search—a woman swathed in sheep-skins, with a child on her arm.

'Good-day to you, mother.'

'Good-day, son.'

'Where are you off to? Going home?' I asked.

'Yes, but why . . . ?' she queried distrustfully.

'Would you come to the station with me?'

The country woman halted, her face pale and her honest eyes dilated with fright. She was certain that she was talking to a secret agent. If she met the devil on her way she would cross herself, but at sight of a Soviet agent she dare not even do that.

'What have I done wrong that you want to take me along there?'

'I'll give you thirty roubles.'

This was quite beyond the woman's comprehension.

'What for?' she asked, calming down slightly. 'What for? Can't you find your own way to the station? It's along there.' She nodded in the direction I'd come from. 'You go right, then straight on. Follow the lines.'

'But I want you to come with me—so that I can take the child.'

'Oh, my God,' she wailed. 'What is all this?'

'Nothing at all. Anyone with a child can buy a ticket without having to queue for it. That's all. I'll give you the money I promised and the bread I've got here as well.'

The last argument did the trick. The woman as a citizen of a country in which anything may happen, understood without further explanation. We walked along together in the direction of the station buildings.

'And you're not a scoundrel?' she asked when we had gone a little way.

'Of course not, but if you don't believe me, I'll pay in advance.'

'Oh no, that's all right. There's no need to,' she protested, ashamed of her suspicion.

'Why? I'd even prefer it, so that people won't see.'

The black lump of bread and the red bank-note with its likeness of Lenin changed hands—as did a small creature asleep in its wraps. I walked carefully with the child in my arms, so as not to slip on the ice protruding from the well-trodden snow.

'I'll wait here,' said the woman, as we approached the ramp which marked the beginning of the station proper. 'If they see us together they might smell a rat and then we'd both be in for it. Sasha, as well.' She pointed at the infant. 'Why should he be taken away from his mother and put in an orphanage? What's he done?'

Her warning was apt. I hurried along to the station-master's office. When, panting and puffing out clouds of frosty air, I at last found myself in the waiting-room, there were only a couple of people left. The others had apparently bought their tickets already.

I was the last. The door of the office opened and out came three women with children. They had their tickets in their hands. The station-master was letting in three at a time so as to have witnesses to the fact that he was not accepting bribes. For all the world like a proud, tender father, I walked in carrying Sasha and, a little while later, re-emerged with the coveted ticket. I left the building and went back to the ramp, intending to return the gentle burden which I had borrowed.

When I got there—my hair stood on end. There was no sign of the mother! 'She's dumped the baby on me!' I thought to myself in a panic. Drops of icy sweat broke out on my forehead as I dashed blindly down the road, searching right and left. Then I caught sight of the dark kerchief worn by Sasha's mother—in the distance. Finding it inconceivable that anyone could be dealt with promptly in an office, she had preferred to go for a walk rather than wait about in the cold. She had less than half the bread left.

I returned Sasha with my own hands. Then, as light-heartedly as a student at the end of an examination, off I went as fast as I could. There was heavenly bliss in my heart, a ticket to Orenburg in my pocket and a damp stain on my coat.

Having the ticket was not everything. It is easier to travel without a ticket, provided there is a train, than with a ticket when there is no train. And there were no more trains. Those green coaches which had pulled out of Kotlas station the previous day were the last. On the other hand, drafts of liberated prisoners from camps up north were arriving several times a day. In consequence, the air of gloom which hung over this sub-arctic township was entirely dissipated. The merry voices of excited men in rags and tatters could be heard on all sides; their clothes may have been in shreds but the wearers were shaven, their hair neatly trimmed and their spirits excellent. Even the very ill, leaning heavily on sticks, hobbled about, smiling happily as they coughed. Many a man died in the morning with that same smile on his face—out in the park, on the station, queuing for bread or waiting for a ticket.

The town seemed to swell hour by hour as it filled with these poor wretches. Then the rumour got about that the sanitary commission was afraid of an epidemic and, if no other means of dispersing the crowds could be found, they intended to re-direct the newcomers to the camps from which they had only just arrived. Everyone was seized with immediate panic.

After several fruitless days, the homeless wanderers witnessed the arrival of a very long train consisting of more than two hundred goods wagons. It came in about

midnight. Those who were down to go as well as others
who had never asked anybody anything—people who had
bought a ticket and others who had not a farthing in the
world—were all free to board it and travel away. It was
obvious that there would not be room for everyone and
there were few friends sufficiently devoted to risk passing
on the news for fear they might themselves be left behind.
So people who were asleep were not woken up but left to
slumber on, dreaming perhaps of the journey away from
this no-man's-land between freedom and imprisonment.
Bundles were snatched up and the crowds stampeded towards the endless string of black trucks which stood silently waiting in a siding some distance away. The commotion which had at first been limited to a few people had
succeeded in provoking a veritable human avalanche. A
herd of dark shapes, bumping and colliding, as they slithered across the frozen snow, raced for the trucks, clam-
bering into their black interiors and occupying the most
comfortable positions on the floor. The floors were covered with coal dust which smothered the clothing of the
passengers, filtered into their kit-bags in which were
stowed their spare set of underwear, and thoroughly black-
ened their faces and hands.

In the first rush the trucks nearest were filled to
overflowing, while those further away gaped emptily.
After some brief but bitter skirmishing and a few tussles,
to the inevitable accompaniment of oaths and blasphemies,
the crowd filled the train and the passengers began to
settle down for the long journey. Someone had brought
along a few planks, ripped from a nearby fence, so as to
make bunks, while somebody else had managed to get
hold of an iron-stove pipe. There was plenty of time, for
the driver assured us that the engine was not connected
and the train would not leave before dawn. In view of

these assurances several people got out with tin cans to
go and draw drinking water which had been specially
boiled and was now being distributed. The kitchen where
they were boiling the water was situated at the far end of
the station. To get to it one had to cross several tracks
under the wheels of stationary trains.

The water seekers jumped down from their trucks
and squelched away into the inky blackness. They were
no sooner gone than the train started—southwards, to
freedom.

Day and night the train thundered along the endless
track. Now and again it slithered to a halt beneath the
iron branches of a signal, like a serpent under a tree, and
lay still as though dead for hours on end. But at other
times it only stopped for a moment or two. There was no
knowing how long it would rest at any particular stop. We
were told that the train stopped at points on occasion to
let through truck-loads of important supplies or coach-
loads of the more distinguished Soviet refugees from war-
threatened towns.

During such halts people got out to collect handfuls
of snow for water or else to search for food. It was always
as well to keep an eye on the train at such times in case it
ran away, as it might do at any moment right under your
nose. At the least sign that this was about to happen everything was dropped and the passengers dashed back in
breathless haste, terrified at the thought of being left
behind in that silent wilderness.

We had been travelling a week since the day, or
rather the night, of our departure, and, apart from the
bread and soup issued at the one official stopping-place,
Kirov, every man had had to feed himself as best he could.
Jumping in and out of the trucks en route was difficult,

exhausting and dangerous. It was much better to wait till
the train came to a station where it would stop for a
reasonable length of time. One of the passengers had a
map, a small-scale affair, torn from a schoolboy's atlas. He
had traced the route on this map—from Kirov to Perm,
Perm to Chelabinsk, Chelabinsk to Orenburg, Orenburg
to Buzuluk.

That fabulous Buzuluk was situated in the region of
the Urals, and in order to get from there to Siberia it was
necessary to describe a semi-circle. The map was passed
from hand to hand, the owner keeping a careful watch on
it all the time to prevent its disappearance. It was a good
thing to commit the main places on the route to memory—
Perm, Chelabinsk, Orenburg.

Late one night the train pulled into a huge junction
and came to a halt in the impenetrable blackness. We
might have been standing in a mountain tunnel. It was
bound to stop there a long time. The station was very big
and crowded. People began emerging with their buckets
to go in search of food. It was no easy matter to find
one's way to the station. There was a maze of tracks to be
crossed, with a train standing on each. If it was a goods
train, it was comparatively simple to climb up on the open
platform and jump down on the other side, but in the case
of a passenger train, the doors were usually locked so that
one had to crawl under the coaches. This was an unpleasant
business—the lines being fouled with excrement. Besides,
one never knew when one of the trains might start. Luckily,
the station building showed up white in the distance and
behind its glass doors, in front of the kitchen where barley
was being issued, stood a row of men holding containers.

When a ladleful of barley landed in my can, my first
thought was to eat it and then return to the train. It was
not hunger that provoked this decision, but the fact that

I knew what it would be like getting back; I would never be able to swallow a mouthful of it after crossing those tracks. The hot barley burnt my mouth and throat and, despite the desirability of haste—in the blissful hope of getting a second helping—it was an utter impossibility to eat quickly. They closed down the kitchen before I had emptied the can. There was nothing for it but to go back.

Having climbed over dozens of sleepers, coal tenders, locomotives, tank wagons, platforms, rails and points, I found myself back where my train ought to have been. There was nothing to be seen but the empty rails stretching away into the blackness. Perhaps I had missed my way or the trucks had been shunted into a siding, I thought. Surely the train was bound to be stopping some time. But no. It had simply left. There was another man standing there besides myself. He was equally helpless, and holding a bucket full of barley intended for his fellow passengers—thirty-six rations.

'We've been left behind,' he said, coming up to me.

'So it seems,' I admitted.

'They've gone.'

'It looks like it—and with all my things . . . the bundle with my ticket in it.' I sighed.

'What do we do now?'

'We might as well eat the barley you were going to give your friends.'

'You're right. We'd better empty the bucket.'

We put down the bucket on a sleeper and, having seated ourselves opposite one another on the tracks, took out our wooden spoons and commenced eating. We worked hard in complete silence till we could see the bottom of the bucket.

It is no easy matter to eat thirty-six rations of thick barley-oats.

*

The place where the train left me standing, like a rider whose horse had bolted, was called Glazov. It was an important junction. It would not have been so bad had it only been possible to buy a ticket for Buzuluk, but, unfortunately, Glazov was a strange station. There was no booking-office. It was hard to imagine how anyone could ever travel beyond it. The station-master informed me that he had not heard of any train going in my direction. It was up to me to find a way of reaching my destination. The line on that map had led first to Perm, so that was the place to make for. When I woke up the next morning, after spending the night on a bench, I found that my companion in sorrow had flown, taking his bucket with him. He had probably found the train during the night and, being a kind-hearted fellow and loath to wake me, had gone off quietly without saying good-bye.

Round about dawn a long train of goods wagons drew in. They were full of Russian refugees bound for Perm.

The commandant in charge of the draft let me into the last truck which was empty. It was a dirty truck lined with wet straw, the floor full of holes, the iron stove smashed and boards missing from the walls.

The train remained at a standstill all day and did not leave till night-fall. I had nothing to eat while I was waiting, but at least my mess-can served as a pillow for my head. During the night, the train was more often stationary than not, for it stopped at every halt.

The passengers were poor, working-class people— women, children and old men from districts threatened by the surge of war. They were travelling complete with all their belongings and the provisions necessary for a journey lasting months. I, being without food or a change of clothes and obliged to report at a certain place within a given time, under pain of arrest for vagrancy, could not permit myself such leisurely progress. During one of those halts in open country, as the train which was being given priority over us came past, I left my truck and climbed on to the rear platform of the 'special.'

A rapid journey in winter-time through the snow-clad fields of Russia—and on an open platform—is not to be counted a major pleasure. Even though you curl up, press your shoulders to the wall, turn up your collar, let down your ear-flaps and slide your hands into your sleeves, you still stand a good chance of freezing to death. Despite hunger and exhaustion, it is much better to stand up and ward off the persistent onslaught of sleep by slapping your frost-bitten cheeks with your hands. Luckily, during one of the compulsory halts, I was noticed.

Two men, well wrapped in furs, approached the platform on which I was standing. One was the commandant of the train, the other, his second-in-command. I greeted them, told them how I had missed my own train and stressed the urgent necessity of my getting, at least, as far as Perm. They informed me that the station was no longer called Perm but Molotovsk, adding that the train would pass through there on its way to Novosibirsk. After that they gave me permission to remain on the platform, provided I got off immediately on arrival at Perm. I solemnly promised to do so, whereupon they went away.

At the next stop, they reappeared, but not of their own accord. They had been sent. They invited me to come and have a bowl of soup. Their tone was less official than on the previous occasion. There was no doubt they had been sent by a woman. Not only are women on the whole more kind-hearted than men, but they are more apt to re-member that a man may be hungry and exhausted.

I got into the train accompanied by my hosts and found myself in a goods wagon converted into a two-room dwelling with a kitchen. An elderly lady was lying on the bed reading, while a young one was busy at the stove. The commandant of the train was the director of a heavy industrial factory being evacuated from Moscow and the second-in-command was his son-in-law, while the two women, mother and daughter, were their wives.

They entertained me at dinner and let me pass the night by their stove. When evening came and the doors had been closed, the oil lamp extinguished, I slept soundly on the floor—warm and no longer hungry. The next morning, I thanked them for their hospitality and, armed with my faithful mess-can, slipped off the train at Perm, which station bore the name of the former Minister for Foreign Affairs.

My run of good luck persisted. A train, drawn by two engines and consisting of a series of splendid coaches belonging to the Moscow Underground, had just arrived. A young girl, poorly dressed, got out to stretch her legs on the platform. I asked her whether the train was bound for Chelabinsk. She told me that it was and added that I could travel by it, but advised me to wait till it started before getting in, just in case the other passengers might object. Somebody yelled, 'Take your seats!' The girl went back to her carriage with the air of a conspirator and stood watching through the half-open doors. A moment later, as the train got under way, I sprang in, slamming the doors.

We travelled fast. Standing in the warm corridor, I got into conversation with the girl, from whom I learned that there were some important personages on board. She, herself, had only been given a seat on the train by virtue of the fact that she was employed as a domestic worker by one of the travelling dignitaries.

'Not as a servant,' she emphasized proudly, 'but as a domestic worker.'

I replied that the designation 'domestic worker' was likewise current in my capitalistic country—and not the word 'servant.' I felt like adding that such domestic workers were far better dressed in my country, only I was afraid of hurting her.

The hours and kilometres would have passed much more quickly had it not been for the growing pangs of hunger. A tall, generously built woman slid open the glass doors of the compartment. She had a packet in her hand which she was going to throw out the window, for the large ones inside the compartment would not open. Fortunately, the windows in the corridor were also jammed and I offered to help. She handed me the packet and returned to the compartment. There was some bread in the packet, slightly mouldy, but soft and white. Once the green spots were picked out, it would be quite edible. I stood with my back to the door leading into the compartment and flung the packet out—but only the paper and the mouldy crumbs. The remaider of the bread I slipped into my coat pocket. But I was seen doing it. A short while afterwards the woman came out again and invited me to share come refreshments. I accepted and was introduced to some of the passengers. The woman herself was the wife of a young dramatist. Her husband, who was travelling with her, had made a great success of writing propaganda plays for the Red Army. In addition to this couple, there were three of their friends—high officials in Communist Party uniforms—a university professor, an aeroplane designer, a chief surgeon of a hospital in Moscow, the directress of the public library in Moscow, and the children of two generals, six girls and youths of eighteen or nineteen, one of whom, a girl in trousers and a leather jacket, might have stood as the classic example of Slav beauty.

They were all wearing well-cut clothes of good-quality material as well as expensive furs. They had with them elegant travelling bags, colourful woollen blankets, costly jewellery, gold watches, silver cigarette-cases, up-to-date cameras, Thermos flasks and gramophones complete with excellent records. During the journey, they helped themselves to wine, chocolate and high-grade tinned goods. The servant, or rather the domestic worker, was not exaggerating in the least when she referred to them as persons of note. They were in fact representatives of that select band of Party members, the new-style Soviet aristocracy, those who live in luxury while the mass of the people go ragged and hungry. (The sight of a man lying under a wall in the street and starving to death is by no means uncommon in Russia. I drew the attention of a militiaman in Kotlas to one such case. 'Well, what of it? Let him die!' was the answer I got.)

During our conversation, they were all pleasant and direct. They tried to make me stay after we had eaten, but I felt out of place in my dilapidated boots, my galoshes tied with wire, my tattered trousers and my no less ragged jacket which I was vainly attempting to conceal under a civilian overcoat that had seen better days.

I excused myself accordingly and went out in the corridor. I was not alone for long, however. Two serious-looking dignitaries came out for a chat. They gave me a cigarette and we started to talk. They were cultured, polite, intelligent, educated and quite *au fait* with politics, literature and art. One of them, anxious to know in what part of Siberia I had been, went into the compartment and brought out an encyclopædia with the request that I should point out on the map the exact position of my polar camp.

Then they both asked me about conditions in the deportation camps, about which they knew little and that only by hearsay. Afraid that they might just be pumping me, I answered with reserve, declaring that the camps being designed equally to reform the deportee and to exploit the natural resources of the Urals, the worker who is to be utilized but not destroyed enjoys tolerable conditions and is well fed. In short, I lied and spun as good a line of propaganda as any Soviet Education Officer. While one of the gentlemen was away replacing the encyclopædia, which was a heavy volume, the other, who had been listening to my account of the delights of Siberia, took advantage of the absence of his friend to edge closer to me and whisper,

'That's all very fine. Only I don't think I heard the beginning of your story, so I haven't the remotest idea why on earth you ever came to this nightmarish land of ours.'

Night was approaching and the passengers settled down to rest, spreading their blankets and pillows on the benches. I lay down on the floor with my mess-can, draped in my cap, under my head. The other passengers, doubting that I could possibly sleep on the floor, invited me to occupy one of the vacant benches. I was amazed that they could possibly have any doubts about anything so obvious.

The journey lasted some days and nights. The train raced along smoothly with scarcely a rumble or rattle, till it reached the outskirts of Chelabinsk and entered the goods station where passenger trains, as a rule, did not stop. On this occasion, however, the authorities were making an exception so that the distinguished refugees would not be inconvenienced by the mob of would-be travellers who always stormed the coaches of a passenger train.

To get to Orenburg I had to change here, so I said good-bye, got out and in no time at all found myself waiting for a tram which took me to the right station. The train for Orenburg, a line of green passenger coaches, was drawn up near the pump which was watering the locomotive. The train was packed full and conductors stood threateningly on the steps of each coach. They were surrounded by a crowd, but were letting nobody on to the train.

I kept well clear of the crowd pestering the conductors. The sight of the pump continuing to water the locomotive was an assurance that the train would not move for some time. Then, on the other side of the station, a hissing stream of boiling water gushed down the wall from a brass tap gleaming against the whitewash.

'Hot water! They're giving out hot water!' came the cry from all quarters.

A few score of passengers emerged bareheaded from the coaches with cans and mugs and raced to the tap. I joined them in the queue, stuffed my cap into my pocket and, with no luggage save my mess-can full of hot water, I likewise returned to the train.

'Let me come past,' I shouted to the crowd surrounding the conductor. 'I've got some hot water for the sick man!'

'Step aside there!' yelled the conductor to the mob. 'Be human. You see the fellow's bringing some hot water for a sick man!'

I was on the train. I elbowed my way along the packed corridors, passing through a number of carriages and trying to lose myself as fast as possible in the throng of passengers. The train left an hour later. About time, too.

Heaven alone knows how, but I managed to find room on a bench in a crowded compartment. I sat down beside a middle-aged man with a prematurely ravaged face. He was going to join his wife and had with him his son, Sioma, a sturdy fourteen-year-old with flaxen hair and red spots. His Adam's apple jutted out over the open collar of his shirt, bobbing up and down whenever he said a word. Not that Sioma was talkative. He preferred to lie on the upper-shelf and sleep.

Russian carriages are all triple-storied. The first story consists of benches on which the passengers sit during the day-time, while the second and third stories are shelves intended for sleeping. The shelf immediately above my head was occupied by a bearded old man who never moved from this position throughout the entire journey. Sioma had appropriated the upper-shelf.

'Let this comrade sleep for a bit, now,' said the boy's father, nudging the lad and pointing at me.

With silent indifference, as though totally unconcerned, the boy lowered his long thin legs and obediently, if sulkily, climbed down from his perch.

'Get up then,' he said sleepily.

I needed no second bidding and was soon sound asleep. I was re-awakened by a sharp tug on my leg. I opened my eyes. It was completely dark.

'You've slept long enough,' said the voice of Sioma. 'Let me lie down for a spell.'

'All right. Thanks.'

I slipped off the shelf. The boy clambered up at once. Although it was night, the boy's father was not asleep but sitting hunched up in his corner. I sat down beside him and we struck up a conversation. There was not much to talk about. I did not conceal the fact that I was a released prisoner, but I did not tell him in so many words that I had gate-crashed the train. My questions, however, concerning the conductors and whether they carried out ticket inspections, automatically gave me away and it was easy for my new acquaintance to guess that I was travelling without a ticket.

The train thundered along the rails through the black night. Suddenly the door opened and two conductors, flashing their torches, entered the dark compartment.

'Tickets please.'

'Well, I'm glad your wife is better now,' said I, winding up a conversation which had never begun, and easing myself closer to my fellow traveller. 'By the time we get there, she may have recovered completely.'

My neighbour understood me perfectly. In the Soviet Union, where the citizen is obliged to deceive the authorities at every step, people, provided they do not denounce one another, very often understand each other perfectly without exchanging a word.

'Yes,' he said, pulling from his pocket an old-fashioned wallet with a metal clasp, 'it's a good thing we caught the train in any case.'

He took two tickets out of the wallet, Sioma's and his own, as though they were his and mine, and handed them to the conductor, who, by the light of a lamp hooked to one of his coat buttons, punched each of the grey, rectangular cards with his clippers, flashed his torch on the snoring man, who, fortunately, looked too old to be trying to cadge a lift and, not wishing to wake him up, left the compartment with his companion. Sioma, unobserved, slept on sweetly.

At dawn the train reached Orenburg—also known as Tchkalov, in honour of the Soviet flier.

FOURTEEN

The Handkerchief

Orenburg marked the second-last stage of my journey and was rather less than a hundred miles from Buzuluk. I went into the town to visit the mother of Lonka, my friend in the camp. My reason told me to get on a train going in the right direction with as little delay as possible, the sooner to get to my destination and the end of my uneasy wanderings. However, the thought that in this town there lived a mother who could not sleep at night through worrying about her son who had been spirited away into the Unknown, compelled me to keep my promise.

First of May Street in Orenburg is one of the main thoroughfares and I had no difficulty in finding the address. I climbed the three steps to the door of a wooden outhouse in the yard, and knocked.

I was answered by a buxom young woman.

'You are the sister of Lonka Shapochkin?' I asked.

'I am,' she admitted reluctantly, her face showing clearly that she was afraid.

She stared wide-eyed at the stranger in felt boots and galoshes, one of which was held on by a piece of string, the other by wire, his coat thrown open to reveal a prisoner's suit consisting of a padded jacket and torn trousers, a fur cap with ear-flaps on his head, ragged gloves on his hands and carrying an iron mess-can.

'I bring greetings from your brother.'

'Oh!' She sighed, a sad sigh almost of aversion.

She did not know what to say. If it were a beggar standing before her she could drive him away and slam the door. But she could not do that in this instance, although the spectral visitor from the world of white death from which no man returns, coming back here to haunt her with greetings from a brother on whom lay the curse of the law, was far more dangerous than any tramp or bandit. She did not want to drive the caller away, yet dared not ask him to come inside. The wisest thing for me to have done was to have said good-bye, turned round and hurried back to the railway station. I was on the point of doing so, when, behind the woman's broad shoulders there appeared a tiny, wrinkled old lady to whom poor Lonka bore a striking resemblance.

'I've brought greetings from your son. I'm his friend from the camp,' I introduced myself.

The mother, hearing news of the lost child she had given up for dead, forgot her own safety and defied the gossip of neighbours as well as the risk of arrest and interrogation.

'Lonka is alive?'

'Alive and well. He asked me to greet you.'

She still could not believe her good fortune. Maybe the stranger was lying in order to trick her into parting with food or money. She stood there silent and uncertain.

'Perhaps I've made a mistake,' I said. 'This is Number 7, First of May Street, where Leonidas Wasilievitch Shapochkin, the agricultural engineer, used to live?'

'Yes, he lived here,' she whispered, holding her yellow hand to her heart. 'Come in, please.'

The young woman dared not oppose this. She would have to be utterly shameless to drive away the friend of her unhappy brother. Hearing the baby crying in its cradle, somewhere inside the house, she at once beat a diplomatic retreat.

'Come inside, my son,' invited the mother. 'You can't stand out there in the cold.'

I went through the parlour where the young woman was hugging the weeping child and sat down by the stove in the bright kitchen, with its large window looking out on the snow-covered garden. The old woman set down a mug of tea in front of me and drew up her stool as close as possible so that we could talk in whispers.

'You say Lonka is well? How's he feeling?'

'He's well and feeling all right. He asked me to let you know.'

'And they've let you out?'

'Yes. I'm joining the army at Buzuluk.'

The old woman sighed. If only her son could do the same.

'How is he living there?' she asked. 'Do they get food and clothes? Has he a proper house with a bed and bedding?'

My recent recollections produced a mental picture of the barracks I had just left, the wooden bunks, the walls your hair might freeze to, the morning wash when you filled your mouth full of water which you spat on your hands before rubbing your face with them, the men sleeping in their clothes, unable to take them off more than once a month when they were taken to that cellar-like cave called a bath. The words 'bed and bedding' seemed so strange in that connection as to be comic. What did this unhappy mother whose eyes were red from weeping know about conditions in deportation camps?

A great gulp of hot tea and a mouthful of bread puffed out my cheeks and hid my embarrassment.

'Oh, yes, of course,' I consoled her. 'Your son is working as an engineer. His studies at the university weren't wasted. He's in a dry, warm office and not out in the forest or on the river.'

'Oh, thank God, thank God!'

'He's got proper clothes; everyone there gets proper clothes. Look, mother, a jacket and trousers like mine. True, they're not very beautiful but they keep the frost out and that's the main thing, isn't it?'

'True, my son, true. God take care of you. Tell me some more about Lonka.'

'What more can I tell you? He's well—not hungry. He's got everything he needs and more besides he's thinking about you, mother, and his only worry is your grief.'

'But he didn't give you a letter or any sign,' she said, wiping the tears from her bare eyelids.

'He gave a sign, but he was afraid to give me a letter. There might have been a search and then we'd both have been in trouble.'

She nodded her head understandingly.

'And he didn't ask about Tania? He loved his wife so much. Pity she's not here now. I'm sure she'd have been delighted.'

'Who knows? Perhaps she wouldn't.'

'You think so, son? Perhaps you're right. Girls are different nowadays. When Lonka was arrested, Tania went off somewhere and we never saw her again.'

'Maybe it was all for the best. You can never tell. It's true, nowadays girls are different,' I agreed, and said no more.

I was afraid it would be too painful a blow to the unfortunate mother to learn the whole truth about the beautiful Tania, her son's beloved.

From an adjoining room came a cry.

'Mamma! Come here, please!'

'Excuse me, my son,' the old lady apologized, 'I'll be back in a moment.'

She got up—so small it was hard to tell whether she was standing or sitting. With her yellow, wrinkled face and her ancient black dress, she looked like a Chinese figure. She disappeared through the half-open door, and exchanged a few whispered words with her daughter. It seemed they were in disagreement. Then she came in again with deeply flushed cheeks, having been rebuked and admonished.

'I'd invite you to dinner,' she confessed, looking down in her embarrassment, 'but my Katia is so strange. She says she wasn't expecting a caller and times are so hard, she has nothing ready.'

'Don't worry, mother.' I thanked her, getting up to go. 'I'm not hungry and as a soldier I'll get served quickly at the station restaurant: cheap and no waiting. I know I'm an uncomfortable guest. A visitor like me attracts too much attention.'

'Yes,' she admitted, still ashamed. 'Katia is afraid of everything.'

'The important thing is that Lonka is well, sends greetings to his mother and hopes to see you again soon. Well, I must go.' I picked up my cap. 'All good wishes to you, good-bye.'

'Just a moment!'

She took my iron mess-can and went to the porch. She brought it back full of tomatoes and small cucumbers.

'Take these with you.'

'God reward you.'

I left the warm kitchen, passed through the room where Katia was nursing the baby and walked down the wooden steps leading from the small balcony into the snowy yard. As the doors closed behind me, I could almost hear Katia's sigh of relief.

I walked quickly through the town towards the railway station, but as I was turning a corner I heard someone call after me.

'Hey, there, wait a moment, son!'

I looked round and halted. Lonka's mother was running behind me with small quick steps. She was very much out of breath.

'Take this, son, it will come in handy,' she said, pressing a green, three-rouble bank-note into my hand. 'You always need money on a journey. Sorry I haven't more. But times are bad,' she explained helplessly.

Three roubles was a ridiculously small sum although, no doubt, to the poor old woman it was a very considerable amount. Moreover, I had money enough. But to refuse this gift, a portion of the old lady's cherished savings, might have been to offend the mother of my friend.

'Thank you,' I said, pretending to be overjoyed.

I bowed and kissed her hand. She pressed my head to her bosom.

'God be with you. You brought me such good news. My Lonka is alive and well. What else can I give you except my blessing? Here take this.'

She gave me the handkerchief with which she dried her tears, just an ordinary square of coarse cloth.

'Thank you,' I repeated. 'And now I'll be going because people are beginning to look at us and I'm wearing a pretty suspicious suit! I'm safe enough, but it might do you some harm, mother.'

'God be with you.'

'And keep you well.'

I kissed her hand again and walked on quickly, but when I was already yards away I looked round and saw her still standing where I had left her. The Russian Mother of Sorrows whose son had been led away to the Golgotha of the Urals.

The old lady waved her hand in final farewell. I pulled the fur cap from my head and holding it high waved it in the air. Then I hurried on.

My iron can swung merrily on its metal handle, full of tomatoes and cucumbers, which together with my bread ration provided a sumptuous repast before nightfall.

The handkerchief, that little square of sacking, I keep as a treasured souvenir. I have it to this day, hidden away at the bottom of a suitcase.

Leaving Lonka's mother I began making my way back to the railway station. As I was walking through the town, I noticed a small kiosk standing at a cross-roads. It was surrounded by a crowd of people buying glasses of iced beer. It was the month of November and frosty, a thoroughly Russian November, yet people were buying glasses of iced beer, for the simple reason that it happened to be available.

They told me at the station that the train for Buzuluk was due to leave the following day. Obviously, the first thing to be done was to obtain a ticket, though this appeared an unlikely achievement. Thousands of people, whole families who had been living on the station for weeks, were laying constant siege to the ticket-office and always in vain. Moreover, to get permission to travel, one had to be in possession of a medical certificate declaring one to be clean and free from infections and insects. The railway doctor was responsible for issuing such certificates and he was nowhere to be seen. Orenburg looked like a complete dead end from which there was no obvious escape.

Before dawn came again I had to find somewhere to rest my head. On every Soviet station there is a propaganda centre—a large waiting-room hung with portraits of leaders and Ministers, in addition to propaganda posters. The tables are covered with red cloths and littered with periodicals and pamphlets. There are armchairs instead of benches, and their upholstery which is red accommodates bugs of a similar hue.

Priority of admittance was given to soldiers and those who were about to become soldiers. This was indeed a great privilege, for civilians were left to freeze outside on the platform. In addition, those who were entitled to enter also received a ration of black bread.

I went in along with the rest. Unfortunately all chairs and tables were already occupied by Soviet soldiers who were lounging asleep with their legs spread out in front of them in their grey puttees and muddy boots. They were snoring open-mouthed, their weary heads in thick cloth caps thrown loosely back or resting on their hands, while all around them an odour of sweat and dirty clothes pervaded the air. In the darkness, I stumbled over the bodies of several men lying asleep on the floor, until at last I found a space close by a pedestal on which stood an oleander bush. I lay down far enough away from this exotic piece of shrubbery to obviate the possibility of anyone who chanced to bump into the pedestal upsetting the pot on my head.

At dawn when I went into town to buy food I saw a curious scene. In front of a large store stood a great queue of children below school age, a line of boys and girls aged from four to seven, clad in shiny coats or muffled up in shawls and kerchiefs. Each child was clutching an empty bottle and some paper money. The line was moving quickly and as each youngster came out of the shop with his or her purchases, away they ran through the frostbound streets, their feet hammering on the frozen pavements. I saw that each carried in one hand the bottle, now filled with some dark liquid. It appeared that the town had just received an allocation of paraffin. At once queues of people had assembled, waiting, bottle in hand, to purchase the fuel as soon as the shops opened the next morning. The following day, however, the people had to go to work, hence parents had been relieved by their young children below school age.

I returned to the station, where I came across a group of young men talking Polish. I went up and joined them. They were going to some place beyond Buzuluk. To join the army? Their answers were evasive and I came to the conclusion that such was not the case. Had they got tickets? Certainly they had—a communal ticket for six persons. When I asked whether I could add my name to theirs, they answered politely that they already constituted the number of persons provided for on the ticket; in fact, they even exceeded it, for the wife of one of them had an infant with her. I begged pardon for my importunity but did not leave them. I clung to them the whole day, keeping the conversation going as best I could till at last the train came at dusk. My new-found acquaintances then called up their wives whom they helped carry suitcases, chests, crates, boxes and bags. The train was hardly at a standstill before the crowds hurled themselves upon it. The conductors, posted on the steps, however, managed to keep them at bay and only admitted those in possession of tickets. The latter were very numerous, and experienced considerable difficulty in forcing their way through the struggling mass of those who were attempting to travel free of charge.

I kept close to the group of six people. The father of the infant, a lanky, helpless individual wearing glasses, and weighed down with luggage, was clearing a way for his wife and child, with the communal ticket clenched between his teeth. There was every chance that he would be trampled underfoot in the crush and the precious document might be lost.

'May I?' I asked, taking the ticket from his lips. 'I'll lead the way.'

Grasping the ticket for six persons in my hand, I flourished it over my head and shouted to the conductor,

'Here's a communal ticket for seven persons! Let's come through, please!'

The conductor glanced at the form, but it was already too dark for him to read what was written on it. Besides which, he was having to contend with the onslaught of a human wave and hence was in no position to bother about lesser details.

'Get in!' he shouted, only too glad to see the crowd reduced, even if only to the extent of seven.

Using my elbows, head, chest, stomach and knees, I fought a path through the multitude on behalf of the six accredited passengers. The conductor counted seven persons as they entered the train in turn. I, myself, in the lead, made so much noise that I aroused not the slightest suspicion. In addition to which I was holding the ticket.

The carriage was empty—until it was swamped by a flood of people. My six recent acquaintances occupied two benches, while I took a single seat by the window in front of a small table on which I laid my mess-can. I then returned the ticket to its rightful owners. They thanked me as effusively as though I had been instrumental in saving their lives. When I got back to my seat, I found that my mess-can had disappeared. I sat down at my little table, intending not to vacate my seat again in case that, too, should be taken. Suddenly I caught sight of a burly individual forcing his way along the corridor outside, holding my mess-can over the heads of the crowd.

'Hey, you!' I shouted angrily. 'You've pinched my can! Give it back and don't try to tell me it's yours! It's got my initials scratched on the bottom!'

I caught up with the fellow, looking like a professional thug, with my unshaven face heavily bearded and moustached, and my ragged coat half open to reveal my prison-jacket. The hapless passenger returned my mess-can without a word of dissent, mumbled something about only borrowing it and melted quickly into the crowd. I put my recovered treasure down on the table. It was filled with soup, steaming fragrantly. Thus, when the train started in the direction of Buzuluk, city of my dreams, I was sitting at my table—I might have been in a restaurant-car—enjoying an excellent meal.

I spent the night in my seat, my head resting on my folded arms, which were in turn supported by my faithful mess-can. When I awoke it was early morning and the train, with a rhythmic sway, was racing smoothly through snow-covered fields impeccably white and bathed in sunlight. I rejoiced in the thought that another few hours would see me safely at the end of my journey. Just then, the doors at either end of the carriage slid open and conductors approached from both sides at once. It was a ticket inspection and a man hunt at the same time. I was no longer afraid of officials, for there was now only a few score of kilometres between me and my destination. When they came to where I was lounging in my seat, I addressed them nonchalantly.

'I'm on my way to Buzuluk—to join the army. You know there's a new army being formed there. I'm on a communal ticket—they've got it,' I said, pointing to the group seated on a neighbouring bench.

The conductor who had questioned me remained standing beside me as though keeping an eye on a highly suspicious individual, while the other turned aside to follow my indication. The young man in glasses produced his travel document, made out for six people. The conductor counted the group carefully. Unfortunately they numbered exactly six.

'They're all right,' he said to his colleague who was standing guard over me, 'but him,' pointing to me, 'they haven't any ticket for him.'

At that my guardian turned to me with the brief but explicit injunction.

'Come with me !'

He took me by the sleeve and led me slowly to the door. We stopped in the corridor where the official, still holding me by the arm, opened the door with his other hand and gave me a push. Luckily the train had slowed down to take a bend. I thought the conductor was only trying to frighten me, but, when I looked into his eyes, it was obvious that he was far from regarding the matter as a joke. He was a half-savage Tartar, with a yellow, pock-marked face, prominent cheek-bones, a short, square nose and slant eyes, glowing red with anger like the eyes of a wolf. His long black coat and black cap with a locomotive superimposed on a five-pointed star made him appear even more sinister. If he had had a scythe in his hand, he would have looked like the personification of Death enraged by the resistance of a victim attempting to slip through the fingers of Destiny.

I stood out on the lower step, hoping he would desist

once having got me out of the corridor. But the conductor began to thrust at me with his knee, at the same time beating my hands as I clung desperately to the rail. The train was crawling round the bend, but once it was on the straight and gathered speed again my life would be in danger. So I jumped off.

The conductor crumpled up my documents in his fist, flung them after me into the snow, then slammed the door shut and disappeared inside. I picked up the papers and took a quick look round. The green train was very long and, having been flung out of the tenth coach, I was able to climb on again at the fifteenth. The train had rounded the bend and was now travelling fast. Provided the conductor had already inspected all tickets in the carriage I was hiding in, he would not be coming back. The train was tearing along, but now, as I watched the telegraph poles streaming past in our wake, every one of them marking a stage nearer to my goal, I felt safe. Sneaking along the corridors, in search of some place out of harm's way, I came across a small side door which led into a round cell, about the size of a toilet. It was where they usually put the stove by which the whole coach was heated.

I locked myself in, feeling certain that nobody would find me. I breathed on the frozen window-pane, and wiped off the layers of frost so that I should be able to see Buzuluk station when we came to it. It could not have been very far off then. Every time we stopped, whether at a station or to let another train pass us, I was stricken with terror. Suddenly the door moved a fraction and an eye gleamed in the narrow slit, low down, at about the height of the keyhole which was blocked up. I held my breath, keeping the door shut with my knee. The eye vanished. Presuming that it could have seen nothing suspicious, I heaved a deep sigh of relief. Soon, however, the door was again pushed gently and the eye reappeared. This time the eye took a good look inside to see whether anyone was there or whether the door had just jammed. I leaned my back against the door, determined to barricade it with my own body. The attacker persisted, but timidly, as though more afraid of me than I of him. I looked through the crack and saw a small creature in red. I opened the door, surprised. A little girl in a torn red dress leapt inside like a dog. Like myself, she was travelling without a ticket and hiding from the railway officials who would hand her over to the militia who, in turn, would have her locked up in an orphanage where homeless children were subjected to prison discipline. The girl was unhealthily thin and fearfully dirty, as though she had never washed in her life. Her ears, nose and shoulders—which showed through rents in her dress—were clotted with blood and her hair, rich and tousled, was matted like a cowl. She told me her mother had died of typhus on the journey and that she was on her way to an aunt living at Tiflis. She was no more than ten years of age but there wasn't much she didn't know about life. When I shared a slice of bread with her, she pressed against me, giving me to understand in no uncertain manner that she was prepared to demonstrate her gratitude in an adult fashion. When I pushed her away, she laughed unpleasantly.

It was dusk when the train drew into the station. The yellow glow of the lamp at the entrance lit the inscription on the board—'Buzuluk.' I left the unfortunate orphan in the stove cupboard and got out of the train. I had reached my journey's end—at last. Soon, I would be a soldier, bathed, fed, in uniform and amongst my own people—really free. I stood on the platform looking about me, for I felt certain there would be other volunteers alighting from the train and we would be greeted by a duty officer with instructions and a car to take us to the barracks.

But there was not a soul. No one but Russian civilians got out, as at any other railway station. Somebody was wheeling a barrow, others were hurriedly getting aboard, while a few Soviet soldiers, shouting to each other, were carrying armfuls of rifles and boxes of ammunition. Then the train pulled out and I was alone on the empty platform.

Although it was a November evening and in the region of the Urals, it was warm, almost warm enough for a thaw. Light, wet snow was falling, its dampness as penetrating as Scotch mist, and there were black puddles of slush on the ground. I passed by the station building, behind which I was overjoyed to catch sight of a Polish officer with a red and white band on his sleeve.

'I say!' I called happily as I ran towards him.

The officer looked round. He was a young second-lieutenant, not more than twenty-five years of age, tall, slim and childlike, full of pride in his own position and admiration for himself; to him were entrusted the responsible duties of a movements officer.

'I'm for the army,' I said, as I got near him.

'Then what do you want here?' he shouted fiercely. He spoke in a sharp, high-pitched voice. 'Can't you read?' He pointed with his cane to a placard on the station fence. 'Can't you see what it says? Anyone going to join the army via Buzuluk has to go to Tashkent.'

My hands dropped to my sides in despair. It would take another six weeks or more to get to Tashkent. I would never make it without food or a ticket.

'Yes, I see that,' I agreed, 'only that's got nothing to do with me; I'm not joining *via* Buzuluk, I'm coming *to* Buzuluk, in accordance with instructions. Is there a headquarters in this town?'

'Yes, but they wouldn't let you in.'

'That's my business. Please give me the address and I'll find my own way there.'

'They'll kick you out on your neck!'

'How dare you speak to me like that, you young puppy!' I roared, stamping my foot in its one galosh tied with wire. 'You don't know who you're talking to, you snivelling brat! I am a colonel!' I lied, looking the officer straight in his childish eyes.

The lieutenant froze in terror. He saluted and begged my pardon. And yet again he begged pardon and once more saluted, explaining that as he had not previously met Colonel Wittlin, he had not realized with whom he had the pleasure of speaking. After which he disappeared like a streak of lightning into the darkness which, a moment later, resounded with the noise of a lorry being driven away at breakneck speed.

I went back to the station and into the restaurant, where I saw a soldier on duty sitting on a bench by the wall. He had a Polish Eagle in metal pinned to a Russian sheep-skin cap. I went up to him and, continuing to play the role of a high-ranking officer, asked whereabouts the garrison was situated. The soldier told me, but advised spending the night in the station and going along the next day. It was sound advice. Fortified by a mug of hot tea, I decided to have a shave and a haircut at the railway barber's, whose saloon was on the other side of the wall.

There were three girls employed in the establishment. Several Soviet officers, airmen and soldiers were waiting their turn and I joined the queue till at last I found myself seated in the chair in front of the mirror. The hairdresser, a young, pretty girl with large, thoughtful eyes, threw a white apron over my shoulders and began preparing the lather. Then she sliced through the jungle of beard and moustache, which had covered my face for many weeks, and trimmed my matted hair, asking whether I wanted it washed. I consented to vacating the comfortable armchair and approached the old-fashioned, wooden washstand with its huge porcelain bowl, like a round pond, dotted with blue flowers.

The girl filled it full of water from a metal jug. I lowered my head and closed my eyes to keep out the soap while she lathered my hair. Then I felt her working the suds with her hands, swishing the water over my head, washing away the soap. I must have been very dirty and unkempt for suddenly the girl, with the gentle care of a sister, began to wash my neck, face and ears, as though I were a little boy.

I felt strangely sad. There was a lump in my throat and all my determination, swagger, aggressiveness, resistance, humour and impertinence—strained by those weary months of prison, deportation to Siberia and adventurous travel—seemed to have vanished, put to flight by the touch of that warm water and the tender fingers of the girl.

I thought I was going to burst into tears—like a little boy.

FIFTEEN

In Evening Dress

Frost glittered through the grey mist of a winter's day, spangling eyebrows and lashes with silver—even the fur band round my cap to which was now pinned the Polish Eagle. The slippery snow crunched under the rubber soles of my army boots. You had to plant your feet firmly on the treacherous rink that was Buzuluk or it was only too easy to take a toss and become a laughing-stock.

I was returning from the market to the barracks, which were some distance away, clad in a pair of black padded trousers tucked into knee boots, and a warm jacket, over which I wore an army greatcoat with silver badges of rank on the epaulettes. In one frozen hand I clutched my mess-can full of milk. The can swung blithely from its handle, but I could hurry along without fear of spilling the milk for it had frozen into a solid block of white marble.

A large group of soldiers in uniforms similar to my own were just emerging from a bookshop close by. Their arms were full of newly purchased copies of *The History of the Bolshevik Party*, *The Problems of Leninism* and the *History of the Revolution*.

'Anyway,' said a Soviet major walking behind me to his companion in a leather coat, 'the training those Poles got in our prisons and labour camps has done them some good. It's nice to see them taking such an interest in our political literature.'

Had he followed those purchasers of Soviet political literature as far as their quarters, he would probably have changed his opinion. The books, each of which was several hundred pages in length, being propaganda, were on sale at a ridiculously low price, and, being newsprint, they were eminently suitable for rolling cigarettes. There was no difficulty about getting tobacco. A glassful of home-grown shag cost very little, but cigarette papers, or indeed newspapers, were quite unobtainable. So the book-shops came to the rescue. Tobacco could be bought, as could milk, on the 'square,' a spacious suburban heath where, on a hillock in the middle, stood a massive church with its onion-like domes thrusting skywards. The church had been closed and converted into shops and stores, the crosses having been long since removed from the spires. The cornice alone still showed traces of its gilded frescoes.

The fields were covered with snow and the peasants brought their produce to market on sledges hauled by camels. Those camels, now dragging sledges across the snow against the background of the Urals, instead of loping in caravan across the scorching desert, looked a trifle odd.

I passed by the bookshop and turned down a side street where stretched a long queue of young women, patiently freezing in their ragged coats and their white or coloured berets, which left their crimson ears exposed. These local belles were waiting outside a hairdresser's displaying the sign 'Manicure.' There was to be a dance that evening.

The thought of a warm stove in front of which I could toast my hands and thaw out the milk lent me wings.

Then, not far from the town theatre, I caught sight of a poster advertising a concert by the Moscow Symphony Orchestra. Russian orchestras are, perhaps, the best in the world, so I was unwilling to deny myself this treat. I bought a ticket at the narrow entrance to the box-office and returned to camp in good spirits. Later that evening I found myself sitting in the theatre.

The auditorium was filled to capacity. High-ranking officers of the Soviet Air Force in dark blue uniforms, wearing all their decorations and Sam Browne belts, sat with their wives who were dolefully clad in skirts of coarse material with kerchiefs wrapped round their shoulders. Many of them clung to their husbands' arms with both hands. In the boxes and the orchestra stalls sat a few men in evening dress and women in sadly outmoded gowns. Their dresses were made of some unusually heavy material, as though they had once been curtains. With their golden fringes, they reminded me of the costumes worn by an amateur opera company. The men in their short, shiny dinner-jackets looked strangely solid. I only realized the cause of their astonishing bulkiness somewhat later in the cloak-room. There I noticed that the gentlemen in evening dress were wearing woollen sweaters under their starched fronts and collars. It was quite understandable, too. Without them they would certainly have frozen to death in the streets, if not in the concert hall itself.

The concert was excellent. The audience knew good music as only Russians do, and demonstrated its appreciation. At the conclusion of each item there was a long moment of silence followed by a veritable storm of spontaneous applause. During the programme they played Rimsky-Korsakov's 'Scheherazade' and Tschaikovski's 'Violin Concerto.' Before the latter commenced, when there was still at least an hour to go before the end of the concert, I noticed that the audience was leaving the hall. Beginning in ones and twos, they were soon trooping out in groups.

The auditorium, so recently packed full, began to gleam bald in patches, whole rows of seats having emptied completely. I could not understand why. The performance could not have been of a higher standard, the evening was still not yet far advanced and no one needed to hurry home, since, the town being small, no one had far to go.

Together with a small group of musical enthusiasts, I sat it out to the end and only on leaving the hall did I gather the reason for the earlier mass desertion. Men in dinner-suits, ladies in evening dress, youngsters in woollen sweaters under jackets too small for them by far, officers and soldiers—all were queueing in front of the buffet in the smoking-room—the only place in the whole town where white rolls and tangerines were on sale. Each customer was allowed one roll and one tangerine—thanks to which the concert was concluded in an empty hall.

That evening at the concert encouraged me to make several visits to the theatre. Not long afterwards, Buzuluk was visited by a company of theatrical performers from Kiev, who were to present a work entitled, *A Young Man from Our Town,* after which there was to be a dance.

I went to the first night. It was a propaganda play. In one scene the hero—the young man from our town— an officer on leave, had decided to learn French, and on being asked by his teacher the reason why he was interested in that foreign language, he replied with an eloquent smile,

'Who knows, maybe it won't be so very long before French stops being a foreign language?'

The audience applauded, there were numerous curtains and when the show was over the hall emptied quickly, for it had to be cleared of chairs in preparation for the dance. I put my overcoat in the cloak-room and left the building. In the doorway, on the stairs and in the surrounding park with its dwarf trees, I passed clinging couples wandering along on their way to the dance.

Alone and deep in thought, I strolled about in the dark blue light of evening. Beads of frost, gleaming like fire-flies, were falling slowly upon the snowy mantle of the earth—silver crumbs let fall from the pale stars above. It occurred to me that if one could put on some sort of a satirical show at that theatre it would be a first-class leg-pull. The question was, how to set about it? The idea did not seem quite practicable, but, all the same, I was so taken with it that I could not get it out of my mind.

The next morning crowds gathered around the notice-board in the mess. During the night someone had stuck up a copy of our wall news-sheet, illustrated with colourful sketches. The funny caricatures were so realistically executed that they reminded one of creatures in a silly symphony. I thought of the political puppet-shows which I once used to write with my friends. A puppet-show is the easiest of all to produce, and is the perfect vehicle for political satire. The flowers of genius often bloom in the most prosaic circumstances: Watt conceived of the locomotive while waiting for a kettle to boil, and I, engaged in eating peas from a tin bowl, made up my mind to write a puppet-show.

I had no difficulty getting hold of the artist who illustrated the wall news-sheet and together we decided that the puppet-show must see the light of day. The artist set to work with a will, enlisting a few women to make the necessary costumes, while I, by day during drill or by night while the others were asleep, busied myself writing songs.

In no time, the offices of the Cultural Section were trans-
formed into a tailor's shop, a studio, a property-store, a
carpenter's workshop, an electrical department and a dolls'
hospital. Unfortunately it was so cold that, despite the
sacrifice of a few chairs to feed the stove, we were obliged
to work in caps, gloves and greatcoats. We were also badly
off for material. Paper and paints were obtainable, but
we had to contend with a tragic lack of plaster and plasti-
cine, without which it was impossible to produce the masks.
As a last resort, the artist decided to model the dolls out
of bread. So the dolls' heads were not made of plaster but
from precious loaves of brown bread, swathed in thin
strips of paper—like an Egyptian mummy. Once dry, this
expedient proved more indestructible than cement.

Those dolls survived a great deal until at last the
mice were attracted by the bread and gnawed the nose off
the President of the United States, and the tail off the
British Lion.

An even more serious problem was the lack of wood,
without which we could not build the stage itself. As the
artist and I were returning from the workshop to the barracks, thinking how we could overcome this particular
difficulty, he drew my attention to the heavy wooden gates
of the Garrison Headquarters. The gate was generally
shut, being only intended to let through vehicles. A sentry
sitting by the pedestrians' entrance was responsible for
opening it. In a flash we hit on a plan of action. I walked
into the sentry-box and showed the sentry not only my
pass, but also a few illustrated weeklies. The painter,
meanwhile, detached two massive planks from the main
gate and made off with them. In the course of a few weeks,
the main entrance gate of the Polish Army Garrison in
the Soviet Union was completely stripped and consequently
open night and day. For lack of some place else to put it,

the grotesque structure of our puppet-theatre was accommodated in the court-martial room and the judges pronounced sentence within its confines. But at last came the day of the première. The revolving stage of the theatre which had so recently presented *A Young Man from Our Town,* now displayed a thatched roof surmounted by a gigantic stork. There were two other storks on the blue curtain, so constructed that, when the curtain swept back, they leapt up and flew away. The auditorium was packed. In the front row sat General Anders with several Soviet dignitaries, amongst whom was Colonel Volkovyski, the Soviet Liaison Officer from Moscow. Backstage, the performers were lined up and ready to start singing as soon as the puppets appeared.

Gong—lights—and away flew the storks. In turn puppets, representing the British Lion, the French Cockerel, the Earth's Drunken Sphere, Oil the Omnipotent and the Yellow Peril, trod the boards. The first two acts went smoothly. Later on, when Hitler was shown dancing with Mussolini, Colonel Volkovyski stamped his feet with delight. Then, suddenly, there appeared on the stage a prisoner from a Russian camp, in rags and tatters, his cap in shreds and the inevitable mess-can in his hand. He bowed to the Soviet officers and danced as he sang a song in which he thanked them for his pleasant stay in Siberia. In reply, the envoy of the Kremlin, Colonel Volkovyski, rose ostentatiously from his chair, stamped his heels loudly and, holding himself as straight as a ramrod, left the theatre.

From where I was standing in the wings, I saw Major Kozhushko, the Soviet Security Officer, begin scrutinizing the programme. Then he underlined my name with a pencil. The rest of the show was performed without further incident and the curtain had no sooner fallen than a host of people crowded on to the stage with congratulations. Outside the theatre, I heard some Russian children singing one of the satirical numbers from the show.

The next day I was called to the adjutant's office. It seemed there was trouble brewing. The Soviet Security Police were not only interested in the text of the puppet-show, of which they were demanding a copy for submission to the censor, but also in the author. The copy of the manuscript was delivered on the following day, I having spent the whole night cutting out pages, revising songs and sticking in fresh verses. Happily, this deception went undiscovered. The whole affair was smoothed over and the show allowed to continue.

SIXTEEN

Three Women

Every morning as she went by train from Krasnovodzk to Ufra on her way to work, Tamara used to pass the camp to which I had been transferred from Buzuluk. The camp, a good distance outside the town, stretched along the stony shore of the Caspian Sea at the foot of some limestone hills far from civilization and any other human habitation. The climate was bad: oppressive heat by day, and by night sudden fierce winds that swept our tents away and bombarded us with a hail of pebbles, sand storms and clouds of dust that settled everywhere.

As far as the eye could reach there was not a tree to be seen, not a blade of green grass. It was a sad, empty area, and the bad food—bad because cooked in sea water—and constant fear of being bitten by a scorpion or tarantula did nothing to improve our spirits.

I had known Tamara a long time and we had become very close friends. One day, when I called to take her out for our usual stroll, the girl laughingly recounted an amusing adventure which had befallen her. As she was dressing in the morning to go to the office, one of her shoes seemed to have disappeared somewhere under the bed, and she had hunted for it in vain. Afraid of missing the train, she had gone off to the office in her bare feet.

'I'd have looked even more ridiculous in one shoe, don't you think?' she remarked.

'Yes,' I agreed. 'But the trains run every fifteen minutes, so if you were a quarter of an hour late . . .'

'I'd get six months in jail,' she explained, with the same carefree smile. 'Don't you know that the first time we're late without good reason they give us six months, the second time it's a year and the third time—you go up north?'

'Oh, I didn't know,' I confessed, ashamed at not having been aware of something so reasonable and obvious. 'Anyway, even though you don't go behind bars if you're late for the pictures, you'd better get a move on, or we won't see "Peter the Great" to-day.'

Tamara liked reading till late at night so she did not find it easy to get up at dawn and go to work.

A similar incident to that of the shoe—but less amusing—occurred shortly afterwards.

As I was waiting for her at the entrance to the park, in which stood a dance-hall, she appeared, smiling as usual, in a green beret, from under which escaped unruly wisps of flax-blonde hair. But her right hand was bandaged and supported by a sling made from a white table-napkin.

'What's happened to you?' I asked.

'Just imagine,' she said cheerfully, as though announcing a piece of particularly good news. 'The train came in a few minutes late this morning, and, as a result, if I'd gone to the office the usual way, I'd have been late. You know what that means.'

'I know.'

'So I crawled under the carriages to get across the line, but the train started and my hand got caught.'

'Broken?'

'No, just a sprain. I'm absolutely delighted. Everything's turned out splendidly,' she went on, beaming with pleasure. 'I got there on time and the doctor gave me three days off. Wonderful stroke of luck, isn't it?'

'Yes, it certainly is. Only the dancing's off for to-day, so let's go for a walk.'

As we strolled through the streets, we passed by the so-called 'Universal Stores' where you could buy a highly imaginative scarf, a guitar, gramophone records, embroidered caps, ties or a cheap brooch with artificial gems.

'Let's go in,' I said. 'I'd like to buy you a little souvenir.'

'Why?' she asked, opening her eyes wide in amazement. 'You're not leaving us already?'

'No. I'd tell you if I were. Only I'd like to get you some small thing as a present. Something you'd like.'

'If I didn't like going out with you, I wouldn't, so why bother about presents? Just leave me your photograph when you're going away, that'll be souvenir enough.'

'You're awfully sweet, Tamara, but, you know, I can't even speak Russian properly.'

'I'm a Ukrainian, so I don't know Russian properly, myself,' she answered with a shrug.

Luba was walking along in front of us. She was Tamara's neighbour and had been at school with her— ruddy-complexioned, strong as a man and the driver of a heavy truck. She'd already heard about Tamara's accident and evinced no surprise.

'I'm dead tired,' she said, greeting us. 'I had an extra job to do to-day.'

'How's that?' I asked.

'We had to go up the mountains and bring down the engine of a wrecked car.'

'Accident?'

'Yes.'

'Occupants all killed?'

'Don't know,' she answered, with an indifferent toss of her head. 'Probably.'

'It's not that important?'

'Not really,' she said, sinking her white teeth into the apple she held in her hand. 'That car piled up twenty years ago and it's been lying on the road since 1920. Nobody felt like clearing up the mess until now. Have an apple—they're very sweet.' She held out the bag.

'Thanks.'

I took one. It was very sweet.

*

If you catch the six o'clock train from Ufra to Krasnovodzk, you are sure to see Sonia in one of the carriages. She always went to work about that time. She was a slim brunette, with long, gleaming hair, black eyes and a dark complexion. She was graceful and good-looking. Ten years earlier she must have been very beautiful. Then, at thirty, she no longer looked young—hard work in the port scarcely assists the preservation of beauty. Ever since that day, two years before, when her husband was called up, she had been all alone except for her sturdy, nine-year-old son, Mischa. The day her husband left, she swore to herself, not to him, that she would faithfully await his return. Lipstick and powder she threw out of the window and unstrung her guitar, for she wanted neither music nor song.

She stayed in mourning a long time—till she met a Polish soldier to whom she gave her whole heart, so long starved of affection. When he first came to see her, paying a sort of official tongue-tied visit, not knowing quite where to sit, how to behave or what to talk about, young Mischa, a bare-footed urchin in short pants and a green shirt but-

toned round the neck, took a fierce and instant dislike to
the newcomer. He squatted in the corner on a low stool
and, with his lips grimly pursed in a sullen line, stared
fixedly at the intruder. The grown-ups took little notice
of the child's presence, though they did nothing of which
they need be ashamed. They sat at the table and drank
glassfuls of the cheap red wine which the soldier had
brought in his water-bottle. They did not even speak,
but just sat and looked at one another, smiling at their
own thoughts which they both knew so well.

They imagined the child was paying no attention, but
Mischa understood everything. He saw quite plainly how,
when they just seemed to be looking at each other calmly
enough across their glasses, they were actually squeezing
each other's hands under the table. He never took his eyes
off them, like an intrepid puppy ready to spring at a
stranger's throat. Glowering, sullen and furious at his own
helplessness, he was painfully conscious that his father was
being done an undeserved wrong, and, in defence of his
rights, he slid forward on his stool a couple of times, significantly—so that the floor creaked.

The soldier, from the height of his chair, looked
down at the little chap. He let go the woman's hand.

'Mischa, d'you like the pictures?' he asked.

The boy was silent.

'Well, answer!' urged his mother.

Mischa remained stubbornly silent.

The soldier took his army pay-book out of his pocket,
extracted a green three-rouble note and went up to the
little boy.

'Here, take this and go to the pictures. Have a good
time!' he said.

It was too large a sum to refuse. Mischa took the
money, but stayed where he was.

'Say "Thank you," get dressed, comb your hair and go along with you,' said the mother in a strained voice, attempting to hurry him up. 'Tell us all about it when you get back.'

The soldier thanked the woman for her support with an eloquent wink. Sonia's neck and cheeks flushed red and there was a pounding in her temples.

'Well, why don't you get along?' she shouted at the child. 'You haven't had a whipping lately. If you don't go at once, I'll get the strap, bolt the door, tan your hide and take the money away from you!'

The final threat was the most severe. Mischa got up slowly, then crawled under the bed on all fours to find a pair of shoes. Without hurrying he slid his bare feet inside them, then thrust his arms through the sleeves of an overlong jacket. From the bucket by the stove he scooped up a handful of water and poured it over his head which he began to tidy with a comb full of grit, standing in front of the broken mirror on the window-sill.

'Hurry up, or you'll be late,' said the woman impatiently.

'I won't be late,' mumbled the child, taking his time.

At last he was gone. He walked slowly at first, then, as country boys do, he started to run. He was running off to enjoy himself, though his heart was heavy as a stone. The injustice being done to his father in his absence was more than he could bear. That affection for his father whom he missed so much—a strange compound of male solidarity and an instinctive sense of honesty—choked him so that it hurt. He did not go to the pictures. He did not feel like it, and besides he was not keen to change the green note. He ran down the alley which led to the sea. He would sooner bathe, go for a swim. Then he would play ball with his friends, or maybe go for a sail, and he

would be home sooner than if he went to the pictures. He
felt subconsciously that by so doing, he would interrupt
his mother and perhaps help his father a little. He was sure
his mother was kissing the foreigner at that very moment.
Perhaps she was even sitting on his knee, with her arm
round his neck, looking into his eyes—the way he had
seen Wania's elder sister, Grischa, do with Alosha, the
tractor driver.

Nor was he mistaken. He was no sooner out of the
room than Sonia jumped up and bolted the door. The
soldier, too, stood up and before she had even finished
with the door, he took her in his arms and began to kiss
her. Sonia, thirsting for affection, drank in his powerful
kisses, spiced with the masculine scent of tobacco. Then
she slipped from his embrace and went over to the wide
bed, lifted the pillows in their white cases and laid them
carefully on a bench. With equal care she folded the embroidered bed-spread, her hands trembling with nervous-
ness. At last, she began to unfasten her blouse.

From that day onwards the soldier came whenever
he was off duty, and often he stole out of camp at night
with a ration of bread, a flask of wine or a tin of preserves.
He could never get on the right side of Mischa, however,
despite the fact that he gave him sugared dates, a penknife
and money for the pictures. The boy was a dumb, helpless
witness of the infamy inflicted upon his father. He understood in his childish way and, with all his soul, he detested
this man who had come to rob the house of its homely
quiet. He grew indifferent towards his mother, though she
was kinder to him now than before, did not punish his
every little transgression and looked after him better.

Sonia, enchanted with the magic of love, grew more
beautiful, gay, swift, eager and full of song. The bloom
of peaches lit her dark Cossack skin. Her dull eyes glowed

afresh with the joy of living and her full lips, ripe with the excess of her happiness, readily parted in a smile, to reveal her strong white teeth. Her bowed shoulders straightened. She was like a pine tree from whose branches under the sun's rays in spring a heavy burden of snow had swiftly melted. Work was a joy to her. She found she could get on more quickly and often helped her companions. She went to work better dressed and her appearance was far more becoming. Her workmates might have wondered at the sudden transformation had they not known the reason for it. Sonia bloomed and became so youthful that, even in the eyes of Mischa, she ceased to be a mother, and was more like some girl he knew, so that several times, quite unconsciously, he called her 'Sonia' instead of 'Mummy,' as he had always done hitherto.

You can get used to anything—even to a foreign soldier, who sits in the room like father, without his tunic, just in trousers, shirt and boots, rolls cigarettes, spits on the floor, pats the woman on the back as though she were his wife, kisses her on the mouth and lays her on the bed. But it cannot last for ever. Father will come back in the end, chase the scoundrel away, give Sonia the sound thrashing she deserves, and restore order. In the houses of his friends whose fathers had gone to the war, the mothers were doing exactly the same thing, with only one difference: Russian soldiers were paying them visits, and not foreigners.

Sonia adored her young lover and, as she waited for him in a strange frenzy of impatience, she was ready to tip the sky for anyone. She would come straight home from work, sweep the room, put a clean white cloth on the table, singing all the time. Mischa followed her every movement with his clear blue eyes, but, although she looked prettier and she was kinder and more cheerful, he did not like her. It was as though she were some strange, different woman.

One afternoon as she was preparing fish for supper, there came a knock at the door, a short, quiet, dry sound. Mischa went to the door and opened it. Outside stood a small man, young but with a faded, wrinkled face and wearing a black coat and a checked cap. His hands were buried deep in the pockets of his greatcoat. He glanced round the room, then, looking down indifferently at the ground, he said, as it were, to his own feet:

'Sonia Amoskinov?'

'Yes,' she answered, petrified, with the plate in front of her.

'Will you come along to the office with me, please. There's a telegram from your husband. You've got to sign for it.'

Sonia knew there could not be any telegram. Why should her husband send a telegram when he never even scribbled a line to her? Nevertheless, she asked:

'He's alive?'

'He's alive.' The stranger echoed her words casually.

'Wounded?'

'No, not wounded. You'll hear all about it in the office. Let's go.'

There was no question about it. She was not being summoned there on her husband's account. She threw a kerchief over her head, tied it under her chin and went out with the official. Mischa was delighted. Father would surely be back soon and then everything would be like it was before. What if he did on occasion take off his belt and measure its length on Mischa's back? After all, that was a father's right. Same all over the world.

A quarter of an hour later his mother's lover appeared. He was surprised to hear that she had gone to the post-office, but he made himself comfortable in a chair, got out his tobacco, lit up and whistling through his teeth, waited patiently for her to return.

Sonia did not get back for a few hours. She looked sad and gloomy, but, at sight of her lover, her face brightened and she set about preparing the evening meal.

'Been to the post-office?' he asked.

'Yes,' she answered, slowly and uncertainly.

Mischa in his corner pricked up his ears and held his breath. He was waiting to hear whether his father would be back in one week or two, and when the intruder would have to clear out for good and all. But he was disappointed. His mother, bending over the stove, just shrugged and said lightly, over her shoulder,

'Nothing important. They get you all upset for nothing these days.'

Soon all three of them sat down to the meal. They had bread, fish, crabs, prepared by Sonia, tinned meat from the Argentine and Australian butter which the soldier had brought. They drank red wine with the food and even Mischa got half a glass. They finished up with hot tea and sugar cut into large, irregular cubes.

Sonia cheered up completely thanks to the wine and every now and then as she got up to fetch the tea-pot, salt or a plate, she kissed her lover's cheek or the nape of his neck. After the meal, they cleared away and washed up together. Mischa undressed, climbed into the cot which had long been too small for him, and pulled the torn cotton quilt up over his head. Sonia took down the paraffin lamp from its nail in the wall, turned down the wick and blew out the light. Mischa turned over on his stomach, buried his freckled nose in the pillow, curled up and soon fell asleep. The soldier and the woman undressed in the dark. That night, Sonia smothered her lover with wild and

feverish caresses, as on the day of their first kiss. Then
she told him the truth about where she had been earlier in
the evening. She had been taken to the militia post where
she had been told that, if she must have a boy friend, he
must not be a foreigner but a Soviet soldier. But she did
not care two hoots about orders and she was not afraid of
anything. They could not do anything to her and, in any
case, she was ready to make any sacrifices, even to die,
for her lover.

The next day the soldier, who was my batman, told
me the story as he was tidying up the tent. He asked
whether he was likely to suffer any unpleasant conse-
quences as a result of his actions.

'Not you,' I reassured him. 'But Sonia most certainly
will. They will come along one night, take her away and
she will be sent to Siberia, while the child will be put in
an orphanage. You will lose your woman, the son will
lose a mother and she will lose her freedom.'

The soldier was worried about his mistress, promised
to stop calling on her and kept his word. Thenceforth,
young Mischa could run down to bathe on the sea shore
as happily as ever and could enjoy himself with his friends,
sailing wooden boats. When his father came back, he
would not have to chase Sonia away, for she had once
more become a good mother and a faithful wife.

It was evening. Dark and cold. Out of the far blackness came the smell of the sea blending with the odour of
oil and paraffin and the tang of seaweed. I was working
in the tent, preparing the bulletin which contained the
latest news received over my field radio set. The tent,
which was dug in to protect it from the nocturnal squalls
of Turkestan and fastened by a stake attached to the canvas door flap, rumbled and cracked under the onslaught
of the wind, like the taut skin of a tom-tom. My batman

was struggling with a tin of corned beef, which he was trying to force open by means of a service jack-knife with a massive black handle. Suddenly, we heard the thud of bare feet on the wooden steps leading down to the tent and a small creature slid under the flap.

By the yellowy-red gleam of the carbide lamp, I made out a tousled flaxen mop of hair wreathing the sooty face of a small boy in long shorts, very ragged, and made from a pair of man's trousers cut down.

'Mischa!' cried the batman.

'Oh, I am glad I've found you!' exclaimed the boy, putting his arms round him and pressing his head trustingly against the soldier's belt. 'I was afraid I would not see you.'

'What about your mother?' asked the soldier, giving me an uneasy look, as though I knew what had happened to her. 'Is she at home?'

'Yes, at home,' nodded the boy, 'only . . .'

'Only what?'

The boy stammered, let his eyes rove round the tent, fixed his gaze on me, then looked up at the soldier's face once more.

'Since you stopped coming to see us,' he began, 'Sonia is very sad. She can't eat or sleep. She's cried so much that her eyes are all swollen. I hear her sighing all night and she's got so thin. She's wasted away. I'm afraid she's going to die. I didn't like you before, because I saw how you were stealing mother away from father. I understand everything, just the same as if I was grown-up. But, you see, Daddy's a long way away at the war. He may get killed, then he'll never come back to us and all the time mother's just crying. I tried to cheer her up, but I'm only a small boy. What can I do? I'm so sorry for her, I can't bear it any longer. Please don't leave her. Come and see us to-morrow, like you used to, when it's evening and she gets home from work, though she doesn't rush home any more now like she did when she was going to see you. Please come, she's so sad!' He looked beseechingly into the soldier's wide eyes. 'I promise not to worry you any more. I won't even ask you for money to go to the pictures. Just come,' he repeated, 'but don't say I was here and asked you to. Make it look as if you thought of it yourself. Say you'll come. Do, please!'

He seized the soldier's hand which was still clenched around the handle of the jack-knife, kissed it and ran out of the tent. He vanished so suddenly he might never have been there at all. But for a little while we could just hear the drumming of his bare heels on the sand as he galloped away in the distance.

SEVENTEEN

Hospital

As I was tidying the papers in my tent one day, I came across a sheet torn from an exercise-book, on which were written a few sentences in Russian. It was a letter in a neat, even hand from some sick Russian soldier by the name of Tadeusz. I was puzzled about the identity of my Russian namesake, and I had to read the letter a second time before it dawned on me. That sick Russian was myself.

During a recent illness, I had been placed in a Russian military hospital in which iron discipline prevailed. Visitors were not allowed to talk freely with the patients and I was only permitted to communicate with the friend who used to come and see me either by sign language through the window or by letter. Letters, written in Russian for the benefit of the censor, were delivered to me by Sister Nadzieya. Instead of writing back, I used to ask the sister to tell my waiting friend what food or other things I was in need of. One day, Sister Nadzieya brought me the following letter:

'*Dear Tadeusz—Sorry that this is the last time I can come to see you but to-morrow I'm leaving for Head-*

quarters, where I've been transferred at my own request.
Hope to see you well again soon,

Yours,
Jan.'

Jan was my best friend and workmate. The above letter convinced me that, now that I was in hospital, my friend, instead of taking over my duties, was deserting not only his post but me. I was being left here among strangers in anything but congenial surroundings.

'Sister Nadzieya!' I shouted. 'Get pen and ink! I'll dictate a letter. You know, I'm not fit to hold a pen.'

'I know,' she said. 'Only don't excite yourself. I'll get everything we need. Just lie quiet.'

She went away and came back with paper, pen and inkpot. Then she sat down at the table by the window.

'I'm ready,' she said, arranging herself in the chair, like a schoolgirl preparing to take a dictation.

'Only write down exactly what I say,' I warned her.

'Of course. Go ahead.'

' "You old scoundrel!" ' I began.

' "You old scoundrel!" ' echoed Sister Nadzieya in her gentle, sing-song voice, starting to write.

' "If you're not willing to take over for me while I'm lying here sick or even to come and see me, then go to hell you blighter, and damn your eyes!" ' Such was my fury as I said these words that it lifted me up in bed.

'Steady now,' begged Sister Nadzieya. 'You can see I'm taking it all down, "If you're not willing to take over for me while I'm lying here sick or even to come and see me, then go to hell you blighter, and damn your eyes!" I've got it all,' she added, looking up from the paper.

'Carry on, then! ". . . and if I were writing this letter myself instead of getting the Sister to do it, I'd really tell you what I think of you. I don't want to know anything more about you, you swine!—TADEUSZ." '

Breathing heavily with anger, the effort and a high temperature, I fell back on the pillow exhausted. The sister obediently finished writing my last words and conveyed the letter to Jan.

I saw her give it to him outside the window, and soon he was reading the note I unearthed amongst my papers. It ran as follows:

'Hello, old man. Thanks for remembering me. I'm feeling a lot better. Sorry to hear you're going away and won't be able to come and see me again. I dare say, when I'm fit, we'll be seeing each other again and working together as before. Sincere thanks once more for all you've done for me. All the best for the time being,

Yours,
Tadeusz.'

*

In that hospital I had a room to myself. One day, as I was vainly trying to get to sleep, the door opened and in came Kulinina, attended by the doctor.

Kulinina, a tall, slim, middle-aged woman and a native of Turkestan, was an inspector at the local Department of Health. With the doctors, as well as their hospitals, she did exactly as she liked, though she had no medical qualifications whatever. As a good Party member she was temperamentally allergic to foreigners representing the capitalist democracies and the degenerate West. She threw an unfriendly glance at me as she came in, then turned imperiously to the doctor.

'This patient must be removed at once to the general hospital.'

Where I was, the doctors were good and the conditions perfectly adequate. It would be a pity to have to leave.

'Citizens,' I said, 'I've a high temperature. Just let me stay here for a few more days, anyway.'

'I'm extremely sorry,' she answered drily, 'but in our Soviet State, everything happens according to plan. If it weren't absolutely necessary to move you, I certainly should not. Have the ambulance come at once and take the patient away,' she snapped to the doctor, who immediately left the room to comply with his orders.

'They'll take you along in an ambulance,' she told me. 'Wrap yourself up well and you'll be quite all right.'

'Oh, well,' I consented. 'Only my things will be a bit of a nuisance. The few books are nothing. I can carry them, but I've got butter in that paper on the table—and a packet of sugar. My friend brought me so much I don't know what to do with it. The butter will melt in the car, and the sugar'll get spilt. Perhaps you'll be kind enough to accept them?'

'You're sure you don't want them?' she asked, trying hard to sound quite indifferent.

'Certain. Do have them. They'll only get spoilt or the orderly will take them.'

Kulinina went over to the table and with a swift movement wrapped the hunk of butter and the sugar in a newspaper. When the doctor returned, she was calmly holding the parcel.

'How is his temperature, actually?' she asked the doctor.

The doctor came over to the bed and took down the temperature chart. The graph paper showed what looked like an Alpine landscape—a chain of mountains, deep valleys, towering peaks, crags, chasms and summits. The inspector surveyed the diagram, shaking her head in feigned interest mingled with sympathy.

'Hm . . . yes. Perhaps it would be better to keep him here a few days longer, till he shows some improvement and his temperature goes down.'

'Maybe it would,' agreed the doctor obediently. 'I'll cancel the ambulance.'

'Well, get better soon,' said Kulinina as she went, taking with her the price of her sympathy, a pound of sugar and the slab of butter with which I had so effectively spread her heart as to soften it to the point of sabotaging the plans of the Soviet State.

She went out with a smile and behind her the servile doctor slipped away, silently closing the door.

*

My fevered blood seemed to be forcing my temples apart and running needles into my eyes. The doors were wide open and I could look straight through into a ward full of cheerful convalescents. Young lads were playing fiddles, accordions and balalaikas, or fighting duels with their crutches. The fencers were each minus a leg. Supporting themselves with one crutch, they wielded the other like a rapier: whoever fell over first lost the match. It was an excellent pastime and, since a man with only one leg takes a long time to stand up again, it provoked plenty of laughter.

With as happy a smile on his face as any of them, Matwiej in his wheelchair sat watching the fencers. He was a handsome, well-built man in his early twenties, with pale blond hair and a small moustache, neatly clipped, which gave him a cross, quick-tempered look. Fate had played Matwiej an exceptionally dirty trick. The ship in which he had been travelling on draft to Baku had been bombed by enemy planes. Matwiej escaped with his life, but he had been so badly jammed in the wreckage of the ship that his body was mangled and his bones shattered. The poor fellow had had both arms and legs amputated, and all that was left of him was a head and trunk. After a few weeks, there he sat or stood in his chair, having been washed and shaved by one of the nurses, looking just like a dummy in the window of a hairdresser's shop. The unfortunate lad had a wife whom he had married in Tashkent shortly before embarking. As soon as he recovered from the operation he asked to be allowed to see his wife in hospital. The hospital office telephoned the appropriate authorities in Tashkent, explaining the case.

Matwiej's wife was summoned to the Security Headquarters in Tashkent and told that, if she wished, she would be given leave from the factory and a permit to buy a return ticket to see her husband. Except in unusual circumstances, such as the evacuation of refugees, travel in the Soviet Union is strictly forbidden to individuals and no booking-office will sell a ticket unless the purchaser can produce an official permit.

The young wife seized the opportunity of seeing her husband and after a three-day journey she reported to the hospital, where they told her about the misfortune which had befallen Matwiej.

'He's a hundred per cent. disabled. He's got no arms or legs. If you want to take him home with you, you can.'

'Of course I want to. After all, he's my husband,' she replied, not grasping the extent of his tragic plight.

'In that case, just sign this declaration to certify that you're taking him with you.'

The woman appended her signature and was taken to the visitors' room. An orderly wheeled in Matwiej through another door.

After loud expressions of joy at their reunion and tearful embraces, Matwiej's wife came to her senses and went to see the commandant.

'Comrade Colonel, what's to become of him? Matwiej needs constant attention. He'll have to be washed, fed, taken to the lavatory; he couldn't even be left alone in the house. If there was a fire or the ceiling collapsed, for instance, the poor boy would be quite helpless. I have to work practically all day in the factory and he's only twenty-four with a sound heart and good lungs. He might live for another sixty years.'

'Certainly, he might, but what about it?' said the Colonel.

'Well how can I take him?'

'You signed to say you would.'

'I know I did, but I'd no idea how bad he was.'

'But we told you he was a hundred per cent. disabled.'

'Yes, but I didn't understand.'

'I suppose you understand Russian?'

'I understand Russian, but I wanted to see him so badly I didn't hear what was being said. I just had to get to him.'

'You shouldn't have signed the undertaking.'

'I know, but now that I have signed it, I'd sooner take in two homeless orphans instead. While I'm at the factory, the children could go to school and I could pick them up on my way back from work. And it'd be safer to leave two children alone in the house than a poor cripple like that.'

'Hm. I see. So you don't want to take him?'

'I can't.'

'Wait a minute while I think. We shall see.'

The Colonel went back to his office where he telephoned to the militia. Shortly afterwards, a black van drew up in front of the hospital and two officials got out. One was wearing uniform, the other plain clothes. First, they went to the office and then along to the waiting-room where, having concluded her visit to her husband, the wife was waiting for the wise Colonel to change his mind. The officials informed her that she was under arrest. She could not believe it, and when they laid hold of her to take her away by force she resisted and began to struggle.

A terrible cry rang out in the silence of the hospital, a sharp, broken scream which dissolved in a spasm of weeping that drowned the woman's helpless pleas as she was dragged away. Soon, a deathly white hush once more enveloped the hospital.

It would be years before Matwiej's wife, who had travelled several hundred miles on a week's leave from distant Tashkent, would return to the capital of her native Uzbeckstan—if, indeed, she ever returned. She was placed in a Turkestan prison to await trial, while Matwiej, who sat in his wheelchair and watched the chivalrous antics of the duellists, was bound for a long journey—to the home for totally disabled veterans.

EIGHTEEN

Vera

After a time, I was transferred to the general ward, in which there were sixteen beds. It was brighter and pleasanter there than all alone in my single room. The patient young sisters were worthy of admiration. They were underfed and paid starvation wages, for which they had to work twelve hours a day, but they tended the sick with genuine devotion and when a transfusion was required they gave their own blood.

In the Soviet Union, the home of paradox, where the life and liberty of a man in good health are in no way protected, where there are no pensions, insurance schemes or financial provision made for old age, where a healthy man is an insignificant pawn—all medical facilities are available to a man who is sick. He is surrounded by attentive doctors and nurses and is at perfect liberty to heap upon them the most vulgar abuse, if it contributes at all to the relief of his suffering. And, indeed, it must contribute thereto, for Soviet citizens avail themselves of this privilege to the full.

I was in the last bed by the wall. In no less than an hour's time the maid was due to bring in my lunch. I was not expecting to see Sister Vera Ivanovna to whose care I had been committed. It was Friday and having been on duty all night, she had the day off. There was silence in the ward, broken only by the monotonous snores of the patients. Flies were buzzing round the white lamp in the ceiling.

'How do you feel?' asked Vera, bending over me with her serious, pretty face and kind, thoughtful eyes.

She wore a pink dress with sky-blue flowers on it, instead of the usual white smock. It was cheap, market calico and badly printed, yet it was colourful, gay, spring-like. Her hair was arranged with more than customary care and she seemed taller than usual, for she was not wearing her working sandals but high-heeled shoes.

'Quite well, thanks,' I replied, raising my head and propping myself up on my elbow, against the pillow. 'I thought you had the day off. You were working all night and I expect you'll be on again this evening. I thought you'd be fast asleep.'

'Well, I should be, but they were giving out sweets at lunchtime so I went along and stood in the queue. I got some. You've no idea how good they taste.' She smiled greedily. 'That's why I came along to give you a few.' She laid a scrap of newspaper containing a few caramels on the blanket. 'I know in your country of capitalist oppression you never get anything like that to eat.'

Vera was far from stupid. On the contrary; but being barely twenty-five years of age, she was entirely a product of the Soviet State which had brought her up and educated her.

'Thank you.' I pressed her hand. 'It's awfully nice of you to share them with me. I must tell you, though, that in my country every child could buy sweets like those whenever he wanted and however many he liked.'

She nodded her head in agreement and smiled her understanding.

'You only say that because you're patriotic, but I know it's not true. It can't be. Since you're ill, I'm not going to quarrel with you. Anything you say,' she conceded indulgently.

A Polish soldier who was seriously ill started to moan loudly from a nearby bed. Vera went over to him, to straighten the pillow under his head. The sick man opened his eyes and recognized the girl.

'Sister,' he whispered, catching her by the hand.

'What is it, my dear?'

'Help me.'

'What do you want?'

'Sister,' he begged, like a small boy afraid of being left alone in the dark, 'I don't want to die here on strange soil and amongst strangers.'

'What do you mean "strange soil"?' Vera asked, surprised by his words. 'You are an ordinary farmer, so the soil of the Soviet Union is no stranger—rather a friend.'

Vera, who was not just an ordinary hospital nurse, but also a medical student, did not stop to reflect, for all her education, that this ordinary farmer had arrived on this strange but friendly Soviet soil by a roundabout route through Siberia, whither he had been transported after having been torn from the bosom of his family.

'I'll have to go now,' she said to me. 'I've got a lot of work to do at home. Bye-bye.'

That afternoon, with a blue dressing-gown thrown over my underclothes, I was sitting outside on a bench, basking in the warm rays of the Turkestan sun. On the stone steps in front of me a young Ukrainian girl with fair hair and wearing a white smock was washing her feet. She stood on one foot and raised the other as though dancing a minuet, while douching it in water poured from a clay jug. She looked like a vestal in an ancient Greek myth.

A bell rang for dinner, reminding me that I had to return to the building. I was no sooner inside than Marfa the maid entered, carrying a tray laden with bowls. She who usually wore a happy smile, to-day looked gloomy and sullen.

'Why the long face, Marfa?' I asked.

'Because I'm annoyed with all these doctors and commandants,' she replied, releasing some of her pent-up fury. 'I wanted to ask the matron for some clean sheets. I went along to their room and there they all were, sitting quite happily round the table drinking tea. They told me to get out and not to disturb them. Just say a word and they'll suspend you and maybe have you tried for insubordination.'

'You see, Marfa, if we foreigners sometimes complain about conditions here—that's one thing. We didn't ask to come here. But your brothers, your father, husband, nephew or cousin have fought, shed their blood and died, to preserve these conditions and this liberty of yours.'

Marfa made no reply. More furious than ever, she passed round the bowls of soup in silence and went out quickly with a rustle of her wide starched skirt.

A few days later, quite fit again, I was standing in the tunnel of an empty corridor waiting for the car which was to take me back to the camp.

'Will you come and see us sometimes?' asked Vera.

'Of course. But bring a couple of glasses, will you? Let's drink up this wine I've got here.'

'No, thanks.'

'Don't you drink?'

'Very little and rarely.'

'Yes, but you'll drink my health?'

'No, really, thank you.'

'If you won't even drink to my health, why should I come and see you?' I asked with forced jocularity.

Vera shrugged her shoulders.

'If you want to drink, I'll get you a glass,' she said, evasively.

'I'm not going to drink all by myself, but if you won't drink to my health let's drink to yours.'

'Please, no.'

'Then to the health of Stalin,' I provoked her.

'My dear boy,' she begged in a whisper, 'if anybody saw us and reported that a nurse was drinking wine in the hospital with a patient—and a foreigner at that—they'd not only sack me, but send me to Siberia into the bargain. They have hospitals there too, and they need nurses. If you like to come and see me privately, at home, you'll be very welcome to tea and I'll dig up some cake from somewhere.'

A car roared up outside and stopped at the gate.

'Where do you live?' I asked.

'No. 5, Chapayeva Street. Ask for Vera Ivanovna, or just for Sister Vera.'

The driver sounded his horn impatiently. I slung the flask over my shoulder—that flask of wine which Vera feared to drink, even to the health of Stalin.

'I'll be round to see you,' I said, as I ran outside.

'I'm free on Friday,' she called after me.

'Yes, I know; see you Friday.'

Only four days to go till Friday, then three and two —until at last the day came when I was to visit Vera Ivanovna.

Krasnovodzk was a small provincial town, half built of timber and desperately depressing. It was just like thousands of other such towns in Russia and I had no difficulty in finding Chapayeva which was one of the main streets.

Sister Vera lived in a small low house, a hovel almost, with a porch leading out on to a dreary back yard. She was waiting for me dressed in her white holiday frock which was not much different from her hospital smock. Her room was a large kitchen, divided in two by a grey blanket, on one side of which stood a bed, chair, table and chest of drawers with a yellowing fly-blown looking-glass. There were faded photographs pinned to the wall with drawing-pins and embellished with artificial flowers made of wire and blotting-paper. In one corner over the bed was a plate-shaped loud-speaker.

Wretched it was and lonely, and inevitably sad.

Vera had put on the kettle while she was waiting, and when I arrived she was in process of sewing a skirt.

'I see you're making a new dress,' I greeted her.

'No. It's not for me,' she said, fixing her needle in the material and laying the work aside. 'It's for sale,' she continued, as she took out a couple of thick glasses on chipped saucers. 'It wouldn't be easy to keep going on nothing but a nurse's pay. The wages aren't high and subscriptions to the library, sports and the Red Army, as well as the special tax I pay because I haven't a child and am twenty-five, account for a fair amount of my cash. If I didn't do some sewing and knitting so as to have a few things to sell, I'd never make ends meet.'

The kettle by this time was puffing clouds of steam. Vera lifted it off the fire and made two glasses of tea.

We sat down at the table which was laid with some home-made cake and a tin of cube sugar.

'It's rather odd,' I said. 'You're such a good person, Vera, pretty, sensible, young and very sweet, yet you go through life all alone.'

She shrugged.

'Do you really think I'm good and sweet?' she asked.

'I'm certain of it. After all, I was your patient and I'll never forget how well you looked after me when I was sick. You were very patient and understanding, not only with me but with all the sick and wounded under your care.'

'It's the duty of any nurse,' she answered evasively.

'Maybe, but I've seen other nurses, and I'm sorry to say they don't all show the same devotion to duty.'

'Oh, yes, I know,' she said, nodding her head thoughtfully.

'Quite a lot of them behave differently according to whom they're dealing with. They're helpful and pleasant and all smiles to some and they've no time at all for others. But you were good to all of us, though I never once saw you smile. Were you always the same?'

'No, but some years ago I forgot how to smile.'

'I'm so sorry. I didn't mean to hurt you. I understand, you suffered some tragedy.'

'It's all right. I'm not angry with you. You're quite right. I did suffer a tragedy, but it wasn't the kind you imagine. Nobody ran away and left me. More water? The tea seems a bit strong.'

'No, thanks. It's fine.'

'You've just said that I'm a good person. Do you think anyone can be good who has killed a fellow human?' she asked in her usual even, melodious and slightly constrained voice.

Her question took me by surprise.

'Yes, I think so,' I said, when I'd got over the first unpleasant shock of bewilderment. 'It all depends on the circumstances. On occasion the best of men are driven to commit murder, while a lot of people who have never committed murder are nevertheless thoroughly base and evil.'

'I agree,' she replied.

'For example, I don't regard myself as particularly wicked, but I killed a few men at the front—men against whom I had no personal ill-feeling whatsoever.'

'Ah, war—that's different,' she objected.

'Yes, but a life taken comes to the same thing in the long run.'

'You see . . .' she began, then broke off, stood up and, in order to hide the emotion she could not control, she turned away pretending to do something in the kitchen.

'Before I became a nurse,' she went on after a short time, 'I used to work in the Security Police. One day, I was ordered to a place near the Chinese frontier, where I was to investigate a certain matter. Exact details as to what and how were to be given me later, so I was told. When I arrived at my destination I reported to my new chief. I hadn't been working with him long before I had fallen in love with him. I was very young at the time; I'd never been in love before, and you know how it is with a girl's first romance.'

'I know.'

'After a time, I got my instructions. The person I'd come to get was the man I'd fallen in love with. I did my duty and accomplished my mission.'

'Your story, Vera, sounds like the plot of a sensational film.'

'Maybe it does, only a film like that would be banal and artificially drawn out and therefore rather improbable. But in real life such things happen.'

'Unfortunately they do. But you chose to take on that kind of work,' I couldn't help remarking. 'Is it true, by the way, that even in a hospital ward there's one sister specially detailed by the authorities to report what the patients discuss?'

'Yes,' Vera admitted, and added, as though suddenly perturbed at the question, 'Why do you ask?'

'Simply because in an access of sincerity I told one of them rather more than was necessary about my humble self.'

'Which one?'

'Natasha.'

'Oh, she's all right,' said Vera reassuringly. 'You can say what you like to her. No need to worry. She won't make use of it. It's only the senior sister—the ward-matron so-called—who, being officially appointed, would report to the authorities.'

The evening was already well advanced. Vera stood up and pressed the wall switch which lit the electric bulb in its papier mâché shade. Then she turned round to look at the alarm clock on the chest of drawers.

'Eight o'clock already,' she said, breaking a silence which had begun to grow rather long. 'I'd like you to stay, but I'm afraid you'll miss your last train.'

'Yes, I must be going.' I stood up. 'Thanks a lot, Vera, I've enjoyed myself. Good night.'

I put on my cap, as I turned to go.

'Good night,' she said as we shook hands. 'Drop in again some time,' she added without enthusiasm, 'and remember, don't say too much about yourself particularly to people in responsible positions, even if it's only a humble senior sister in a hospital ward.'

I went out on the veranda and the door shut behind me. I heard the key scrape in the lock, and, when I looked back, I could see the shadow of her head with its thunder-cloud of hair outlined against the wall.

I went down the steps with a strange inexplicable feeling of sorrow, as though I had lost someone dear to me.

Vera, you see, was the senior sister in the ward.

NINETEEN

Happiness and a Thermometer

It was a scorching Sunday in July. A white sun gilded the grey, sandy crescent of the bay in which lay a string of sailing boats, like the beads of a necklace, gently rocking. The slim, graceful pencils of their masts sketched broad arcs upon the clear, blue sky, measuring the quiet rhythm of a peaceful day. The green pier, supported by ancient tree trunks covered with mould, moss and seaweed, thrust deep into the mirror of the Caspian Sea. As I sat there on the edge of the pier, the water below me was far beyond the reach of my bare feet. It was a secluded spot, quite deserted. Even the fish were not biting. It did not matter how often I changed the bait, replacing a crust of black bread with a white roll or a sardine soaked in oil, there was not a fish to be caught. In my mind's eye, however, I was floating away, far beyond the silver rim of the horizon. Time stood still, in this place, from dawn till dark.

Suddenly, my peaceful meditations were interrupted by the creak of footsteps on the rotting planks. Someone was coming. Afanazy. He was coming slowly and carefully, so as not to twist his ankle in one of the many, treacherous holes, or tear his boot on a protruding nail.

He was better dressed than usual. A shirt with a small, tight collar, fastened at the side, white with blue stripes, well laundered and held at the waist by an army belt, was evenly draped above his navy riding-breeches, tucked into black top-boots. The latter, made out of fibre or some other leather substitute, had rubber soles cut from motor-car tires, and they gleamed like an advertisement for boot polish.

He came up to me, smiled with affected geniality, displaying the two rows of metal teeth, and sat down beside me.

'Good morning,' he began.

'Good morning.'

Silence. It was such a warm, lazy day that I did not even feel like talking.

'You're fishing,' he said, directing a powerful and accurate spit at the surface of the water, as though he were flinging a bean at a window-pane.

A small circle appeared on the still expanse, then vanished as though rubbed from a blackboard.

Afanazy was the political director of the Military Hospital. That was how he had come to know me. Every morning, he used to bring me a copy of the *Red Star,* which he distributed free of charge. Once a week he showed a film in the hall, sometimes he managed to drag books, draughts, dominoes or chess out of the library, and lent balalaikas, violins or guitars to those who were musically inclined. He knew the history of the Revolution and the Party by heart, but he never delivered lectures. That was what hurt him most.

'If only I were educated,' he would whisper, sad and hopeless.

One day, he had brought in some illustrated pamphlets. Aeroplanes were depicted on the cover, winging their way through crimson skies above the heads of Soviet soldiers marching victoriously. Inside, there were dozens of photographs depicting the heroic achievements of the Workers' and Peasants' Army by land, sea and air. The time, place and choice of literature were rather unfortunate. Wounded men or legless cripples, men with their arms in slings or heads swathed in bandages, went beserk at this reminder of the delights of war. The propagandist was unanimously declared an unnatural brute, and his mother a lady of easy virtue.

When the astonished political director tried to explain away his error, beginning his peroration with the time-honoured, 'Comrades, Brothers, Eagles!' the brothers and eagles subjected him to a hail of spittoons and chamber-pots, and Afanazy retreated behind the door without further argument. He did not put in an appearance for the next few days. And then, one morning, as though nothing had happened, he was back again, distributing newspapers. The patients, likewise, greeted him as though nothing had happened.

On this particular day, a Sunday, he chanced to be walking past the pier and had just come up to chat for no particular reason. He explained, as if by way of self-justification, that he just wanted to talk—man to man. His wrinkled face was anxious and thoughtful.

We sat there in silence. What was there to talk about? And the peacefulness of the place was extremely delightful.

'Trying to catch a few fish for yourself?' he repeated.
'Yes.'

There was another long silence. Afanazy spat again, further than before, not down at his feet but right out in front.

'Tell me, do you like it with us?'

'It's all right.'

'Would you like to stay here? Tell me frankly. Don't shrug your shoulders as if you didn't know. You must know. Life with us here is different from other countries. You're not used to it yet, so you'd find it hard at first. But people in other countries aren't happy. Here, they are. Don't smile—I know what I'm talking about. It doesn't matter if certain things are hard to come by, but you will admit that we've done a lot and made great progress in the twenty years since the Revolution. It's true, isn't it? There you are, you say so yourself. And in the next twenty years we'll do a lot more and advance still further. Why? Because our people are happy—not like in those countries of yours. Why do you look so surprised?' He pushed back the peak of his checked cap and spat once more through his metal teeth. 'Yes, indeed. A man can only be happy in our country. Take England or France or America. Millionaire sits in his palace. Sits there bored to tears. For the simple reason he's got everything his heart could wish for —palace, car, aeroplane—everything. And is he happy? Course he's not. He's no sooner got them than he's fed up with his palace, car and aeroplane. But the car factories are thinking up new models every day—green, blue, glass here, bit of glass there, cars with a radio, and so on. So they send him a coloured catalogue and he picks out a fresh model. Being a millionaire, he can't be bothered to go to the factory and take a look at them. Anyway, that's why they sent him the coloured catalogue—so that he wouldn't have to tire himself by going along in person. The millionaire just rings an electric bell and in comes a secretary in a black coat, or a pretty young typist, slim and blonde with pink cheeks and a shapely little bottom like a mandolin. The millionaire doesn't say anything, just points to a number in the catalogue. The secretary or the blonde knows what to do. They grab the 'phone and ring up the factory.

' "Please send along a car. It's number so-and-so in the catalogue—latest model. The money will be paid to you by our bank to-morrow."

' "Very good. Thank you very much," says the factory. Minute later the car he's chosen is standing in front of the palace. So what? Think the millionaire is happy now? Not a bit of it. He's not happy and why should he be? He's been a millionaire a long time. He's quite used to it, so what's he got to be cheerful about now? No. The millionaire carries on sitting there bored and fed up. That's what it's like in England, France or America, and you don't have to be a millionaire either. I only brought in the millionaire so as to exaggerate a bit. It's enough in those countries to buy a bicycle and you want a motor-bike. You get a motor-bike and you want a house. You're never content. But here, in the Soviet Union . . . ?' Afanazy, with a superior smile, scratched his head once again, this time behind the right ear, pushing his cap over to the left as he did so. A gleam of victory shone through the slits of his small, unintelligent eyes. 'With us—you want a smoke, let's say, you'd do anything for a cigarette. But you haven't got one. You've not had one for a long time. Then you hear that a consignment of tobacco's come in and it's being distributed, three packets per man. You're happy. You make up your mind to go and stand in the queue that evening, so as to be near the shop when it opens the next day. You stand there all day till you get results —it might be your free day. But before you're out of the factory other people with the same idea have got there first and the queue's a mile long. You join on the end and after a while it stretches out behind you with all the people who've come along later still. Then you're happy because you're further up in the queue than they are. You talk to your comrades in front and behind and you're all laughing and joking. It gets cold before sunrise but that doesn't matter—the shop will soon be open. So you all cheer up and start joking again. The assistants get there just before eight. There's excitement in the queue. They're just going to start selling. As soon as the shop opens the people start to go in, one after another, in an orderly fashion. Then you see that it's quite true—what they were saying in the town. They are giving out tobacco, three packets per person, at the State-controlled price of six roubles per packet and you can get a couple of boxes of matches to go with them. Everything's going nicely. After two or three hours, however, it becomes apparent that there are more prospective customers than there are matches to serve them with. So the thousandth man, perhaps, gets no matches. But the tobacco's there and that's the main thing. So they go ahead giving out three packets per person but without any matches. About midday, the manager realizes that there may not be enough tobacco for everyone. Hordes of people are waiting. So he orders the allowance to be cut to two per person. The queue is moving quickly and there are fewer people in front of you now. You'll soon be in the shop yourself. When you look round, you see a great, long, black line stretching into the distance—all the people who got there after you did. You cheer up at the thought that if all those people are waiting in the hopes of getting tobacco, you've got even better reason to hope.' Afanazy paused, pondered, as if he had just remembered something, then spat again. 'You get me?'

'I do.'

'And so it goes. But the manager of the shop takes another peep outside in the street and when he sees all those people waiting, he orders the sale of only one packet per person. So the queue moves along more quickly still. All of a sudden, when there's only about three hundred in front of you, the supplies run out completely. Everybody's mad at this, but they see that the people in front are still going into the shop and buying something, so they carry on waiting in the queue just to see what comes of it. Then it turns out that although the tobacco's all gone like the matches before it, there's still something else. Oh, I don't know what—a thermometer, for example. You know, thing for taking temperatures. Everyone's allowed to buy two. It's not an expensive thing—only costs nine roubles and it's always coming in handy. So the people buy them and the queue moves on ahead of you. And then at last, it's your turn. So in you go like all the rest and ask for two.

'"You're late, comrade," says the assistant, "you can only have one thermometer. Otherwise there won't be enough to go round."

'"Well, just give me one, then," you say.

'You pay your nine roubles and off you go with a medical thermometer, made in Moscow. The doorway's chock-a-block with people trying to force their way inside. They don't know whether there'll even be one left for them. But you go home quite satisfied and you wrap up that thermometer in a piece of cloth so that it doesn't get smashed, and you put it away in the cupboard. What happens then? You've been standing out in the cold a whole evening, all night and half the day. You feel a pain in your chest, you've got a bad cold and a hacking cough. You rush off to the factory doctor in a panic. He —or it may be a young woman even prettier than the American typist—examines you, listens to your breathing and reassures you.

' "I can't see anything much the matter with you," he says. "You've simply caught a cold. Take a rest. I'm giving you three days off."

'You go home, make some hot tea—and you're sure to find yourself a drop of vodka. Then you get your thermometer out of the cupboard, go to bed and take your temperature. Then you really feel happy.'

Afanazy stopped and looked at me out of the corner of his eye, in the certainty of seeing me deeply moved.

'You say you've had no education and you can't lecture and yet, look how well you told that story,' I congratulated him.

Afanazy relapsed into despondency.

'Everyone knows that story,' he said quietly, hunching his shoulders and hanging his head. 'I didn't make it up. They gave us that on our introductory course as an example of how to begin the first talk. But if I had not only courses but an education behind me, why, I might even be able to give lectures on international politics.'

The knowledge of his educational shortcomings was really distressing to the ambitious Afanazy. His lined face looked even greyer, almost the colour of ashes. He sat silent, deliberating hopelessly. Finally he changed the subject.

'Been sitting here long?' he asked.

'Quite awhile.'

'What do you use for bait?'

'Bread.'

'Funny you haven't caught anything up to now. Why not try an ordinary cork for a change. You sometimes catch them with the most ridiculous bait.'

'Sometimes, but not always.'

On the grey-blue horizon there appeared a little ship,

a steady stream of smoke rising from her squat funnel. She might have been tracing her route with a piece of charcoal on the great empty map of the sky.

A ship bound for Persia, the green land—the free.